D1573038

(re)DESIGNING

NARRATIVE WRITING UNITS

for Grades 5–12

Property Of
Jeffry B. Fuller

KATHY TUCHMAN GLASS

Solution Tree | Press a division of
Solution Tree

Copyright © 2018 by Solution Tree Press

Materials appearing here are copyrighted. With one exception, all rights are reserved. Readers may reproduce only those pages marked "Reproducible." Otherwise, no part of this book may be reproduced or transmitted in any form or by any means (electronic, photocopying, recording, or otherwise) without prior written permission of the publisher.

555 North Morton Street
Bloomington, IN 47404
800.733.6786 (toll free) / 812.336.7700
FAX: 812.336.7790

email: info@SolutionTree.com
SolutionTree.com

Visit **go.SolutionTree.com/literacy** to download the free reproducibles in this book.

Printed in the United States of America

21 20 19 18 17   1 2 3 4 5

Library of Congress Cataloging-in-Publication Data

Names: Glass, Kathy Tuchman.
Title: (Re)designing narrative writing units for grades 5-12 / Kathy Tuchman
   Glass.
Description: Bloomington, IN : Solution Tree Press, 2018. | Includes
   bibliographical references and index.
Identifiers: LCCN 2017027069 | ISBN 9781942496786 (perfect bound)
Subjects: LCSH: English language--Composition and exercises--Study and
   teaching (Middle school) | English language--Composition and
   exercises--Study and teaching (Secondary) | Narration (Rhetoric)--Study
   and teaching (Middle school) | Narration (Rhetoric)--Study and teaching
   (Secondary)
Classification: LCC LB1631 .G557 2018 | DDC 428.0071/2--dc23 LC record available at https://lccn.loc.gov/2017027069

Solution Tree
Jeffrey C. Jones, CEO
Edmund M. Ackerman, President

Solution Tree Press
President and Publisher: Douglas M. Rife
Editorial Director: Sarah Payne-Mills
Art Director: Rian Anderson
Managing Production Editor: Caroline Cascio
Senior Production Editor: Suzanne Kraszewski
Senior Editor: Amy Rubenstein
Copy Editor: Miranda Addonizio
Proofreader: Jessi Finn
Cover and Text Designer: Abigail Bowen
Editorial Assistants: Jessi Finn and Kendra Slayton

Acknowledgments

Writing a book is an enormous undertaking. Although I have a well-defined vision of what I want to impart, articulating it clearly and concisely and organizing it well inevitably prove challenging at certain times during the writing process. I've welcomed input from others who have played vital roles at pivotal points and graciously lent their talents and input. Within my sphere of supporters, I have many to thank.

This book would not have come to fruition if it weren't for the dedication of the staff at Solution Tree. I'm grateful to those who worked behind the scenes whom I've not met in addition to those whom I recognize here.

Douglas Rife, a longtime friend and colleague, always offers prudent advice, caring support, and lively conversations. I am glad he invited me to hop on board so we can work together again and am grateful that he championed what I envisioned for this project.

Claudia Wheatley, an instantaneous friend from the get-go, helped shape the proposal until it was just right. She listened, researched, provided suggestions, and weaved her magic to ensure it was ready for prime time. I'm especially grateful to both Douglas and Claudia for helping secure our alliance for a long time to come.

Amy Rubenstein helped me as I stepped out of the gate, providing nascent feedback to launch the project in the right direction. She invited Tonya Cupp early in the process to offer necessary insight and to do what was in the best interest of my project. I appreciate their judgments and salient feedback about direction at the early stages to launch this endeavor properly.

Thanks to Rian Anderson and his team for being receptive to my suggestions and producing an eye-catching cover that beautifully integrates with the text design and visuals. I also appreciate their careful attention to design throughout the book.

I am grateful for the hard work and dedication Sue Kraszewski devoted on my behalf to make this book the best it could be. It is an arduous task she undertook, and her keen eye and remarkable skill contributed greatly to this final product.

Technology is a vast new domain still with so much to explore. I'm grateful to Nancy Akhavan and Keli Kinsella for helping me find ways to explain the complicated world of technology in a coherent fashion so educators can access and extend their offerings to students.

I'm always indebted to Johnna Becker and Nancy Rhodes, my dear friends and go-to girls from way back when I first started my consulting career. I admire their continual willingness to maximize their own potential so they can pass on the very best in curriculum and instruction to their students.

No matter how immersed in a project Nicole Vagle is, she always lifts her head with a smile to offer feedback. She helps me tease out confusing parts that seemed clear one day but somehow not so much the following day. Offering valuable insight, she sets me in a new and wonderful direction that supplies me with more information to share than I thought I had in me.

Lynn Erickson has been an inspiration to me and undoubtedly countless others. Her work challenges my thinking, and her professional advice has helped to fuel a whole new venture.

For my health and well-being, I have Matt Black to thank. He listens to me fret about another deadline, keeps me on track, finds time in his schedule to train my weary body, and makes me smile.

The proverbial last but not least, I owe a debt of gratitude to my family. With my children now launched, my heart is full of pride and my attention clear to focus on this book. My husband, Mike, is forever my lead champion and constant advocate, always proud and understanding of the path I've chosen. His steadfast encouragement, backing, and confidence spur me on each and every day. And he makes a perfect latte!

Solution Tree Press would like to thank the following reviewers:

Dee Grimm
English Teacher
Turner Ashby High School
Bridgewater, Virginia

Marlene Hosmer
Eighth-Grade Gifted Language Arts Teacher
Northwestern Middle School
Milton, Georgia

Bradford Lardner
English Teacher
Kinard Core Knowledge Middle School
Fort Collins, Colorado

James McCrink
English Teacher
Ransom Everglades School
Coconut Grove, Florida

Blair Perzentka
English Teacher
Marshall High School
Marshall, Wisconsin

Jani Sparr
English Teacher
West Middle School
Sioux City, Iowa

Molly Uppena
Language Arts Teacher
Mineral Point High School
Mineral Point, Wisconsin

Visit **go.SolutionTree.com/literacy** to download the free reproducibles in this book.

Table of Contents

About the Author

Kathy Tuchman Glass, a consultant, is an accomplished author and former classroom teacher with more than twenty-five years of experience in education. She provides professional development services to K–12 educators with a focus on areas concerning curriculum and instruction.

She is recognized for her expertise in differentiated instruction, standards work around English language arts, literacy, instructional strategies, assessments, teaching methods, and backward planning for unit and lesson design. She is a member of the International Literacy Association, the National Council of Teachers of English, the Association for Supervision and Curriculum Development, and Learning Forward.

She earned a bachelor's degree from Indiana University–Bloomington and a master's degree in education from San Francisco State University.

To learn more about Kathy's work, visit Glass Educational Consulting (www.kathyglassconsulting.com).

To book Kathy Tuchman Glass for professional development, contact pd@SolutionTree.com.

Introduction

If you're reading this, you may have already read *The Fundamentals of (Re)designing Writing Units* (Glass, 2017a), the foundational book to this *(Re)designing Writing* series. If so, you already understand the critical importance of writing to enhance student learning, no matter the subject. The second book in the series, *(Re)designing Argumentation Writing Units for Grades 5–12* (Glass, 2017b), continues that discussion, emphasizing devising and conducting units of study centered on students writing an argumentation piece. This book, *(Re)designing Narrative Writing Units for Grades 5–12*, is all about writing a form of narrative and all it entails to produce a well-crafted piece. Although students can write an informational or argumentative piece based on narrative text, such as a literary critique or an essay, this text focuses on generating a narrative fiction or nonfiction written product.

Authorities in the field of writing have espoused the need for teaching narrative writing. In Carol Lee's foreword to George Hillocks Jr.'s (2007) book *Narrative Writing: Learning a New Model for Teaching*, she encapsulates this importance:

> Learning to write rich narratives offers access points for understanding the rhetorical moves employed by writers of great fiction, expands what students understand about rhetoric more broadly (i.e., critical semantic manipulation, functional uses of sentence structures, elements of narrative genres), and shows how this can transfer to writing in other genres. (p. vii)

In his text, Hillocks (2007) provides this compelling reason for teaching narrative writing:

> First and perhaps most important, work on narrative, if we make it personal, is a way to examine the stories of our lives. Beyond that, it allows students to contribute to the body of literature they will study, understand more fully how the works of professional writers are constructed, and learn techniques that will be useful in other kinds of writing. (p. 1)

In English language arts, students might craft a contemporary realistic fiction piece with invented characters, setting, and plot. However, opportunities for crafting a narrative abound within many disciplines—not just English class. For example, in social studies, students can write historical fiction to demonstrate their understanding and educate readers on a particular time period with factually accurate events and characters. In science, students can compose science fiction to explore and speculate about topics such as environmental issues and natural disasters. They can also write detailed descriptions to accompany a model, such as one that describes the ways the geosphere, biosphere, hydrosphere, and atmosphere interact. In mathematics, students can write a biography about a famous mathematician and the impact of his or her work.

About (Re)designing

I title these books *(Re)designing* because my goal is to help you rebuild or newly design and develop writing curriculum and deliver instruction with depth, rigor, and clarity. These books give you the guidance, tools, and wherewithal to be judicious and intentional about the following.

- **Designing new units:** Some of you may read these books and develop a writing unit from scratch. In the case of narrative writing, the work can focus on writing in a language arts class, align to a content area, or follow an interdisciplinary unit that culminates in students writing a genre within narrative, such as a mystery, realistic fiction, memoir, or biography.

- **Revising existing units:** Others may redesign an existing unit. This means you have taught a unit in the past or have one at your disposal and feel the need to revise all or part of it. Maybe you need to tweak lessons, make the culminating assessment more rigorous, add more engaging activities, write or revise guiding questions, and so forth.

- **Critiquing a new or previously adopted textbook or curriculum:** You may use what you learn to ensure the published material satisfies the need for rigor and aligns to standards and other goals. Some resources might include an overwhelming amount of effective (and ineffective) strategies, activities, assessments, pedagogy, writing ideas, and so on. With new knowledge, you can critique what is available and make conscientious decisions, such as revising, augmenting, or bypassing mediocre material you encounter.

The aforementioned foundation book, *The Fundamentals of (Re)designing Writing Units*, is a recommended prerequisite for each book in the series, including this one. The following briefly summarizes that book; if you are familiar with its topics, you might choose to forgo reading it and dive into this book's focus on narrative.

- Chapter 1 summarizes the research related to writing and provides recommendations for instruction; an overview of the different writing types (narrative, descriptive, expository, persuasive); and their characteristics, purposes, and associated genres. It also features a writing continuum to vertically and horizontally plot standards.

- Chapter 2 focuses on the stages of the writing process, various instructional strategies, and resources for digital communities and technology to be used throughout the stages.

- Chapter 3 tackles the backward-planning approach to unit design with attention to the beginning stage—identifying standards and using them to articulate what you want students to know (K), understand (U), and

be able to do (D), plus unit- and lesson-guiding questions.

- Chapter 4 focuses on evidence of student learning, particularly culminating writing assessments. It features types of performance assessments, writing prompts and examples, student writing checklists, and rubrics. This chapter also includes suggestions for using student writing models, grading, calibrating, and determining anchor papers.

- Chapter 5 moves to lesson design, specifically the gradual release of responsibility model for teaching a new skill, strategy, or process. It explains each phase of this lesson approach, a concrete lesson example, and ideas for differentiating instruction.

- Chapter 6 is all about launching the unit. The text describes piloting the unit and reflecting on lessons to perfect the design and provides revision suggestions for the next time you teach this unit.

I intend for each book to guide you in designing and conducting a seamless unit of instruction for writing, one that raises the bar for students and builds teachers' capacity. All books in the series, including this one on narrative, contain templates, checklists, rubrics, writing prompts, assessments, instructional strategies, and more—all couched in a backward-design process—for you to plan a quality-driven unit that guides and empowers students to compose a sound written piece. (Visit **go.SolutionTree.com/literacy** to access materials related to these books.)

Who This Book Is For

This book is primarily for subject-matter teachers, curriculum designers, or literacy coaches who expect students to read and author narrative-oriented content in grades 5–12. The *you* I address refers to any reader invested in delivering or designing curriculum aligned to narrative writing in these grades. Those who serve elementary students may also find this book beneficial, as they can adapt the material as needed.

Although you can read this book independently, I recommend that you work with colleagues to plan the writing unit together. Consider working as a department, a collaborative group within the context of a professional learning community, or an interdisciplinary team, if appropriate.

Although language arts teachers are responsible for addressing a variety of writing and other literacy standards, other subject-area teachers might also ask students to produce a coherent and organized written narrative piece. As stated earlier, social studies, science, and mathematics, for example, present ripe opportunities for students to write. The choices are endless for infusing narrative writing in a single content area, in a core subject (humanities), or in an interdisciplinary situation where different teachers share students from across subject areas.

Consider collaborating with colleagues to identify which narrative writing skills each will target and teach to delineate expectations so teachers are not inadvertently missing skills or overlapping their instruction. For instance, if those who teach science communicate to the language arts teacher that students will produce a descriptive piece to accompany a science model, the language arts teacher can focus instruction on imagery and strong word choice. A social studies teacher can focus instruction around research to accumulate historically accurate facts about content while the language arts teacher can discuss the characteristic elements and structure of historical fiction. Teaming with others to divvy up skills and standards that each will be accountable for will help ensure an optimal written piece.

In *The Fundamentals of (Re)designing Writing Units* (Glass, 2017a), I discuss and suggest creating a writing continuum as part of a curriculum mapping project that a school or district can undertake. The continuum articulates genres and related skills across grades and subjects to provide transparency so you can plan and lead instruction accordingly to expose students to the essential writing practices. Doing so can avoid unnecessary repetition of instruction year after year on the same genre, such as a personal narrative or a realistic short story, focusing on the exact same expectations. You might consider spearheading or suggesting such a curriculum mapping project so students acquire a deep understanding of several genres across the years.

If you teach in a self-contained classroom, collaborate with job-alike colleagues to brainstorm and create a unit together. Logistically, you and others could generate a Google Doc (or utilize another electronic collaborative tool) so each can contribute to the pieces that will eventually make the final product a robust unit. Some of you

may be in a small district, where you are the only teacher for one or more grades or content areas. Try to work virtually with colleagues in other counties or schools. Or consider collaborating with content-area teachers in or across appropriate grade clusters in your school and create a unit together to share. Even if these situations are not feasible, this book can still provide the necessary tools to re-envision what you teach and how you teach writing to your students.

About Timed Assessment

Although this book will prepare students for standardized writing situations that assess their narratives, it is not about students responding to an on-demand writing prompt in a timed situation. You might issue such a prompt for different assessment purposes before or during instruction to gauge what students know and to inform your instruction. This book focuses primarily on designing or redesigning a complete and rigorous narrative writing unit of instruction in which students advance through the steps of the writing process. As such, you can use an analytic rubric as an instructional tool and to score and gather information to improve the quality of students' writing. When students participate in a demanding and engaging writing unit, it prepares them well for a district- or state-mandated test:

> In schools with a major emphasis on standardized tests, teachers are prone to conclude that their own assessments must always approximate the nature of the year-end standardized test so students will be "ready" for that test when it comes. . . . However, we ought not to lose sight of the fact that if all teaching is proscribed by the very limited and limiting format of a particular test, students' learning experiences are woefully restricted. . . . If they learn better because of how we teach and assess them, it's likely they will fare better on standardized tests than if we insist on teaching them in narrow ways that are ineffective for them. When learning "works" for a student, that student is likely to enter a testing situation both more competently and confidently than would otherwise have been the case, and outcomes should be predictably better. (Tomlinson & Moon, 2013, p. 46)

Avoid aligning every task you administer to a standardized test-like prompt or situation. Teaching writing effectively across a range of genres supplies the necessary skills to embolden students to approach any writing situation with courage and assurance.

The Fundamentals of Narrative Writing

The following sections present a brief overview of the fundamentals of narrative writing and describe additional information available in the appendices at the end of this book, specifically:

- Appendix A: Narrative and Descriptive Text Types

- Appendix B: Elements of Literature

- Appendix C: Literary Devices and Figurative Language

If you require more guidance on narrative writing before you begin your work creating unit plans in chapter 1, refer to these appendices. While English language arts teachers and others conversant in narrative and descriptive text types, narrative genres, elements of literature, figurative language, and literary devices will likely find this information familiar, teachers from other disciplines looking to infuse narrative and descriptive writing into their subject areas might find this overview valuable. With that said, however, those familiar with these topics might still like to peruse the appendices to determine how the examples featured might be used within lesson planning.

Narrative and Descriptive Writing

Narrative and descriptive writing are text *types* also known as categories or modes of writing. (Expository and persuasive are the other two text types, the subject of other books in this series.) Any text type aligns to a writer's purpose for crafting the piece—to entertain, inform, explain, and so forth—which in turn dictates other writing factors like audience and style. Various genres reside within text types, which represent different works that are grouped together because they share commonalities—like a distinctive style, form, or element. Table I.1, an excerpt from chapter 1 of *The Fundamentals of (Re)designing Writing Units* (Glass, 2017a), lists the narrative and descriptive text types, their unique characteristics, the primary purposes of each, and the genres and subgenres within narrative writing, essentially serving as an outline for appendix A (page 123). Descriptive writing is interwoven throughout various genres across text types and doesn't necessarily have dedicated genres, which appendix A addresses in more detail. Although this resource provides an overview of the most common narrative genres and subgenres, there are even more that you can find when conducting your own research. Furthermore, there are various definitions, classifications, and nuances within some of them.

Elements of Literature

The elements of literature—or narrative elements—are the heart and soul of fictional narrative. They include *character, setting, plot, point of view,* and *theme.* Without them, a work of fiction seems incomplete, undeveloped, or inadequate. These elements appear to some degree in nonfiction narrative.

Most standards documents list expectations around elements of literature for both writing and reading, including the English language arts Common Core (National Governors Association Center for Best Practices [NGA] & Council of Chief State School Officers [CCSSO], 2010). The genre can affect the treatment, so students need to know which kind of narrative they are expected to write so they can make decisions about elements. For example, in historical fiction the setting is altogether critical to the telling of the story and affects characters, plot, and theme. In myths, the setting might be an ill-defined, amorphous, and remote past, but the principal characters are pronounced and can possess supernatural powers. In mysteries, authors fashion a plotline with a crime that launches the story.

Appendix B (page 131) presents a thorough explanation of each element for those needing this information or a review of it.

Literary Devices and Figurative Language

Authors select and employ literary devices and figurative language to suit the purpose for which they are writing and enhance a work of narration. *Literary devices,* such as allusion, analogy, mood, tone, flashback, foreshadowing, dialect, dialogue, irony, and others, are techniques that writers use to enrich and add dimension to their work.

Table I.1: Narrative and Descriptive Writing Overview

Types (Modes, Categories)	Characteristics	Primary Purposes	Genres and Subgenres

Narrative (Fiction)	• Fictional narratives are based on the imagination.
	• Fictional narratives include elements of literature: plot, character, setting, point of view, and theme.
	• Some subgenres, such as contemporary realistic and historical fiction, include facts.
	• Writers can utilize a variety of literary techniques, such as suspense, foreshadowing, dialect, dialogue, allusion, and so forth, as well as descriptive details and figurative language (such as imagery and simile).
	• Plot forms the basic structure that chronicles how the events unfold naturally and in a logical order.
	  • Plot elements include introduction, central conflict, rising action, climax, falling action, and resolution (denouement).
	  • More sophisticated writers might include flashbacks, flash forward, or parallel or multiple plotlines.
	  • Developing writers can create a beginning, middle, and end or a problem and solution as a starting point for producing a plot.
		• To entertain
		• To describe
			Folktales
			• Fairy tales
			• Myths
			• Legends
			• Tall tales
			• Animal tales
			  • Trickster tales
			  • Fables
			  • Pourquoi (or etiological) tales
			Fantasy
			• High and low fantasy
			• Science fiction
			Realism
			• Contemporary realistic fiction
			• Realistic fiction
			• Historical fiction
			• Mystery

Narrative (Nonfiction)	• Unlike fictional narrative, nonfiction narration is based on facts and is informative rather than fictitious.
	• Genres in this category can include some elements of literature but with a different treatment.
	  • The characters are actual people.
	  • All genres do not include each plot element; for example, a biography may not have a climax.
	• Writers of narrative nonfiction may utilize literary techniques such as dialogue, allusion, and symbolism, irony, as well as descriptive details and figurative language (such as imagery and metaphor).
		• To inform
		• To describe
			• Biography
			• Autobiography
			• Memoir
			• Personal narrative

Descriptive	• Writers describe an object, topic, character, person, place, experience, situation, emotion, or event so readers can visualize it. • Descriptions can stand alone or be incorporated within narrative text (such as describe a setting, character, or individual), expository writing (describe steps to perform a task or describe parts of a plant), or persuasive writing (describe a scenario to establish context for an argument). • This type of writing includes precise and vivid language and relies heavily on figurative language (such as imagery, simile, or metaphor).	• To describe	Poetry and various genres that incorporate descriptive writing for different purposes

Source: Glass, 2017a.

*Visit **go.SolutionTree.com/literacy** for a free reproducible version of this table.*

Figurative language rcfcrs to simile, metaphor, imagery, personification, and hyperbole. It enhances setting, character, plot elements, feelings, ideas, and other content to make the text vivid, realistic or fantastical, and compelling. When authors use figurative language, they want readers to understand the connotation rather than the literal interpretation of their words. As a result, readers must use interpretation skills once they recognize and identify instances where the writer uses these figures of speech.

You can explore the definitions and extensive examples of literary devices and figurative language in more detail in appendix C (page 137) should you need this support or as a tool for planning lessons.

Book Organization and Contents Overview

This book takes a sequential approach to building a narrative writing unit. Therefore, many chapters include exercises suggesting how you can apply what you read, so that by the time you finish the last page you will have a draft of your unit ready to develop and pilot. For this reason, I suggest targeting a particular area of your curriculum in which producing a narrative is the culminating assessment.

Chapter 1 presents a host of options for developing and supporting narrative maps. You can download and use items from the sample template that feature learning outcomes and guiding questions as a resource for developing your own unit. Or use one of the two blank templates in the chapter and start fresh.

Chapter 2 includes suggestions and specific examples for crafting a preassessment and a performance assessment task aligned to narrative writing. In addition, I offer a narrative checklist and rubric to use during instruction that you can adapt for your teaching purposes; the latter is also used to score the final writing piece. Since presenting the checklist or rubric is critical to setting clear expectations, I share strategies for introducing and using these tools with students. The chapter also features grading suggestions.

In chapter 3, you will find a detailed example for teaching students how to write a setting with imagery using the components of the gradual release of responsibility design model. It includes the step-by-step sequence and student materials so you can conduct the lesson.

Chapter 4 focuses on strategies, resources, activities, and assessments specific to teaching skills related to narrative. You can use what this chapter features to redesign or build your own lessons—for example, learning experiences related to writing plot, theme, introductions for narratives, dialogue, and more.

Because reading and writing are intrinsically linked, chapter 5 features various strategies for teaching students to analyze complex narrative text and demonstrate understanding of it. Additionally, it includes ideas for students to study an author's craft as a vehicle to make their own writing more effective.

Once you complete your narrative writing unit, it is time to pilot it and note what worked and what didn't. In this book's epilogue I suggest closing exercises.

As discussed in the previous section, appendices A, B, and C offer a thorough overview of narrative and descriptive text types, elements of literature, and literary devices and figurative language with literary examples respectively should you need more in-depth information. If not, you may bypass these sections or perhaps skim them to find and incorporate any of the material in lessons you devise. If you need a technical overview of dependent clauses and complex sentences to accompany a lesson in chapter 4 on sentence structure, read appendix D.

Next, appendix E lists a compilation of resources for you and your students that I have divided into sections for easy access. This list is a reference for many resources that I mention throughout the book, as well as additional ones you might find useful. As a reminder, the foundational book in the series, *The Fundamentals of (Re)designing Writing Units* (Glass, 2017a), lists general offerings and a comprehensive array of electronic tools and applications.

Finally, appendix F lists figures and tables for templates, checklists, rubrics, student activities, and more. Visit **go.SolutionTree.com/literacy** to access these free resources, which you can use to design your narrative unit and conduct lessons.

Building a Narrative Unit Map

This chapter shows a narrative unit map example that features learning outcomes, specifically what you want students to know, understand, and do (KUD), along with guiding questions to frame your units and lessons. These components represent the beginning stage of backward planning. When you reach the exercise later in this chapter, you may download the featured narrative map (visit **go.SolutionTree.com/literacy**) and make revisions, or refer to it as a guide to develop your own map using the blank unit templates. As you read this book, each chapter will provide resources you can use to continue building this map and begin drafting lessons for the narrative genre you will teach. As mentioned in the introduction, should you need background information on narrative writing and what it entails—or perhaps want material to use within lesson planning—refer to appendices A, B, and C on pages 123–148.

To understand the map and the design process, you need to be familiar with backward planning. If this approach falls outside your knowledge and experience and the following section does not provide you with enough information, please consider reading *The Fundamentals of (Re)designing Writing Units* (Glass, 2017a), which covers each component of backward design in detail, along with examples to illustrate aspects of this approach.

A Review of Backward Design

As a brief review, *backward design* (Wiggins & McTighe, 2005) means that you initiate planning your unit (or lesson or course) by reviewing and grouping pertinent content-area standards. Using these standards as a guide, you will identify learning outcomes (KUDs), craft guiding questions, and determine a culminating assessment with success criteria, specifically a checklist and rubric. You can use analytic rubrics and checklists as instructional tools; the former serves as a scoring mechanism as well.

Developing KUDs and guiding questions allows you to determine learning outcomes based on the content standards your state, district, or province expects you to implement. These components provide clarity and direction for determining evidence of learning and then planning meaningful, effective lessons. In doing so, you can expressly construct and implement classroom experiences to meet the targeted goals that you have articulated in the KUDs. Figure 1.1 (page 8) details the components and a suggested sequence, from top to bottom, for developing your units guided by backward design. After identifying the content standards, though, you may change the order of how you develop KUDs from figure 1.1; just remember that designing lessons occurs after you articulate these overarching learning outcomes.

Group **Standards**
Use English language arts and pertinent content-area standards.

K (Know)
Identify **knowledge** items (factual and foundational).

U (Understand)
Craft essential or enduring **understandings**.

Develop unit- and lesson-**guiding questions**.

D (Do)
Cite skills to state what students will **do**.

Determine **culminating assessments** and **criteria** (rubric and checklist).

Develop differentiated **lessons** and other **assessments**.

Figure 1.1: Unit-planning components of backward design.

*Visit **go.SolutionTree.com/literacy** for a free reproducible version of this figure.*

The Role of Standards

A unit map is a guide for curriculum development that emanates from content standards. Since narrative writing is the focus, input grade-level literacy standards to support students in producing a genre within this text type. For example, table 1.1 shows examples of writing standards for grade 8 from the Common Core State Standards (CCSS; NGA & CCSSO, 2010), the Texas Essential Knowledge and Skills (TEKS; Texas Education Agency [TEA], 2010), and the Ontario Curriculum (Ontario Ministry of Education, 2006).

Some standards, like the first two entries in table 1.1, clearly specify narrative or aligned terminology; others, like the Ontario Curriculum (Ontario Ministry of Education, 2006), are open ended and rely on the teacher, school, or district to determine what the writing focus entails. You will also need to address other writing standards, such as those related to the writing process, development, coherence, style, and organization, as well as considering the task, purpose, and audience. Additionally, add key writing skills related to grammar and conventions that might appear under a strand or category other than writing.

In addition to narrative writing standards, target other literacy expectations, such as reading, listening, and speaking. Because students will read and examine many texts from published authors and students for a variety of purposes, it is imperative to target standards related to these other strands. Furthermore, if you teach a core or humanities class that combines language arts and history, you might ask students to integrate the two. For example, students can demonstrate understanding of what they have read and learned about the events, places, and individuals of a particular time period by writing historical fiction. Or they can compose a myth that represents cultural values of a specific civilization. If this resonates with you as a viable and effective direction for your unit, incorporate relevant history and social studies standards too. Inputting a combination of all applicable standards—literacy and subject specific—will serve to guide you as you design the key learning outcomes and the culminating assessment, which then focuses your lesson design.

If you do not know the content that you are expected to teach well enough, or the standards do not supply enough information (which is often the case), conduct research to increase your own professional expertise. To do so, rely on multiple references, such as textbooks that span different grades. These could include college-level texts and materials, online resources, and colleagues who are more experienced in the area. Additionally, find anchor papers and examine published and student writing samples that exemplify excellence so that you operate under correct assumptions about the quality of writing your students should attain. If you are unsure, ask informed colleagues.

Next, you can preview examples of narrative unit maps as you begin to consider what kind of map to create for driving effective curriculum design.

Table 1.1: Sample Grade 8 Excerpts of Writing Standards

Source	Sample Grade 8 Writing Standards
CCSS (NGA & CCSSO, 2010)	**W.8.3:** Write narratives to develop real or imagined experiences or events using effective technique, well-chosen details, and well-structured event sequences. a. Engage and orient the reader by establishing a context and point of view and introducing a narrator and/or characters; organize an event sequence that unfolds naturally and logically. b. Use narrative techniques, such as dialogue, pacing, description, and reflection, to develop experiences, events, and/or characters. c. Use a variety of transition words, phrases, and clauses to convey sequence, signal shifts from one time frame or setting to another, and show the relationships among experiences and events.
TEKS (TEA, 2010)	(15) **Writing/Literary Texts.** Students write literary texts to express their ideas and feelings about real or imagined people, events, and ideas. Students are expected to: (A) write an imaginative story that: (i) sustains reader interest; (ii) includes well-paced action and an engaging story line; (iii) creates a specific, believable setting created through the use of sensory details; (iv) develops interesting characters; and (v) uses a range of literary strategies and devices to enhance the style and tone. (16) **Writing.** Students write about their own experiences. Students are expected to write a personal narrative that has a clearly defined focus and includes reflections on decisions, actions, and/or consequences.
Ontario Curriculum (Ontario Ministry of Education, 2006)	**Form** 2.1 write **complex texts** of a variety of lengths using a wide range of forms (e.g., a memoir of a significant Canadian; a report comparing the economies of two nations and explaining how a new industry might affect each nation's economy; briefing notes for an oral debate outlining both sides of an argument, including appeals to both logic and emotion; a narrative in the style of a particular author, adding to or extending a text by that author; an original satirical, science-fiction, or realistic fiction piece modelled on the structures and conventions of the genre; a free verse or narrative poem, or a limerick)

Narrative Unit Map Examples

This section features two versions of unit map resources to examine. Later you can begin building your own map using the end-of-chapter exercise to guide you. At that time, you can select your preferred version and use items in the samples I provide as you see fit as well as augment your own entries.

To orient you to these resources, table 1.2 (pages 11–17) represents one format; tables 1.3 and 1.4 (pages 18–19) reflect a different one. Both include components for the beginning stages of backward planning aligned to narrative, such as elements of literature (setting, character, plot, and so forth), figurative language, and some literary devices (for example, dialect, mood, and suspense). However, tables 1.3 and 1.4 (pages 18–19) each show unit map excerpts that include activity ideas, resources to teach the unit, and formative assessment evidence. Sometimes when designing maps, lesson ideas surface; therefore, the format in these tables includes cells to record them. To conduct some lessons, what you record might be enough to lead effective instruction. For teaching new material, though, you can take what you input to later develop into more robust lessons. (See chapter 4 for a discussion about the gradual release of responsibility lesson design approach.) Some of you, though, may not prefer this granular level of detail for a unit map and will design one like the example in table 1.2 (pages 11–17). When reviewing this version and thinking about how you might use it to devise your map, consider these points.

- Although table 1.2 seems comprehensive and complete, you will find that adaptations, deletions, and additions will be necessary based on key factors, such as your targeted genre, content-area standards, the complex text or texts at the center of instruction, student population and characteristics, and other variables—even your teaching style. Your English language arts (ELA) standards will indicate items to add: specific literary devices (irony, foreshadowing, and satire, for example), grammar skills (like active versus passive voice), or sentence structure areas (such as parallelism or compound-complex sentences). In addition, you will likely include English language development or English learning expectations, and perhaps content-area standards if you teach and incorporate disciplines other than ELA for this narrative unit.

- The compilation of items serves as options for your unit, so you'll select those that align to your learning outcomes. For example, you may not need every row I include or you might combine some like setting with imagery and revise accordingly. For each targeted area (for example, character, theme, or dialogue), perhaps choose one essential understanding or wordsmith to combine two, plus use some of the knowledge items instead of all bullet points.

- For lesson-guiding questions and skills, select those that address your students' needs and the outcomes or revise them. Some appeal to reading—as students examine texts—and also guide students' writing. For example, these questions and skills are geared to reading: *How do readers determine a story's narrator and point of view? Identify a narrative's point of view and analyze how it impacts the work and readers' perceptions.* And these for writing: *Who will be the narrator for my story? What point of view will I use? Introduce a narrator and establish a point of view.* I typically enter reading first, followed by writing as students initially examine text and then apply what they learn to their own writing. Alternatively, you can separate reading and writing into their own columns or add subheadings within a column, as you wish.

Return to this section when you begin drafting your unit map to take into full account these points along with the others mentioned later in the chapter.

Before generating a map to develop your unit, there are some matters regarding the unit as a whole to consider, which I detail in the following sections. One involves the unit's organizational structure and another concerns existing resources at your disposal. I also suggest that students keep a notebook (referenced in tables 1.3 and 1.4) throughout the unit and beyond to support their learning.

Narrative Unit Approach

A well-choreographed unit exemplifies commitment to your craft. Your dedication to detailing what matters most in the unit will yield dividends in organizing your teaching, targeting goals along the way, and contributing to student achievement. When you aptly prepare for curriculum design, your teaching will go more smoothly and you will position your students to progress in their learning. A unit map serves this purpose. It guides you in lesson design based on learning outcomes and indicates the sequence of lessons to reflect how the whole unit will flow. For example, at the outset it is prudent to issue one or more preassessments, which I discuss in chapter 2 (page 29) along with examples. Follow the preassessment with a launch lesson to orient students to the characteristic elements of the targeted genre at the center of instruction and to introduce the expectations for their narrative writing task. (You can find details for leading this lesson in the section (Re)design a Narrative Writing Checklist in chapter 2 on page 32.) After conducting a preassessment and initiating the unit, consider continuing in one of two ways.

1. Conduct a lesson on a narrative topic or related topics—for example, setting and imagery or plot with suspense. Then allow students time to produce a graphic organizer or draft of a paragraph based on the lesson focus for their own narratives. They collect this work in a folder or electronically. Conduct another lesson focused on a topic and again give time for students to draft something for their own narratives and add it to their ongoing collection. Repeat this sequence. Later, they use these prewriting pieces to compose their first drafts.

Table 1.2: Narrative Writing Unit Map Item Options—KUDs and Guiding Questions

Standards-Based Items	Knowledge	Essential Understandings	Skills	Unit-Guiding Question	Lesson-Guiding Questions
Narrator and Point of View	• Role of and choices for narrator • Pronouns and points of view: first-, second-, and third-person limited, as well as third-person omniscient • How point of view impacts narrative • Literary devices connected to point of view: satire, irony, or sarcasm	• The narrator and point of view a writer selects help to shape the plot and influence readers' perspectives. • Writers can employ multiple points of view to juxtapose perceptions of different characters and their experiences.	• Identify a narrative's point of view and analyze how it impacts the work. • Introduce the narrator. • Establish point of view. • Write from a consistent point of view.	How does the narrator's point of view impact a text?	• How do readers determine a story's narrator and point of view? • Which narrative genres dictate a point of view? How so? • How does point of view shape readers' perceptions? • How do narrators use their point of view to create satire, sarcasm, or irony? • Who will be the narrator for my story? What point of view will I use?
Setting	• Definition and types of settings • Impact setting has on other elements of literature	• Setting provides a backdrop that can convey mood and significantly influence other aspects of a narrative.	• Use textual evidence about setting to identify mood. • Determine cause-and-effect relationships between setting and its impact on plot and character. • Create a setting for a narrative that evokes mood.	How do authors invent settings?	• Besides time and place, what are other ways writers indicate setting? • How do writers use setting to convey mood? • What are ways that setting plays an important role in a narrative? • What is an appropriate setting for my narrative?

continued ▲

Standards-Based Items	Knowledge	Essential Understandings	Skills	Unit-Guiding Question	Lesson-Guiding Questions
Character and Characterization	• Direct and indirect methods of characterization—what a character says, looks like, thinks and feels, and does; what others say about the character • Different types of characters—antagonist, protagonist, dynamic, static, round, flat, stock, and so forth	• Writers interweave methods of characterization that readers use to make inferences about characters' motives, beliefs, and actions. • Readers make inferences by accumulating and analyzing information about characters through the author's use of characterization.	• Analyze character types. • Critique how authors create multilayered characters through indirect and direct methods of characterization. • Use methods of characterization to invent characters for a narrative.	How do writers develop characters?	• What are different types of characters in a narrative? How are their roles distinctive from one another? • What are the methods of characterization? What can I infer about characters based on an author's use of characterization? • How do writers decide on characters for their narratives? • How can I use methods of characterization to invent realistic and complex characters?
Character and Plot	Character and characterization knowledge, plus: • Plot elements • Interconnection between characters and plot • Contributing factors that lead to a change in dynamic characters	• Characters' traits, motivations, or feelings drive their actions and contribute to plot development. • Characters can change and evolve through interactions with others, personal experiences, and their environment, which can shape the plot.	• Analyze the cause-and-effect connection between character development and plot, including how conflicts affect characters. • Cite textual evidence to support a character's change throughout time. • Use textual evidence to make inferences about characters; identify their traits.	How do characters contribute to plot development?	• What traits describe characters in the narrative? • What evidence supports these traits? • How and why do characters change? How can these changes impact the plot? • How do characters' traits, actions, or feelings move the plot forward?

Historical Setting, Character, and Plot	Character and characterization and character and plot knowledge, plus: • Interconnection among setting, character, and plot • Characteristic elements of historical fiction	• The culture and circumstances of a historical era influence characters' motivations, perspectives, and actions, which ultimately impact the plot. • Writers reveal the political and social tensions of a historical era through characters' interactions, thoughts, and beliefs within the context of the setting. • Historical fiction authors conduct research to create vivid, historically accurate characters and settings depicting life in a given era to compel readers to gain deeper meaning about that time period.	• Use textual evidence to identify a narrative's historical context. • Use context clues to acquire meaning of historical references. • Compare characters' motivations and reactions to historical settings. • Research to collect historical facts about a specific time period. • Write historical fiction that satisfies criteria.	How does historical setting influence aspects of a narrative?	• How do readers detect that a narrative is historical fiction? What are the characteristic elements of this genre? • How does the writing reflect the attitudes and beliefs of people of this era? • What historically accurate details do writers incorporate into their stories? What resources can they use? • How can I write an effective historical fiction story? What resources can I use to collect information?
Plot Sequence and Suspense	• That plot is one of the five elements of literature • Plot elements—introduction, central conflict, rising action, climax, falling action, and resolution • Basic plot diagram • Logical event sequence • Literary devices connected to the plot, such as suspense, multiple plotlines, flashbacks, and flash forward	• To make their work compelling, authors intentionally structure their narratives, sequence the events within them, create suspense, and manipulate time for a desired effect. • Authors organize a well-paced and logical event sequence and present plot elements in a dynamic and sometimes complex way to engage and intrigue readers.	• Identify plot elements. • Critique the way plot elements follow a sequence and advance the action. • Compare and critique authors' treatment of suspense and other literary devices associated with plot. • Develop a narrative plot; include suspense that adds intrigue and tension.	• How do writers develop a compelling plot?	• What are plot elements and examples of each element? • What is a basic plot structure and text examples? What are variations to it? • How do authors sequence significant events to facilitate understanding? • How does cause-and-effect work in a narrative? How does the author address and resolve conflicts? • How do writers create suspense effectively? • Why and how might writers create multiple plotlines, flashbacks, or flash forward? • How do I create a compelling plot for my narrative?

continued ▶

Standards-Based Items	Knowledge	Essential Understandings	Skills	Unit-Guiding Question	Lesson-Guiding Questions
Narrative Introduction	• Narrative introductory elements—narrator, characters, setting, and central conflict • Internal and external conflict	• An effective narrative introduction provides context by establishing the narrator, introducing characters and setting, and presenting a central conflict that sets the story in motion all in an engaging way. • An internal or external central conflict creates the foundation for a storyline that authors seek to develop in a compelling way.	• Critique narrative introductions using textual evidence to assess strengths and weaknesses. • Differentiate internal from external conflict. • Draft a narrative introduction based on criteria in a rubric.	How do authors engage readers from the beginning?	• What components does the author include in an introduction? • What makes an introduction engaging? • How does knowing the characteristics of a genre help writers compose an introduction? • What are different types of central conflicts? How can authors use characters' defects to establish a central conflict? • What central conflict can I use as the basis for my narrative? How can I write a strong introduction?
Theme	• That *theme* is one of the five elements of literature • Definition and examples of *theme*; universal themes • Motif: recurring concept, idea, object, emotion that helps to develop a theme; examples of motif • Textual evidence that supports theme within one text and across many texts	• Writers develop a theme over the course of a narrative to illustrate universal truths about human behavior. • Many works of literature share common themes, which readers can compare to glean deeper understandings of each text. • Writers determine a theme and plant evidence throughout their work to support it using motifs, characters' actions or thoughts, interactions with other characters, or the influence of setting.	• Analyze the development of theme over the course of the text. • Compare and contrast themes across different texts. • Cite evidence to support motif and themes. • Identify a theme and use it as the basis for developing a narrative.	How do authors develop their narratives based on a theme?	• What are themes? What are motifs? What is the connection between the two? • How does textual evidence support a theme? • What texts share similar themes? How so? • How can a narrative's theme mirror human behavior or life? • How can writers identify a theme as the basis for their work? How will this help them develop their narratives?

continued ▲

Dialogue and Dialect	• Purpose and function of dialogue • Meaningful versus superfluous dialogue • Dialect definition, examples, and purpose	• Writers can use dialogue to develop experiences and events and to show characters' responses to situations. • Dialogue helps readers better understand characters and their motivations, and it moves the plot forward. • Writers employ dialect to highlight cultural milieu and establish characters in a particular setting.	• Discern strong from weak dialogue using criteria. • Cite textual evidence of how dialogue and dialect help to develop characters and further the plot. • Interpret and analyze dialogue and dialect. • Write purposeful dialogue to develop a narrative.	How do dialogue and dialect enhance a narrative?	• Why do writers include dialogue? How does it impact the text? • What does dialect reveal? Can it be misleading? • How can I include meaningful dialogue with dialect in my story?
Dialogue Punctuation	• Punctuation and capitalization rules for dialogue or speaker tags • Types of dialogue or speaker tags—beginning, middle, end, or no tag	• Writers employ proper usage of grammar and conventions to support readers in fluidly moving through their work to clearly decipher the text.	• Use proper dialogue mechanics.	Why and how do writers adhere to proper grammar and conventions?	• What are different types of dialogue tags? • What are the rules for dialogue punctuation and capitalization for each type?
Descriptive Words and Figurative Language	• Types, definitions, and examples of figurative language—simile, metaphor, imagery, personification, and hyperbole • Descriptive words and nuances of words • Purpose of figurative language and its intended effect • Inferences and multiple meanings • Tone and mood definition and examples	• Writers select descriptive words and infuse figurative language to enhance visualization, provide fresh insights, and emphasize key passages to enable readers to deepen comprehension. • Authors invent figurative language to create vivid settings, characters, and events that compel readers to connect viscerally with the text and gain deeper meaning. • Imagery can evoke mental pictures and emotional and physical responses in readers, thus adding depth and dimension to an author's work.	• Locate and give examples of description and figurative language. • Interpret and make inferences from figurative language. • Write settings, characters, or events using descriptive words and figurative language.	• How can word choice and figurative language enhance narratives? (Or, Why and how do authors use types of figurative language?)	• What are the different types of imagery and examples for each type? • Why do authors use a particular type of figurative language? What is its impact on the text? • How can readers interpret figurative language and make inferences from it? • How do writers use word choice to develop tone and elicit a mood? • How can I use descriptive words and figurative language to vividly describe settings, characters, or events?

Standards-Based Items	Knowledge	Essential Understandings	Skills	Unit-Guiding Question	Lesson-Guiding Questions
Vocabulary	• Online and print resources for learning new words • Context clues—word parts, definition, explanation, synonym, antonym, example, analogy; grammar construction of appositive • Nuances and meanings • Ways to use new words and synonyms to avoid redundancy	• Authors use precise vocabulary to deepen meaning and convey ideas.	• Use context clues to determine meanings of new words. • Define and articulate nuances of vocabulary. • Use precise words in narrative writing to clearly articulate ideas. • Incorporate new words in narrative; use synonyms to avoid redundancies.	How do writers use words effectively?	• How do writers learn and use new words? • How can precise words make writing more effective? • What are different context clues? How do readers use them to define unknown words? • What words can I use in my story to make it stronger? What synonyms should I use to avoid repeating the same words?
Sentence Beginnings	• Options for beginning sentences—adjectives, prepositional phrases, dependent clauses, subject, or other ways • Purposes and ways for varying sentence beginnings	• Writers conscientiously craft sentences with various beginnings to create cadence, indicate sequence, and transition between ideas, time, and place.	• Identify and critique different ways sentences begin from various writing samples. • Articulate purpose and function of sentence beginning variety. • Write sentences with varied beginnings.	Why and how do writers vary their sentence beginnings?	• What are options for beginning sentences in different ways? • How does the variety of sentence beginnings impact writing? • How can I effectively use sentence beginning variety in my narrative?
Sentence Structure	• Various types of sentences: simple, compound, complex, compound-complex • Construction of sentences • Independent and dependent clauses • Phrases versus clauses • Subordinating and coordinating conjunctions • Parts of a dependent (adverbial) clause: subordinating conjunction, subject, verb	• Writers elect to vary their sentence structure by types and lengths to convey meaning and enhance rhythm, fluidity, and reader interest.	• Compare and contrast types of sentence structures; analyze their usages. • Deconstruct sentences and identify their parts. • Write using varied structures for express purposes.	Why and how do writers use different sentence structures?	• What are different sentence structures? • How do I construct sentences in different ways to achieve intended purposes?

			Why and how do writers use the writing process?	What are the stages of the writing process? How does each stage help to develop and shape the narrative? What does prewriting involve? Why might writers revisit this stage later in the process? At what point do writers create a first draft? How do they solicit and use input from others to revise for subsequent drafts? How do writers edit their work so it is free of errors? How do the rules of writing mechanics and grammar usage facilitate communication? What resources can writers use to edit? How do writers choose what part of their writing needs revision? What are revisionary options and how can writers go about making changes? In what ways can writers publish their narratives? Who are different audiences they might address? How can writers reflect on themselves as writers, collaborators, and researchers and use what they learn for future projects?
Writing Process (See Glass, 2017a)	• Stages in the writing process—prewriting, drafting, revising, editing, publishing, and reflecting • Purpose of implementing the writing process • Options, tools, and resources for each stage related to a writing task and genre	• To produce an optimal final product, students move through the writing process with a clear sense of criteria prior to writing and synthesize all they have learned into their final work. • Writers implement a writing process to systematically improve on each step in writing to ultimately produce their best work. • The process of effective writing requires planning and revising to improve organization, clarity, and detail. • Knowledge and application of standard English grammar usage and mechanics enables writers to communicate more articulately and precisely.	• Develop and strengthen writing using the skills embedded in the writing process—prewrite, draft, revise, edit, publish, and reflect.	

Visit go.SolutionTree.com/literacy for a free reproducible version of this table.

Table 1.3: Detailed Unit Map Excerpt—ELA

Unit: Narrative—The Art of Entertainment		**Unit Time Frame:** Five to six weeks; mid-April to end of May	
Subject: Language arts	**Grade:** Middle school	**Lesson Timing:** Approximately two fifty-minute class periods	

Essential Understanding: Authors use imagery to create vivid settings, characters, and events that compel readers to connect viscerally with the text and gain deeper meaning.

Unit-Guiding Question: How do authors develop descriptive settings?

Imagery and Setting	**Lesson-Guiding Questions**	**L* 1:** What are different types of settings?	**L 2:** How do authors use setting to elicit a mood?
	Knowledge	• Types and ways to express setting	• Definition and examples of mood • Ways authors elicit mood through setting descriptions
	Skills	• Cite textual evidence of various types of settings.	• Draft setting that elicits a mood.

	Activity Ideas	1. **Generate a text-specific list of settings:** Student groups review a complex text and highlight or use sticky notes to indicate passages that include settings. Then they report out to compile a class-generated list.
		
		2. **Categorize list:** Facilitate an activity where students categorize the class list of setting items. If students' lists are not comprehensive, instruct them to return to the text and find other examples where the author writes about setting, specifically:
		  • *Places* (anything someone can sit or stand in, like inside a house or an airplane, or on a road, playground, football field, or roller coaster)
		  • *Location* (such as a planet, universe, country, city, state, or county)
		  • *Time periods* (a clock reading, day, month, year, or century)
		  • *Climate*, *weather*, *season*, and *natural surroundings*
		
		3. **Define setting:** Students review the class-generated list. Together, arrive at a consensus for a definition of *setting* and its attributes to record in their notebooks.
			1. **Identify mood based on setting:** Explain that mood is the emotion readers feel while reading. Authors can create a mood by the way they describe settings. Students return to the text passages that contain settings and identify words and phrases that elicit mood and name the mood. For example, they might identify a setting to be eerie, serene, or frenetic. Ask them to record in their notebooks any words and phrases that elicit mood that impressed them to consider for their own writing.
			
			2. **Find other examples:** Students return to the same class complex text or another one. Ask them to circle or highlight examples of setting that elicit a mood. In the margin, they write the mood they evoke and share their responses with others.
			
			3. **Draft a setting with mood:** Students draft a setting for their narrative to elicit a mood. They exchange their paragraphs with a classmate who reads the draft and determines what mood the student writer intended to evoke and cites textual evidence to support the assertion. The pair discuss if more detail is needed to help readers arrive at a mood and together revise, as needed.

	Resources	• Classroom complex text • Student journals or notebooks	• Classroom complex text • Student journals or notebooks
	Formative Assessment Evidence	• Participation in group and whole-class activities • Notebook entries of setting definition and attributes	• Participation in discussion and partner activity • Notebook entries of words and phrases that evoke mood • Draft of setting that evokes mood

* L = Lesson

Table 1.4: Detailed Unit Map Excerpt—Interdisciplinary ELA and History

Unit: Historical Fiction—Stories About the Past		**Unit Time Frame:** Four to five weeks	

Subject: ELA and history	**Grade:** Upper elementary or middle school	**Lesson Timing:** Approximately three fifty-minute class periods

Essential Understanding: Writers of historical fiction use dialect to capture realistic exchanges between characters in a particular historical era to reveal culture, social status, country of origin, or other information.

Unit-Guiding Question: How do historical fiction authors use dialect to reveal information about characters and setting?

Historical Fiction	**Lesson-Guiding Questions**	**L* 1:** What can dialogue with dialect reveal about historical fiction?	**L 2:** What were the beliefs, customs, and way of life of people living during this time?	**L 3:** How can I use dialect effectively in my historical fiction?
	Knowledge	• Indicators of historical fiction • Definitions and examples of dialogue and dialect	• Aspects of a particular period in history—beliefs, customs, lifestyle, religion, government, economy, family life, and so forth	• Purpose of dialogue and dialect
	Skills	• Cite textual evidence of dialogue with dialect in complex narrative text and use it to analyze characters and make inferences. • Rewrite dialect into standard English.	• Research a historical time period and cull key details.	• Write dialogue with dialect to reflect a historical time period.
	Activity Ideas	1. **Identify dialect:** Find examples of dialogue from historical fiction text. Ask students to circle words and phrases that answer this question: What part of the dialogue reveals clues about a historical era? 2. **Infer from dialect:** Explain that dialect reflects the language characters use. It can indicate characters' country or regional origin, era or century, gender, culture, race, and social standing or group. Ask students to review what they circled and identify what the dialect reveals about characters. 3. **Rewrite into modern language:** Assign different dialogue passages to a student pair that contains dialect. Ask them to discuss the passages and make inferences, and then rewrite their assigned excerpts into standard modern English to demonstrate understanding of the text passages. Students share what they wrote with another partner set and evaluate if each other's translations follow the intent of the author.	1. **Participate in jigsaw activity—Part 1:** Assign each student group a different question about the text's historical time period. Provide resources for them to read and use as the basis for their responses so they become experts on this topic. Tell them to take notes; explain that they will teach others about their topic. Choose from among these or other research questions: What were the political, social, and economic conditions? What was the government and political structure? Was it a thriving economy or not and what attributed to this condition? What geographic features surrounded them? What natural resources did they have and how did they use them? What was family life like? What did they do for entertainment? What kind of transportation did they use? Was one religion dominant, and if so, which one? 2. **Participate in jigsaw activity—Part 2:** When students finish note taking, each group disbands and forms a new group comprising one member from each original group. Students share what they learned about their assigned question to teach others. Classmates take notes on what they learn.	1. **Review dialogue:** Reiterate the purposes of dialogue—to reveal information about characters, move the plot forward, and so forth. 2. **Generate ideas for dialogue:** Ask student partners to review their notes on the historical time period and think about a conversation that two characters would have in this era. Have them share their ideas concerning the purpose for their dialogue with the class. 3. **Use dialogue with dialect:** Partners agree on a situation for an exchange of dialogue, and then draft a passage that includes realistic dialect from that period and a conversation the two would plausibly have. Pairs can share their dialogue with another partnership or with the class.
	Resources	• Text excerpts of historical fiction that include dialect within the dialogue	• Various resources about different topics associated with a historical time period	• Research notes about the historical time period
	Formative Assessment Evidence	• Participation in discussion • Rewritten dialogue	• Participation in group discussions • Research notes	• Draft of dialogue with dialect

* L = Lesson

2. In another approach, lead a series of lessons in succession that introduce all the literary elements, devices, and forms of figurative language. When students prewrite and compose their first draft, they take everything they learned into account and apply it wholesale for their narratives.

Your map should reflect these decisions since it catalogs not only the order for teaching skills to sequence the unit but also the approach for how to write a narrative. The first approach can assist students who are fairly new to narrative writing or less experienced writers because it gives them a place to start their first drafts by accessing various existing prewriting tools they've accumulated throughout the unit as opposed to a blank slate. Students might decide to scrap or completely change any accumulated work when they finally begin the first draft, but at least they have some material to begin the writing process. Either path, however, can produce the same results provided that you devote the necessary time and energy to map out a sound unit and teach effectively.

Consideration of Existing Resources

As you develop your map, scrutinize your existing resources to choose materials that match what you want students to know, understand, and do. To accomplish this goal, review your textbook or other resources carefully if you have not already, and intentionally find the parts that serve the goals of the narrative unit you are building. If you use a textbook or other curriculum, you might change the order of what a writer or publisher thinks is the best sequence and take charge of how you want to teach the unit based on your expertise and preference. For example, you could decide to focus on setting before characters, which might contradict the table of contents in a literature textbook you use.

To determine which texts you will use to teach standards-based skills, scour the resources at your disposal (anthology, textbook, or other materials). Identify which complex texts complement your unit and aptly exemplify what you will teach—elements of literature, literary devices, figurative language, writing style, and so forth. If you use the more detailed unit map (tables 1.3 and 1.4, pages 18–19), record the text resources with page numbers to prime yourself for the lesson design phase. If you use the less comprehensive map (table 1.2,

pages 11–17), consider adding a column for resources or jotting them down on a separate document. By undertaking this exercise, you familiarize yourself with the available resources and prepare for devising your own lessons or revising what the teacher's guide might offer.

Although publishers propose certain elements or devices tied to a story, you are the final arbiter of this decision. For illustrative purposes, I vetted a literature textbook for grade 8 and highlight my findings for two selections: Walter Dean Myers's (1997) "The Treasure of Lemon Brown" and W. W. Jacobs's (1997) "The Monkey's Paw."

"The Treasure of Lemon Brown"

I concur with the publisher's recommendation that character portrayal plays a key role in Walter Dean Myers's (1997) "The Treasure of Lemon Brown." However, setting also deserves attention and warrants students' keen examination, which is not a focus in the teacher's guide. The following quotes supply evidence for the setting's prominence in the story where Myers uses figurative language to describe how this element contributes to the mood.

*   "The dark sky, filled with angry swirling clouds, reflected Greg Ridley's mood as he sat on the stoop of his building" (p. T94).
*   "It was beginning to cool. Gusts of wind made bits of paper dance between the parked cars" (p. T94).
*   "He reached the house just as another flash of lightning changed the night to day for an instant, then returned the graffiti-scarred building to the grim shadows. . . . The inside of the building was dark except for the dim light that filtered through the dirty windows from the street lamps" (p. T95).
*   "There was a footstep on the stairs, and the beam from the flashlight danced crazily along the peeling wallpaper" (p. T99).

Therefore, when perusing textbooks, use your professional judgment and learning outcomes to determine aspects of narrative worthy to target as a teaching focus.

"The Monkey's Paw"

In W. W. Jacobs's (1997) "The Monkey's Paw," the publisher aptly highlights suspense and irony. Like the short story previously mentioned, this text is also ripe for exploring the setting and the mood it creates. These excerpts and others within the story can testify to this.

- "Without, the night was cold and wet, but in the small parlor of the Lakesnam Villa the blinds were drawn and the fire burned brightly." (p. T185)

- "'That's the worst of living so far out,' bawled Mr. White, with sudden and unlooked-for violence; 'of all the beastly, slushy, out-of-the-way places to live in, this is the worst. Pathway's a bog, and the road's a torrent.'" (p. T186)

Both of these stories appear within the same literature textbook about one hundred pages apart. Since they both exemplify an author's use of setting to create mood, I would expose students to each story in succession to illustrate this element and literary device. Additionally, juxtaposing the authors' treatment of language to create different moods would prompt worthwhile analysis. By carefully perusing the entire offerings of complex text in any resource—textbook, anthology, prepackaged curriculum—you can devise a unit map and develop lessons that might prove more effective than if you rely solely on the publisher as the guide instead of your own professionalism.

Student Notebook

Throughout the unit, students will expand their writing capabilities in all sorts of ways as they acquire new skills, processes, strategies, vocabulary, content knowledge, and so forth. To capitalize on their ongoing learning, ask them to create an individual writing resource notebook either in a hard-copy format or electronically, or a combination of both. In it, they can store and continually build on their continuing knowledge base around writing. They can refer to their notebooks—and share them with others—as they write all year long. Students can divide this resource in sections such as these.

- **Vocabulary lists:** As they read salient passages from complex text, students record words and add to their lists consistently. They don't just study words for a particular unit and then leave them behind. Rather, they repeatedly reinforce and use vocabulary to increase their inventory. For each word, they provide examples, explanations, definitions, parts of speech, and nonlinguistic representations (such as illustrations or symbols). To help make

these words part of their lexicon, students should continually use them; therefore, teachers encourage them to access this section and use selected vocabulary in their writing. They can organize the vocabulary section into subsections by parts of speech or by types of words (for example, alternatives to the word *said*; words for personality traits [like *courageous*, *innovative*, *resourceful*, and *selfless*]; and sensory words). If students create an electronic notebook, they can categorize words easily and also keep them in alphabetical order.

- **Genres:** Students can dedicate a section of their notebooks to what they learn about the different writing genres and the unique characteristics of each. They can insert checklists and rubrics that align to specific genres and include exemplary writing samples. These can be their own examples as well as other students' or published ones.

- **Elements of literature:** When you orient students to the five elements of literature—(1) character, (2) setting, (3) plot, (4) point of view, and (5) theme—they will accumulate various handouts and sample excerpts from complex texts that exemplify each element or a combination of them. Instruct students to store anything related to this topic in this section. They can indicate in their binders any overlap with the figurative language section.

- **Figurative language:** Students include definitions and passages of simile, metaphor, personification, hyperbole, and imagery from various authors' works they believe employ figurative language well. Additionally, they brainstorm their own examples to use at some point in their writing.

- **Grammar, conventions, and formatting:** This section consists of any grammar and conventions resources to assist students in creating pieces free of grammar, punctuation, spelling, and capitalization errors. It also includes style guidelines for formatting in-text citations and works cited documents from the Modern Language Association (MLA) or American Psychological Association (APA). Classroom or school directives for headings and other routine formatting expectations can be included, as well.

- **Bookmarks:** Students should keep electronic bookmarks on their devices for sites that support their writing, such as websites for vocabulary, resources for grammar or proper formatting like MLA or APA, glossaries of literary devices, sites that feature writing samples, and so forth.

When introducing the writing resource notebook, you might say something like this: "Throughout the year, I will expect you to keep a three-ring binder to use as a writing resource. I will check it periodically for organization, completeness, and accuracy. Put tabs in your notebook and divide it into these sections: [insert the sections you wish them to include]. All year long, refer to it and add to it to help you become a more proficient writer."

When teaching pertinent lessons, encourage students to make and insert entries into this resource. For example, when you discuss allusion and the class generates a definition and finds examples in text, instruct students to record this information in their notebooks.

Exercise: Unit Map—KUDs and Guiding Questions

At this point, if you haven't already, target a unit of study around narrative. Start by creating or redesigning a standards-based unit map with any of the following approaches.

- **Option 1:** Access **go.SolutionTree.com/literacy** and download table 1.2 (pages 11–17) for ELA. This option is for readers who want to select and adapt existing KUDs and guiding questions, plus augment others as they see fit, to accommodate their teaching situation. (Review the points pertaining to this map under the section Narrative Unit Map Examples.)

- **Option 2:** Access **go.SolutionTree.com/literacy** and download figure 1.2, unit map template 1. This option is for readers who want to create a map from scratch that includes learning outcomes and is a blank version of table 1.2.

- **Option 3:** Access **go.SolutionTree.com/literac**y and download figure 1.3 (page 24). Those who want to build a more comprehensive map should use this template, which is based on tables 1.3 and 1.4 (pages 18–19). Revise this template appropriately as you work with it to accommodate the number of lessons your unit requires to align to each unit-guiding question.

Once you determine your template, read the Exercise Tips that follow. This will position you for starting your own customized unit map.

Exercise Tips

When working on the Unit Map—KUDs and Guiding Questions exercise, heed the following suggestions regarding standards, complex text, sequence, and language.

Standards

Content-area standards—whether national, state, provincial, or district—define goals and expectations that students should achieve by the end of the school year. They are not intended to serve as a curriculum, but rather guide unit and lesson design, which is precisely why you use them to develop your unit maps.

- Each line item on the map links to one standard or a combination of standards. You might combine those that make sense for what you are teaching; for example, connect setting with plot and characters, or setting with figurative language, and so forth.

- Weave content-area standards in with English language arts standards if you are teaching narrative writing in conjunction with another discipline. Tables 1.5 and 1.6 (pages 25–26) are excerpts from interdisciplinary unit maps. The former is a sample English language arts and history map and the latter combines English language arts and science.

continued ➤

Standards-Based Items	Knowledge	Essential Understandings	Skills	Unit-Guiding Question	Lesson-Guiding Questions
Narrator and Point of View					
Setting					
Character and Characterization					
Character and Plot					
Historical Setting, Character, and Plot					
Plot Sequence and Suspense					
Narrative Introduction					
Theme					
Dialogue and Dialect					
Dialogue Punctuation					
Descriptive Words and Figurative Language					
Vocabulary					
Sentence Beginnings					
Sentence Structure					
Writing Process					

Figure 1.2: Unit map blank template (option 1).

*Visit **go.SolutionTree.com/literacy** for a free reproducible version of this figure.*

Unit: _____	Unit Time Frame: _____
Subject: _____	Grade: _____	Lesson Timing: _____

Standard Focus:

Essential Understanding: _____

Unit-Guiding Question: _____

	Lesson _____:	Lesson _____:	Lesson _____:
Lesson-Guiding Questions			
Knowledge			
Skills			
Activity Ideas			
Resources			
Formative Assessment Evidence			

Figure 1.3: Unit map blank template (option 2).

*Visit **go.SolutionTree.com/literacy** for a free reproducible version of this figure.*

Complex Text

Although students produce a culminating written narrative, they will read plenty to examine complex text throughout the unit for a variety of purposes. Therefore, keep these pointers in mind.

- Consider the complex text or texts students will experience and their key elements, figurative language, and literary devices. Make sure the map reflects these aspects of the literature since students can perhaps emulate what they notice and study from authors' models.

- Additionally, you'll want to include learning outcomes about the content of the complex text itself if you are teaching it concurrent with students writing their narratives. See table 1.7 (page 27) for an excerpt of a unit pertaining to Charles Dickens's (1843) *A Christmas Carol* that focuses on key ideas of the text. The Knowledge column is omitted, but would contain factual and foundational information, such as political, economic, and social factors of the Victorian era, social status and acceptance, moral and ethical values, vocabulary associated with the text, relationships among characters, and so on.

- You might very well incorporate informational text in your unit, so account for this in your map. Even though students examine and produce narratives, there are opportunities for them to read informational text. For example, when they conduct research for a biography or historical fiction piece, they will delve into an array of informational text such as interviews, newspaper articles, or primary source documents.

continued ➤

Table 1.5: Interdisciplinary ELA and History Unit Map Excerpt—KUDs and Guiding Questions

Knowledge	Essential Understandings	Skills	Unit-Guiding Question	Lesson-Guiding Questions
• Geographical features and enemies of ancient Egyptian civilization • Map skills • Factors contributing to growth of Egypt	Geography can contribute to and fuel a civilization's growth by providing rich resources and a natural protection that inhibits enemy invasions.	• Cull information from complex text and make inferences. • Analyze the impact of geographical features on ancient Egyptian civilization.	1. How can geography impact a civilization?	• **L* 1.1:** What are the geographical features of ancient Egypt? • **L 1.2:** Why did people settle near the Nile River? • **L 1.3:** Who were their enemies and what did they want? • **L 1.4:** How did geographical features protect them and contribute to their growth?
• Credible sources for researching about ancient Egyptian geographical features	Historical fiction authors conduct research from multiple credible sources to ensure they embed sufficient, historically accurate facts into their narratives.	• Conduct research about ancient Egyptian geography and environment using multiple credible resources. • Write historically accurate narrative settings about ancient Egypt using imagery.	2. How can I search for accurate evidence to satisfy my task?	• **L 2.1:** Where can I go to find credible sources about ancient Egypt's geography? • **L 2.2:** What part of my research will I use to create historically accurate and compelling settings?
• Imagery definition and types • Realistic and historically accurate setting of ancient Egypt	Historical fiction authors use imagery to depict vivid, historically accurate settings that compel readers to visualize and gain deeper understanding about a given time period.	• Draft a factually accurate historical setting using imagery.	3. How does imagery impact historical fiction?	• **L 3.1:** What are types of imagery? • **L 3.2:** What is the benefit of using imagery for historical (or any) settings? • **L 3.3:** What are ancient Egyptian settings? How can I use imagery to vividly describe settings for my historical fiction?

* L = Lesson

Table 1.6: Interdisciplinary ELA and Science Unit Map Excerpt—KUDs and Guiding Questions

Knowledge	Essential Understandings	Skills	Unit-Guiding Question	Lesson-Guiding Questions
• Definition of an urban heat island: hot spot that is created when heat builds up in a city compared with nearby suburban and rural areas • Differences and reasons for varying temperatures in urban versus rural areas • Ways to reduce the heat island effect (such as trees, vegetation, roofs, and so on)	To improve a community's environment and quality of life, humans can actively reduce the adverse impact of atmospheric heat in urban areas.	• Compare and contrast temperatures in nearby suburban, rural, and urban areas. • Cull evidence from sources to determine the causes and effects of urban heat islands.	1. How can human activities impact the surface temperature of specific communities?	• **L* 1.1:** What is an urban heat island? What are the causes and effects of urban heat islands? • **L 1.2:** What makes urban areas hotter than rural and suburban areas? • **L 1.3:** How can communities reduce urban heat island effects?
• Changes of temperature on Earth since the early 20th century • Increase of atmospheric levels of greenhouse gases • Human activities that impact the rise in global temperatures • Positions on both sides of the global warming debate	Human activities, such as the release of greenhouse gases from burning fossil fuels, can contribute to the current rise in Earth's mean surface temperature (global warming).	• Collect and cite textual evidence to support a position about the global warming debate. • Cross-reference multiple credible sources.	2. How does human activity affect global climate change?	• **L 2.1:** What is global climate change? How does global climate change particularly affect urban areas? • **L 2.2:** What human activities are factors in the current rise of Earth's temperature? What changes can we make? • **L 2.3:** What claims do opponents and proponents of global warming make?
• Elements of science fiction and narrative techniques • A science or technology topic on which to speculate ("What if?" topic) and associated research • Types of figurative language	Science fiction authors speculate about what might happen to the world based on a dramatization of a science or technology topic to compel readers to consider alternatives and consequences of human actions.	• Write a science fiction piece adhering to the characteristic elements of this genre; use narrative techniques. • Incorporate science facts accurately within science fiction writing. • Use types of figurative language to engage readers.	3. How can science fiction compel readers to think about the consequences of human action or inaction?	• **L 3.1:** What are the characteristic elements of science fiction? Why is it an important genre? • **L 3.2:** What global warming topic can I address for my science fiction story? What is the *what if*? • **L 3.3:** How can I incorporate the research about this topic into my story to engage and educate readers? • **L 3.4:** Where and how can I use figurative language effectively?

*L = Lesson

Table 1.7: English Language Arts Map for *A Christmas Carol*— KUDs and Guiding Questions

Essential Understandings	Skills	Unit-Guiding Question	Lesson-Guiding Questions
• Societal, economic, and political aspects of historical eras influence a writer's perspective, which future generations can interpret in myriad ways. • A literary work can mirror the social and political climate in which an author lives, fostering analysis and insight about moral values, tolerance, and the human condition.	• Analyze the causes and effects of social, political, and economic situations during the Victorian era. • Identify moral values during the Victorian era and cite evidence. • Compare and justify characters' behaviors based on their beliefs and motives. • Categorize characters according to social status.	1. How do historical eras impact an author's work?	• **L* 1.1:** How did the Victorian era influence Dickens's writing? (Or, How did *A Christmas Carol* reflect the time in which he lived?) • **L 1.2:** How does the historical setting shape the plot and influence characters?
• Authors might produce literary works as a vehicle to expose oppressive societal conditions and issues.	• Cite evidence to reveal the theme of *A Christmas Carol*. • Make text-to-world connections. • Identify topics that reveal oppressive human conditions today and appropriate genres for communicating them.	2. How can authors use narrative writing as an influential tool?	• **L 2.2:** Why did Charles Dickens write *A Christmas Carol*? What message was he trying to convey? Was he successful? • **L 2.3:** How do authors use narrative writing as a vehicle for commentary? • **L 2.4:** Was Dickens's work controversial? In what way? How would (British or American) readers and critics perceive it if Dickens wrote it today? Is the theme still relevant (in England or America)?

*L = Lesson

Sequence and Language

The order of the line items on your map matters so be intentional in your placement of them.

- Organize the line items row by row in an explicit order to show the flow and sequence of how you will teach the unit. If you conduct interdisciplinary lessons, tables 1.5 and 1.6 can prove helpful. In these examples, students acquire and apply information—geography and global climate change, respectively—that they use in their narratives. They will undoubtedly complete assessments in the content areas but will further demonstrate their understanding by creating historical and science fiction narratives.

- Each unit question has a number to reflect a teaching sequence along with associated lesson-guiding questions that are even more specific—lesson 1.1, 1.2, or 1.3. Notice that the lesson-guiding questions, for example those in tables 1.2 (pages 11–17), 1.5 (page 25), 1.6, and 1.7, are situated from less complex to more sophisticated. Once you determine which lesson-guiding questions you will use, sequence and number them to show an order for teaching.

continued ➤

- You can add a final question to pertinent sections to frame learning experiences for students to apply skills they acquire to their own narratives, such as: How do I incorporate allusion into my own story? How can I write using a consistent point of view? What types of figurative language are appropriate for my narrative? Alternatively, consider replacing *I* with *you*.

- In table 1.2 (pages 11–17), I write some lesson-guiding questions in third-person point of view. In your unit plans, write them in first, second, third, or a combination. Additionally, choose to use either *author* or *writer*, as you wish.

- There are instances in which you may repeat essential understandings and unit-guiding questions throughout the unit. While reading a complex text with several settings, for example, students revisit the question, How do authors create descriptive settings? By critiquing each new setting passage that authors introduce, students gain deeper meaning and invent or revise their own settings to apply what they learn. For this kind of situation, insert similar rows in your unit map to reflect elements or devices that students re-examine.

Remember that your unit map is a work in progress. You are just beginning work on it, and as you read subsequent chapters, you will continue to add to it. At any point, you can always return to it and make changes. If you are collaborating with colleagues and create a Google Doc or a similar online tool for the map, invite anyone to edit it. You can even dedicate collaborative team time or department meeting sessions to discuss and work on this project.

Summary

By using the backward-design approach as a guide, you have a clear path to planning a rigorous unit. Comprehensively reviewing the content you are to teach and intentionally planning effective learning experiences increase your own professionalism and teaching ability and impact student achievement.

When creating your narrative unit map, you can plan one from scratch using one of two templates. Alternatively, use the completed map available in this chapter and revise and augment it accordingly. Be sure to begin with standards and consider not only English language arts standards—writing, reading, speaking, listening, grammar, and conventions—but also English learner (EL) or English language development (ELD) standards and any subject-specific content-area standards that are part of the unit. Consider approaching your textbook and materials as useful resources that you intentionally access, augment, and revise, as needed, for explicit purposes to address learning outcomes. Of course, be mindful to operate within the dictates of your school or district so you do not deviate from its expectations.

When building your map, first think about how you want to organize the unit to determine the teaching sequence. Will students have an accumulation of notes and paragraph sketches that they produce all throughout the unit to use when they write their first drafts? If so, incorporate lesson-guiding questions at strategic points for students to work on these pieces. For example, end each appropriate collection of lesson-guiding questions with these kinds of queries: How can I use methods of characterization to develop my protagonist and antagonist? Or, What plot structure can I use for my narrative? Another factor to keep in mind is how you will use existing resources, such as the textbook, in the unit. Also ask students to keep a notebook as a reference tool throughout the whole unit and beyond to support and extend their learning.

Moving forward, you will have the opportunity to use what you developed about learning outcomes to guide the culminating writing task and criteria for success. In the next chapter, I present information and examples for you to write this performance task, and the checklist and rubric that accompany it, for instruction and assessment. You will also have a chance to consider preassessment options and plan an appropriate one to implement.

CHAPTER 2

Formulating a Pre- and Culminating Assessment and Establishing Criteria for Success

At this point, you likely read chapter 1, "Building a Narrative Unit Map," and began or finished identifying what students should know, understand, and be able to do (KUDs) and established guiding questions for a narrative unit. As you continue reading this book, feel free to revise what you have recorded on your map from the exercise Unit Map—KUDs and Guiding Questions on pages 22–28 and add other components as needed. Proceeding with the backward-planning process, this chapter focuses on formulating a culminating assessment and determining the criteria to score it, plus designing a preassessment and ideas for launching the unit. There are four exercises in this chapter. I purposely placed the preassessment after the narrative writing prompt and writing checklist exercises so that you can design it with the foresight of the prompt and criteria in mind.

In this chapter you can (re)design a narrative:

1. Writing prompt
2. Writing checklist
3. Rubric
4. Preassessment

(Re)design a Narrative Writing Prompt

A prompt is a task teachers design that elicits from students the creation of a product to demonstrate what they come to know, understand, and do. For this unit, you will devise a prompt in which students apply what they have learned concerning narrative writing and perhaps subject matter content. In *The Fundamentals of (Re)designing Writing Units* (Glass, 2017a), I discuss curriculum-embedded and complex project performance assessments as the type of culminating project students will produce in response to a task. These assessments rely on an integration of curriculum, instruction, and assessment. They:

> Not only measure learning, as is characteristic of summative assessments, but they are also designed for continuous involvement in learning through a host of meaningful assessment opportunities along a continuum of formality and intensity. Each learning experience you conduct requires students to think, produce, and build expertise to acquire many skills. (Stanford

Center for Assessment, Learning and Equity [SCALE], 2015)

It is about not just the end product of the narrative they compose but also the process of working on the many steps it takes to complete it. Curriculum-embedded and complex project performance assessments immerse students throughout the duration of the unit to acquire skills that culminate in a polished product—in this case, a genre within the narrative text type.

There are innumerable possibilities for generating narrative writing tasks across content areas. In social studies, students might compose historical fiction to demonstrate understanding of a civilization, culture, or situation based on historically factual characters, settings, and events. In science, students might write a biography about a scientist who overcame obstacles to make a discovery that has worldwide implications. During language arts, students might write an original fiction or nonfiction narrative to apply what they learn about genre characteristics, elements of literature, figurative language, and targeted literary devices. Or they can change one or more aspects of a published story and rewrite it accordingly. For example, students can alter the ending, make the protagonist into an antagonist, convert a minor character into a dynamic one, redirect a significant decision, write from a different point of view, invent a new setting, or infuse literary devices like allusion, dialect, or foreshadowing.

Figure 2.1 is a template with specific examples to support you in creating and customizing a narrative prompt for your students as a culminating assessment. Feel free to deviate from the template and access it to foster ideas. Case in point—not every example provided in the figure aligns precisely to the template. As a friendly reminder, use your unit map as a guide for task design because it keeps you focused on what content, material, and skills students can prove they know and understand.

Narrative Template Ideas for Generating Tasks

Design a writing task using any of the options within each part as you see fit.

Part 1: Focus the Task

- Complete this template: "After reading _____ (name the specific text) by _____ (author) . . ."
- Complete this template: "After conducting research on _____ (name the topic) . . ."
- Include a guiding question.

Part 2: Identify the Writing Task

- Write (or rewrite) a/an _____ (specific genre, sequel, alternate ending, or specific text) . . .
- From the point of view or perspective of _____ (a different character or narrator) . . .
- Using _____ (the author's writing style, specific literary device, or type of figurative language) . . .
- With a different _____ (tone, setting, purpose, central conflict, or other) than the author's . . .
- About . . .; based on . . .; that shows . . .

Part 3: Emphasize Something Important

- Use this _____ (checklist or rubric) to guide you while writing.
- Include a works cited document for research you conduct for your _____ (historical fiction, biography, or other).
- Create illustrations, graphics, or visuals to enhance your narrative.
- Organize your events in a logical sequence.
- Be sure to include the characteristic elements of _____ (genre).
- Include figurative language that compels readers to visualize and deepen their understanding.
- Use (or incorporate) literary devices and figurative language _____ (name the specific types) to enhance your work.

Narrative Writing Prompt Examples

Realistic Fiction

Rewrite a classic piece of literature into contemporary realistic fiction. Make it relatable to today by modernizing the characters, setting, and events. Incorporate allusion, dialect, suspense, and figurative language to enhance your work. Use the writing checklist or rubric to guide you as you write.

Write a realistic story of survival from first- or third-person point of view. Include the characteristic elements of this genre and rely on the literary device of suspense among others you choose to use. The central conflict can focus on an internal (protagonist against self) or external (protagonist against nature, society, or other) conflict, but be sure it qualifies as realistic fiction.

After reading Kurt Vonnegut's (2014) "Harrison Bergeron," write a story with new characters and a situation in which people receive handicaps for areas of talent different from what the author features. You can invent a futuristic setting as Vonnegut does to produce science fiction or fantasy, or rewrite yours as realistic fiction.

Historical Fiction

After conducting research on WWII (or another war), write a historical fiction piece based on factual details of the time period. Create an authentic plotline, characters, settings, and dialogue that demonstrate your understanding of the opposing forces and their beliefs; the political, social, and economic climate; and the events of WWII. You may invent fictionalized characters as long as they stay true to the historical setting. Use the rubric to guide your writing so you are clear about the criteria.

How did the debate between Jefferson and Hamilton influence the political system of the United States? Write a historical fiction piece focused on differing sides of the issues involving the Constitution that divided Thomas Jefferson, Alexander Hamilton, and their political allies during the Washington administration. In your narrative, respond to the guiding question and include the personal and political philosophies of key characters. You may write from the point of view of a "Jeffersonian" or "Hamiltonian" or effectively change points of view.

After reading *A Christmas Carol*, write a historical fiction piece in which you reveal the societal, economic, and political aspects of the historical era. Within your story, show the influence of the era on the setting, characters, and events.

Science Fiction

Read informational texts about various habitats and the species that thrive within them. Then write a narrative from the point of view of a scientist, government official, concerned citizen, or organism within a habitat that recognizes an imbalance in an ecosystem and works to solve it. In your plotline: (1) present a disturbance that disrupts the preexisting balance of a population of species in the habitat and (2) revolve it around restoring balance or the effects of permanent destruction. Your story should show your knowledge of the habitat, species that live there, and a solution or the effects of the disturbance.

What dire situation in a future society can result from the lack of attention to a current-day scientific problem? Write a science fiction story that highlights the cause and effect of ignoring scientific facts around an issue you choose. Base your story on researched evidence and use effective narrative techniques and description. Include a works cited document that shows the sources you use to write factually about this potential problem.

After reading "All Summer in a Day" by Ray Bradbury (n.d.), write a sequel from the point of view of the young girl in the closet. Include a complete story arc and begin the plot from where Bradbury's story ended.

Myth

Write a nature or creation myth that explains why something in nature came to be, such as seasonal changes, animal characteristics, earth formations, or constellations. Organize your events in a logical sequence, use narrative techniques, and include the characteristic elements of a myth.

After reading several Greek myths, invent one of your own that explains a natural phenomenon or land formation. Feature Greek gods and goddesses interacting with one another to demonstrate your understanding of their power, personality traits, and relationships. Be sure to apply the characteristic elements of myths, as well as narrative techniques and figurative language to make your story engaging. Feel free to include illustrations to accompany your myth.

Nonfiction Narrative

After reading and discussing Robert Frost's (n.d.) poem "The Road Not Taken," write a personal narrative or memoir about a time you chose an alternate path. Stylistically and creatively address these and other questions in your narrative: What path did you choose? What were the consequences? Did you regret or accept your decision? Use literary devices and figurative language to enhance your work.

After reading *The Curious Incident of the Dog in the Night-Time* by Mark Haddon (2003), write a realistic fiction, personal narrative, or memoir in first-person point of view from the perspective of an individual with a disability. In your work, reveal his or her thoughts, feelings, emotions, and struggles. Infuse your writing with meaningful figurative language that fosters emotional responses. Readers should glean an appropriate tone from your work.

How does the way you handle adversity or a difficult situation reveal something important about you? Write a personal narrative or memoir based on this guiding question. Include figurative language that compels readers to visualize and deepen their understanding of your experience.

Figure 2.1: Narrative template for generating tasks and examples.

*Visit **go.SolutionTree.com/literacy** for a free reproducible version of this figure.*

Exercise: (Re)design a Narrative Writing Prompt

Design a narrative prompt and input it on the unit map that you began in the Unit Map—KUDs and Guiding Questions exercise in chapter 1 (page 22). When you devise a writing checklist in the next exercise, you'll place this prompt at the top of it to make students aware of their assignment. To design a narrative prompt, consider the following.

- To fashion an original prompt from scratch or revise one you already have, use the narrative template ideas and examples in figure 2.1 (pages 30–31) as a resource.

- Search for prompts that align to your unit from the SCALE (www.performanceassessmentresourcebank .org/bin/performance-tasks) resource bank for performance assessments across content areas. Although argumentation and informational or explanatory assessments dominate the site, peruse the various tasks to find those for a narrative. Feel free to edit what you find to align to your unit goals and match learners' needs. Also, consider converting an argument or informational prompt to a narrative. For example, read this "Spreads Like (Exponential) Wildfire" (SCALE, n.d.) prompt on the SCALE website:

  > For this task, students will create and solve a problem that addresses a situation involving exponential growth or decay. Students imagine that the school's math department is conducting a math competition. The problems that they create are intended for that competition. The topic must be able to be modeled by an exponential function. (Examples include rumors, infections, wildfires, and so on.) Their final solutions should include graphs, charts, and other mathematical work supporting the solution.

  You might rewrite this original task so students demonstrate understanding of the mathematical concept of exponential growth or decay by writing a story.

(Re)design a Narrative Writing Checklist

Students can use a checklist as a guide when they write to be sure they fulfill an assignment's requirements. *The Fundamentals of (Re)designing Writing Units* (Glass, 2017a) covers the function, rationale, and suggestions for using a checklist in more detail. In this section, I provide information, examples, and an exercise (page 37) for you to revise or design a narrative student writing checklist. Additionally, I include an activity that you can conduct early in the unit to prepare students for using the checklist as an effective instructional tool.

Figure 2.2 features a generic narrative writing checklist. It covers five categories: (1) general, (2) story elements and literary devices, (3) description, (4) sentence structure and transitions, and (5) grammar, conventions, and format. Each category contains items or indicators describing narrative writing requirements. In the figure, I have combined certain subheadings within the categories (for example, sentence structure and transitions)

because I consider some of the grouped elements intrinsically linked. You can organize categories differently or use alternative ones to those in the figure. Whichever way you choose, work in concert with colleagues to ensure consistency so that students in your school or district see and learn the same or similar terminology and indicators for writing. In the exercise at the end of this section, I share several possible categories as a tool to use when working on your checklist.

As options, you might also add or replace any of the categories and indicators in the checklist in figure 2.2 with any of the following.

- Organization:
  - My story follows a plotline and logical sequence.
  - My story is well developed.
  - My memoir is logically sequenced with a beginning, middle, and end.
  - I clear up questions readers might have or reveal the significance of the event on my life.

Narrative Writing Checklist
Directions: Use this checklist to guide you while responding to the following writing task.   _____   _____

General

- ❑ The *title* captures my story in an original or creative way.
- ❑ I show awareness of *task*, *purpose*, and *audience*.

Story Elements and Literary Devices

- ❑ I introduce the *narrator* and establish and maintain a consistent *point of view* unless I intentionally write from multiple viewpoints.
- ❑ My beginning *engages* readers. I present a *setting*, *characters*, and a *central conflict* that set my story in motion.
- ❑ My *plot* is original; the story is *well paced* and *developed*.
- ❑ I sequence the *events* in a *logical order*. If I use multiple plotlines, flashbacks, or flash forward, readers can follow the storyline.
- ❑ I build gripping *suspense* that creates tension and present a *climax* that shows the turning point.
- ❑ My *dialogue* purposefully moves the plot forward by revealing feelings, interactions between characters, or reactions to setting or events. *Dialogue tags*, when necessary, enhance the dialogue.
- ❑ I use *dialect*, as appropriate, to signify a character's geographical origin, social status, bias, or era in which he or she lives.
- ❑ My *ending* resolves the central conflict and answers questions readers might have.

Description

- ❑ I use precise and accurate *vocabulary* and avoid unnecessary repetition.
- ❑ I compose relevant *figurative language*—such as imagery, simile, metaphor, personification, and hyperbole—to vividly describe events, settings, and characters and to elicit a mood.
- ❑ I include strong *verbs* in dialogue tags and describe reactions, gestures, or movements only as needed (not overdone).

Sentence Structure and Transitions

- ❑ My writing does not include *run-on sentences* or *fragments*.
- ❑ I vary my *sentence beginnings* and use different *sentence patterns* for rhythm and stylistic effect.
- ❑ I include *parallel construction* to enhance my writing.
- ❑ I add appropriate and varied *transitions* to connect sentences so my writing flows, to convey event sequence, and to show shifts in time and place.

Grammar, Conventions, and Format

- ❑ I use proper *grammar* except for stylistic effect, such as writing in the voice of a character who does not speak in standard English.
- ❑ My *conventions* are correct—using correct spelling, punctuation, and capitalization.
- ❑ I use proper *mechanics* for dialogue.
- ❑ I know when to use new *paragraphs* and indent them appropriately.
- ❑ I *format* my paper correctly with proper margins and a heading. If I type, I use appropriate font style, color, and size. If I handwrite, it is legible.

Figure 2.2: Student narrative writing checklist.

*Visit **go.SolutionTree.com/literacy** for a free reproducible version of this figure.*

- Content:
  - I show I am knowledgeable about _____ (*historical time period, text, biography subject, era*, or othe=r).
  - In my biography, I demonstrate understanding of the obstacles my subject faced and how he or she overcame them.
  - In my _____ (*biography, historical fiction*, or other), I write factually about characters (or *individuals*), settings, and events using multiple credible resources that I reference in a works cited document.
  - In my myth, I reflect the culture of the _____ civilization.
- Word choice and description:
  - I use precise nouns and domain-specific vocabulary, as appropriate.
  - I avoid repetition and vague language. I use lively verbs and precise nouns and adjectives.
  - I use synonyms to add variety and avoid redundancy.
  - I avoid forms of the verb *to be* (for example, *is, are, was, were*). Instead, I use action verbs.
  - In my memoir (or *personal narrative*), I use descriptive detail and figurative language to vividly explain how the episode (or *situation, event*, or *memory*) impacted my life.
  - My dialogue is natural and intentional to enhance the plot.
- Grammar and conventions: I edit my writing to ensure proper—
  - Word usage
  - Sentence syntax
  - Paragraph usage
  - Pronoun-antecedent agreement (for example, "<u>Everyone</u> brought <u>his</u> or <u>her</u> book to class.")
  - Ellipses usage
  - Active versus passive voice (for example, "The helpful child washed dishes"

instead of "The dishes were washed by the helpful child.")
  - Conventions for dialogue punctuation

The excerpt for a mystery writing task in figure 2.3 shows a checklist example that addresses skills specific to a genre.

Excerpt of a Student Writing Checklist for Mystery

- ☐ I write a *mystery* about a crime that needs solving.
- ☐ I explain what happens in a *logical sequence* so my mystery makes sense.
- ☐ I introduce a *crime* and *motive* at the beginning of my mystery.
- ☐ I create a *setting* so my readers know where and when the mystery takes place.
- ☐ My *characters* are specific to mystery stories.
  - ☐ Victim
  - ☐ Detective
  - ☐ Suspects
  - ☐ Witnesses
- ☐ I include these *mystery elements*.
  - ☐ Clues
  - ☐ Hunches
  - ☐ Alibis
  - ☐ Distractions
  - ☐ Red herring
  - ☐ Breakthrough
- ☐ My *ending* shows that the crime has been solved because:
  - ☐ I show evidence.
  - ☐ I include a deduction.

Figure 2.3: Mystery checklist excerpt.

After students write their narratives, they can create a PowerPoint, Prezi, or Keynote and present it to the class or read their stories aloud. Either way, they can include something stylistic or visual—for example, a prop or costume—and employ speaking techniques—voice modulation, inflection, tempo, enunciation, and eye contact.

When students share their narratives, ask the audience to critique the presentation using a checklist like the one in figure 2.4, which can promote active listening and engagement. It can also serve as an instrument to guide students as they prepare for their presentations.

Narrative Audience Critique			
Criteria	Completely Agree; Very Strong	Somewhat Agree	Do Not Agree; Weak or Confusing
Story Content			
The *beginning* engages me.			
I clearly understand the *central conflict* and it sets the story in motion.			
I have a mental image of what the *protagonist* looks like and can infer a personality trait for him or her based on story details.			
I have a mental image of what the *antagonist* looks like and can infer a personality trait for him or her based on story details.			
I can visualize the *setting* in my mind.			
The writer has sequenced *events in a logical order* so that I can easily follow the story.			
The story is *well developed*. It does not feel too short, and the writer builds *suspense* to make the story interesting.			
The *ending* resolves the central conflict so I'm not left with questions.			
Meaningful dialogue and *dialect* enhance the story by moving the plot forward, revealing feelings or thoughts, or showing how characters interact.			
The writer uses precise *vocabulary*, *figurative language*, and *vivid details* throughout the story.			
Speaking Techniques			
The speaker *modulates* his or her voice so the *pitch* is just right. He or she also uses *inflection* so his or her voice isn't monotone and boring.			
The speaker uses *tempo* to make the story interesting. I feel he or she slows down or speeds up at appropriate parts to engage the audience.			
The speaker clearly *enunciates* words.			
The speaker uses *eye contact* to make the audience feel included and to show he or she has rehearsed.			
Comments			
What I particularly like about the story and presentation:			
What I would suggest the writer consider for revision:			

Figure 2.4: Narrative audience critique.

*Visit **go.SolutionTree.com/literacy** for a free reproducible version of this figure.*

The writing checklist can serve as an instructional tool to set expectations and the purpose for learning; therefore, it is critical to introduce it effectively so students own it. However, help them become aware of what narrative elements of the genre entail before you introduce the checklist so they are familiar with the terminology. Conduct two activities that serve this purpose—one that familiarizes students with the characteristics of the genre and narrative writing in general and another that orients them to the expectations for what they will eventually write.

First, I'll focus on a lesson you can conduct to present or review the characteristic elements of a specific narrative genre. To implement this activity, find and use differentiated writing models (also known as mentor texts) that give students a clear sense of what the genre entails, as this conveys your expectations for student writing. Later in the unit, you can return to these examples within a lesson to target specific skills, plus juxtapose strong with weak examples for instructional purposes. You can lead this preliminary activity early in the unit by following these five steps.

What the teacher does:

1. Arrange students into small groups differentiated homogeneously by reading levels.

2. Find and distribute at least two exemplary narrative writing samples for the genre students will write that are appropriately challenging to each group. See the Student Writing Models section in appendix E (page 152) and **go.SolutionTree.com/literacy** to access live links to these and other resources in this book.

What students do:

3. Each group reads both writing samples and makes a list of common characteristics that the samples share. (You may elect to tell them both are samples from a specific narrative genre, or allow them to determine it for themselves based on this activity.)

4. Groups report their lists to the whole class as you record these commonalities.

5. Students review the class-generated list and identify common elements among the samples. Make sure to name the genre if students have not already identified it.

At the end of the exercise, students should be familiar with the genre and what it entails. Explain that they will engage in many learning experiences to highlight these elements and support them in creating this type of writing piece. Next, orient them to the details of the writing assignment by following the ten-step roundtable activity that figure 2.5 details.

Orienting Students to a Writing Checklist
Roundtable Exercise

1. **Prepare students for the exercise:** Arrange students into small groups of three or four. Instruct each student to take out a pencil or pen. Ask someone in the group to supply one sheet of paper for the entire group. Or, students can each take out an electronic device and prepare a Google Doc or a similar electronic tool for making a collaborative, synchronous list.

2. **Provide an activity overview:** Tell students they will participate in a group activity that goes like this.
   a. Your group will make a bulleted or numbered list in response to a prompt I will give you shortly.
   b. When responding to the prompt, each of you will enter one to three words each time it is your turn. Avoid sentences because the list should include brief items.
   c. You'll pass the paper around in a clockwise fashion or make online entries when it is your turn to add your item. Read the items before writing yours to eliminate duplicates.
   d. If at some point you are out of ideas when it is your turn, you can say, "Pass."
   e. You have _____ minutes for this activity. (Assign a time limit of about six to ten minutes.)

3. **Make a group list:** Once students are ready with their materials or electronic devices, issue the prompt, "What does a _____ include? Remember to include what contributes to good writing in general too." (Insert the specific genre that is the focus for your narrative unit.)

4. **Report out:** When you call time, each group reports out one line item at a time that you record on chart paper, a whiteboard, or an interactive whiteboard to arrive at a class-generated list.

5. **Review the class-generated list:** Open it up for individuals to add any items a group has not offered. Invite the class to review the accumulated list and do any or all of the following.

    a. Combine items.

    b. Categorize items and add subheadings to the list.

    c. Delete unnecessary or incorrect items.

After the Roundtable Exercise

6. **Cross-reference the class list with your prepared checklist:** Distribute the teacher-prepared checklist to each student (see figure 2.2, page 33). Instruct groups to do the following.

    a. Perform one-to-one correspondence by checking off items on the class-generated list (from step 4 in the roundtable exercise) that match those on the teacher-prepared checklist.

    b. Add missing items to the checklist that you think are important to add.

7. **Consider adding items:** Discuss as a class if the matching items contribute to an effective piece of writing. If students recommend adding any items you omitted, discuss why they are worthy of inclusion. If so, formally add them so they are now an expectation.

8. **Assess writing models:** You might elect for students to examine a student sample and assess it against the checklist. Discuss to what degree the writer satisfies key points on the checklist.

9. **Distribute the checklist:** Give students a clean copy of the checklist to keep in their writing folders or provide an electronic version. Emphasize that they will use it as a guide while writing.

10. **Use the checklist throughout instruction:** Focus on discrete checklist line items or a combination of items along with associated guiding questions to set the purpose for learning.

Figure 2.5: Orienting students to a writing checklist.

*Visit **go.SolutionTree.com/literacy** for a free reproducible version of this figure.*

Exercise: (Re)design a Student Narrative Writing Checklist

In this activity, I invite you to work on a student writing checklist. You may (1) create one from scratch, (2) revise an existing one of your own, or (3) download mine and use it as is or adapt it. To locate my checklist, visit **go .SolutionTree.com/literacy**. The following points can guide you in this exercise; feel free to work collaboratively (in person or virtually) or individually. Once you complete your checklist, you can adapt or create an accompanying scoring rubric (or vice versa), which I detail in the next section.

- Review content standards and the KUDs on your narrative unit template that you crafted as the result of the Unit Map—KUDs and Guiding Questions exercise (page 22) in chapter 1. The checklist should reflect these learning outcomes.

- Include the writing task at the top of the checklist along with a reminder to use it as a tool while writing. Refer to (Re)design a Narrative Writing Prompt earlier in this chapter for examples on this point.

- Write items (or indicators) on the checklist in first-person point of view and with present-tense verbs since students use it to guide them during the writing process. Also, write in language accessible to your students.

- Consider excluding obvious line items that your students have mastered. You might include some generic ones as reminders; others will be specific to the genre and assignment students will complete.

- Concentrate on what you expect to actually see in the paper rather than strategies students use while composing. For example, avoid this kind of statement: *I use print and digital resources to check that my spelling is correct.* Instead, enter on the checklist the evidence of application, such as, *I spell all words correctly.*

continued ➤

- Generally keep line items brief unless you feel examples are necessary. Students can refer to resources or handouts if they need a reminder about what something means. For example, include this item—*I write using different types of sentence structure*—rather than something more involved like, *I write using various sentence structures, such as simple, compound, complex, and compound-complex.*

- Organize related line items under categories for easy readability such as these options for narrative writing. Combine those that make sense as shown in some areas in figure 2.2 (page 33).

• General	• Narrative techniques	• Tone and style
• Development of ideas (or idea development)	• Literary devices	• Vocabulary
• Content	• Organization	• Sentence structure
• Context	• Organizational structure (or text structure)	• Transitions
• Focus	• Description	• Grammar usage
• Incident significance	• Figurative language	• Conventions
• Genre characteristics	• Word choice	• Format
• Story elements	• Language and style	

(Re)design a Narrative Rubric

Like checklists, analytic rubrics can serve as effective instructional tools, but they also function as scoring mechanisms. Rubrics include the following three components.

1. **Scoring criteria:** These are specific elements to assess—such as point of view, central conflict, dialogue, and so forth—grouped under overarching categories, like Story Elements and Literary Devices. Each element includes a brief overview of the skills associated with it—for example, this under Suspense and Climax: "Build tension through well-crafted suspense; present the climax to show the turning point."

2. **Criteria descriptors:** Each scoring criterion includes descriptions along a continuum of quality to indicate performance at different levels.

3. **Levels of performance:** Levels—represented by numbers, words (for example, *advanced*, *proficient*, *partially proficient*, and *novice*), or a combination of both—indicate how well students have performed. Four- or five-point rubrics are common; however, some use three- and six-point scales.

Checklists and rubrics are valuable albeit different instruments that students and teachers use. Refer to *The Fundamentals of (Re)designing Writing Units* (Glass, 2017a) for more information about function, rationale, and suggestions for using a checklist, and also a thorough explanation and instructional suggestions for using rubrics, how to differentiate between analytic versus holistic rubrics, ways to write descriptors for levels of performance, and more.

In figure 2.6 (pages 39–43), I present a complete narrative rubric as an example. The end of this section includes an exercise you can use to devise a narrative rubric for your unit, or adapt the one I share. Like the checklist, my featured rubric reflects characteristic elements for a generic narrative, so you will not find genre-specific items. To arrive at a single score using the rubric, see figure 2.7 (page 43) for information on determining mode and median.

Narrative Writing Rubric

Directions: Score the paper by circling the appropriate rubric scale score for each criteria item. To arrive at a single score, determine the mode or median based on all the scores. For items that are weighted double, input the score twice in your calculations. Then use the conversion scale at the end of this figure to arrive at a percentage score and translate to a grade, if necessary.

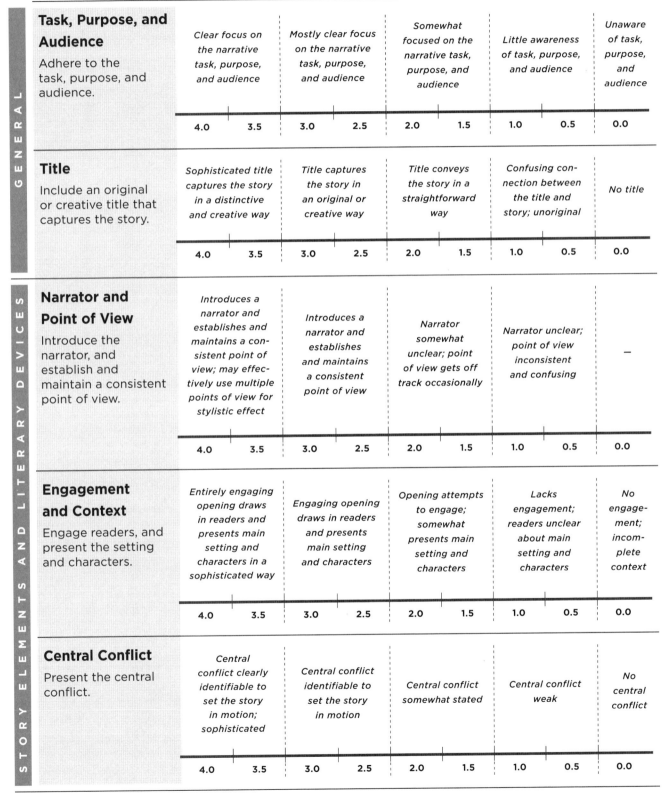

GENERAL	**Task, Purpose, and Audience** Adhere to the task, purpose, and audience.	Clear focus on the narrative task, purpose, and audience 4.0 3.5	Mostly clear focus on the narrative task, purpose, and audience 3.0 2.5	Somewhat focused on the narrative task, purpose, and audience 2.0 1.5	Little awareness of task, purpose, and audience 1.0 0.5	Unaware of task, purpose, and audience 0.0
	Title Include an original or creative title that captures the story.	Sophisticated title captures the story in a distinctive and creative way 4.0 3.5	Title captures the story in an original or creative way 3.0 2.5	Title conveys the story in a straightforward way 2.0 1.5	Confusing connection between the title and story; unoriginal 1.0 0.5	No title 0.0
STORY ELEMENTS AND LITERARY DEVICES	**Narrator and Point of View** Introduce the narrator, and establish and maintain a consistent point of view.	Introduces a narrator and establishes and maintains a consistent point of view; may effectively use multiple points of view for stylistic effect 4.0 3.5	Introduces a narrator and establishes and maintains a consistent point of view 3.0 2.5	Narrator somewhat unclear; point of view gets off track occasionally 2.0 1.5	Narrator unclear; point of view inconsistent and confusing 1.0 0.5	— 0.0
	Engagement and Context Engage readers, and present the setting and characters.	Entirely engaging opening draws in readers and presents main setting and characters in a sophisticated way 4.0 3.5	Engaging opening draws in readers and presents main setting and characters 3.0 2.5	Opening attempts to engage; somewhat presents main setting and characters 2.0 1.5	Lacks engagement; readers unclear about main setting and characters 1.0 0.5	No engagement; incomplete context 0.0
	Central Conflict Present the central conflict.	Central conflict clearly identifiable to set the story in motion; sophisticated 4.0 3.5	Central conflict identifiable to set the story in motion 3.0 2.5	Central conflict somewhat stated 2.0 1.5	Central conflict weak 1.0 0.5	No central conflict 0.0

Figure 2.6: Narrative writing rubric.

continued ➤

*Visit **go.SolutionTree.com/literacy** for a free reproducible version of this figure.*

STORY ELEMENTS AND LITERARY DEVICES

Plot Development and Event Sequence

Create an original plot that is well paced and developed; sequence events that unfold naturally and logically.

Highly original, clearly well-paced, and developed plot; sequence unfolds naturally and logically; may effectively include multiple plotlines, flashbacks, or flash-forward events	Original, clearly well-paced, and developed plot; events sequenced logically	Plot original in some places and predictable in other places; somewhat well-paced and developed plot; somewhat logically sequenced	Restates existing plot, halted pace, undeveloped with many holes, weak or haphazard sequence, and/or difficult to follow	Length not adequate for development

4.0   3.5   3.0   2.5   2.0   1.5   1.0   0.5   0.0

Suspense and Climax

Build tension through well-crafted suspense; present the climax to show the turning point.

Highly effective and sophisticated use of suspense to build tension; captivating climax represents clear turning point	Somewhat suspenseful; climax shows the turning point	Attempts suspense and climax	Little suspense; climax unclear and weak; somewhat monotonous or flat	No suspense or climax

4.0   3.5   3.0   2.5   2.0   1.5   1.0   0.5   0.0

Dialogue and Dialogue Tags

Use purposeful dialogue to move the plot forward by revealing feelings, interactions between characters, or reactions to setting or events; include dialogue tags, as needed, to describe reactions, gestures, or movements.

Meaningful, sophisticated dialogue moves plot forward by developing events or characters' reactions, actions, thoughts, and feelings; dialogue tags enhance the dialogue and serve a clear purpose	Uses dialogue to meaningfully and adequately move the plot forward; uses dialogue tags to enhance the dialogue	Sometimes includes unnecessary dialogue, too much dialogue, or not enough; dialogue tags weak	Little dialogue that fails to move the plot forward or confuses readers; perfunctory, confusing, or irrelevant dialogue tags	No dialogue

4.0   3.5   3.0   2.5   2.0   1.5   1.0   0.5   0.0

Dialect

Use dialect to reveal information about a character, such as geographical origin, social status, bias, or era.

Effective and sophisticated use of dialect reveals information about characters	Uses dialect to reveal information about a character	Attempts dialect	Incorrect or confusing dialect	No dialect

4.0   3.5   3.0   2.5   2.0   1.5   1.0   0.5   0.0

Resolution

Resolve the central conflict and answer questions readers might have.

Central conflict resolved completely; sophisticated	Central conflict resolved with no unanswered questions	Central conflict mostly resolved	Weak ending or appears abrupt	No resolution

4.0   3.5   3.0   2.5   2.0   1.5   1.0   0.5   0.0

DESCRIPTION		4.0 3.5	3.0 2.5	2.0 1.5	1.0 0.5	0.0
	Vocabulary Use precise and accurate vocabulary; avoid unnecessary repetition.	*Consistently precise and accurate vocabulary; sophisticated language; little or no repetition unless used for stylistic effect*	*Precise and accurate vocabulary; minor unnecessary repetition*	*Adequate choice and usage of words; some unnecessary repetition*	*Rare use of precise words; instances of inaccurate word use; noticeable unnecessary repetition*	*Replete with simplistic language, inaccurate word usage, and repetition*
	Figurative Language and Description Use relevant types of figurative language—imagery, simile, metaphor, personification—and description to vividly portray events, settings, and characters.	*Varied, sufficient, and sophisticated use of relevant figurative language and descriptive detail for events, settings, and characters*	*Generally varied and sufficient use of relevant figurative language and descriptive detail*	*Limited, superficial, or repetitive (such as only similes) use of figurative language or descriptive detail*	*Rare, confusing, or irrelevant use of figurative language and descriptive detail*	*No figurative language or description*

SENTENCE STRUCTURE AND TRANSITIONS		4.0 3.5	3.0 2.5	2.0 1.5	1.0 0.5	0.0
	Complete Sentences Produce complete sentences void of run-ons and fragments.	*Minimal or no errors; may have intentional use of run-ons and/or fragments for stylistic effect*	*Minor errors*	*Some errors*	*Serious errors hinder reading; unaware of sentence structure or transitional use*	—
	Sentence Beginning Variety Include a variety of sentence beginnings.	*Thoughtful, consistent, and sophisticated use of a variety of sentence beginnings (for example, subjects, prepositional phrases, adverbs, and dependent clauses)*	*Uses a variety of sentence beginnings*	*Begins some sentences in the same way*	*Begins most or all sentences in the same way with either the same word or the same type (for example, all subjects)*	—

continued ➤

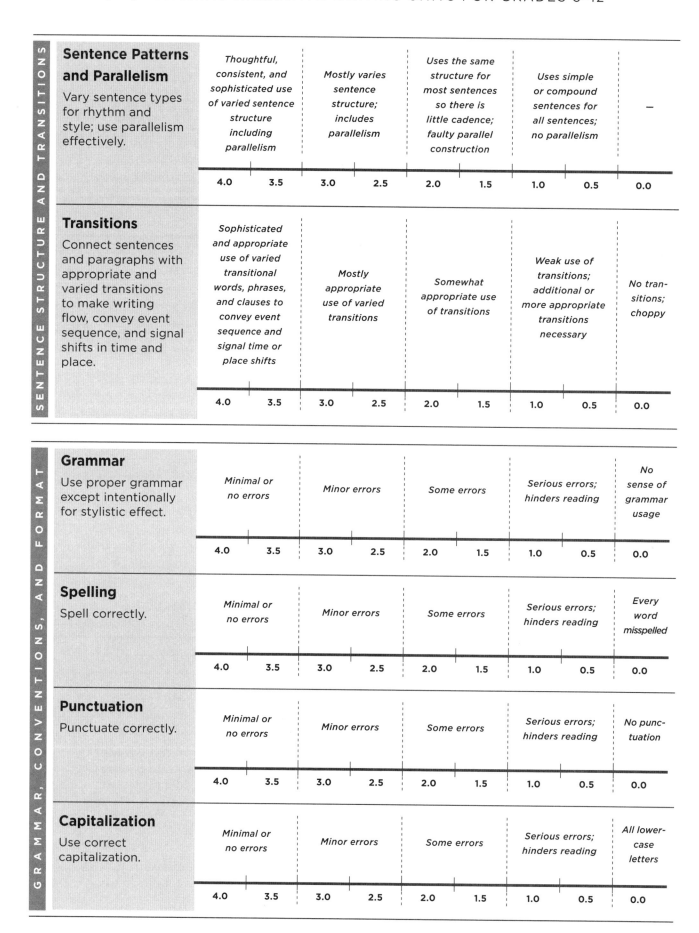

SENTENCE STRUCTURE AND TRANSITIONS

Sentence Patterns and Parallelism

Vary sentence types for rhythm and style; use parallelism effectively.

| Thoughtful, consistent, and sophisticated use of varied sentence structure including parallelism | Mostly varies sentence structure; includes parallelism | Uses the same structure for most sentences so there is little cadence; faulty parallel construction | Uses simple or compound sentences for all sentences; no parallelism | — |

4.0 3.5 3.0 2.5 2.0 1.5 1.0 0.5 0.0

Transitions

Connect sentences and paragraphs with appropriate and varied transitions to make writing flow, convey event sequence, and signal shifts in time and place.

| Sophisticated and appropriate use of varied transitional words, phrases, and clauses to convey event sequence and signal time or place shifts | Mostly appropriate use of varied transitions | Somewhat appropriate use of transitions | Weak use of transitions; additional or more appropriate transitions necessary | No transitions; choppy |

4.0 3.5 3.0 2.5 2.0 1.5 1.0 0.5 0.0

GRAMMAR, CONVENTIONS, AND FORMAT

Grammar

Use proper grammar except intentionally for stylistic effect.

| Minimal or no errors | Minor errors | Some errors | Serious errors; hinders reading | No sense of grammar usage |

4.0 3.5 3.0 2.5 2.0 1.5 1.0 0.5 0.0

Spelling

Spell correctly.

| Minimal or no errors | Minor errors | Some errors | Serious errors; hinders reading | Every word misspelled |

4.0 3.5 3.0 2.5 2.0 1.5 1.0 0.5 0.0

Punctuation

Punctuate correctly.

| Minimal or no errors | Minor errors | Some errors | Serious errors; hinders reading | No punctuation |

4.0 3.5 3.0 2.5 2.0 1.5 1.0 0.5 0.0

Capitalization

Use correct capitalization.

| Minimal or no errors | Minor errors | Some errors | Serious errors; hinders reading | All lower-case letters |

4.0 3.5 3.0 2.5 2.0 1.5 1.0 0.5 0.0

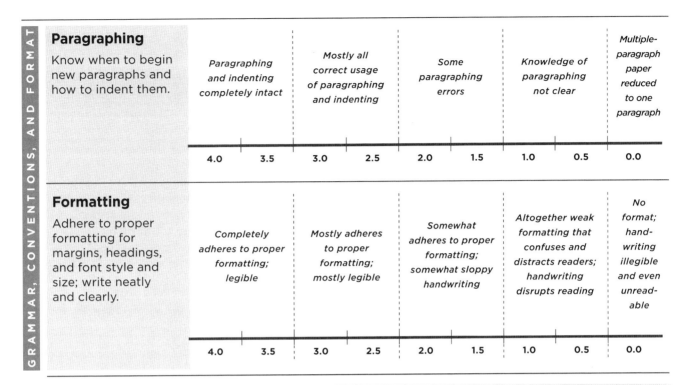

After determining the mode or median, identify the corresponding percentage and issue a grade based on your preferred scale of what constitutes an A, A–, B+, and so forth. You may alter the correspondence between percentages and rubric scores to reflect the meaning of grades in your context.

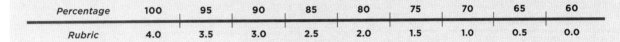

Percentage	100	95	90	85	80	75	70	65	60
Rubric	4.0	3.5	3.0	2.5	2.0	1.5	1.0	0.5	0.0

Determine Median and Mode		
For illustrative purposes, a student earns these scores on eleven criteria items on a four-point scale: 2, 2, 4, 3, 4, 2, 3, 4, 3, 3, 1. Here is how to calculate the median and mode.		
Definition	**How to Do It**	**Example**
Median The middle value of a set of numbers	• Rewrite the list of numbers in order from smallest to largest. • Select the middle one. • If there is an odd number of items, the median is the middle entry after sorting the numbers in order. • If the list of numbers is even, calculate the median by adding the two middle numbers and dividing by two.	1, 2, 2, 2, 3, ③, 3, 3, 4, 4, 4
Mode The number in the list that is repeated more often than any other	• Rewrite the numbers in order. • Determine the number that is repeated most frequently. • There can be more than one mode.	1, 2, 2, 2, ③, 3, 3, 3, 4, 4, 4

Figure 2.7: Process to determine median and mode.

Exercise: (Re)design a Narrative Writing Rubric

Design (or revise) a rubric to assess the narrative genre students will write making sure it aligns to the checklist. Visit **go.SolutionTree.com/literacy** to download and alter the rubric in figure 2.6 (pages 39–43), revise one you already have, or create a rubric from scratch. You might gather feedback from colleagues or create this scoring guide with them. The following is intended to guide you in this exercise; if you need more direction, consider accessing the information about rubrics in *The Fundamentals of (Re)designing Writing Units* (Glass, 2017a).

- **Include scoring criteria and group them under categories:** Write elements for the selected genre along with those for general writing that you included on the checklist because they are companion pieces. Also use the same overarching categories on both assessment instruments; for suggestions, refer to the list of category options within Exercise: (Re)design a Student Narrative Writing Checklist (pages 37–38) or the 6+1 Trait® Writing Model of Instruction and Assessment from Education Northwest (www.educationnorthwest.org/traits/traits-rubrics).

- **Write descriptors for what you are assessing on a continuum of quality for each level of performance:** Aim for clear language, although some descriptors will be subjective. For example, for the element of *significance* within a memoir, you might include the following descriptors.

  - 4—Significance and its impact altogether clear whether implied or stated; sophisticated insights well integrated into paper

  - 3—Significance and its impact clear whether implied or stated; insights mostly integrated into paper

  - 2—Unclear significance or impact; brief insights may be tacked on as an afterthought or are unclear

  - 1—Significance and insight omitted

- **Avoid quantitative descriptors:** Rather than using numbers to score, such as *one or two* or *three to five dialogue mechanical errors*, keep descriptors more open ended. Use these kinds of descriptors, which are associated with levels of performance: *few or no dialogue mechanical errors, some errors, many errors,* and *no dialogue or no mechanics applied to offset dialogue.* With papers of varying lengths and levels of sophistication, this provides a more accurate impression of skill application.

- **Avoid redundancy and overlap:** Dedicate each line item to a specific criterion.

- **Use a consistent performance-level scale across a school and even a district:** The criteria will naturally vary depending on content area and task, but if the point system is familiar to students, it will help them understand the values associated with different criteria items.

- **Weight scores, as appropriate:** Not every line item needs to have the same scoring structure. Consider doubling the weight of some skills that are more challenging, like for logically sequencing events.

- **Find and use anchor papers for scoring and instructional purposes:** Although a rubric includes clearly written expectations describing how the teacher will assess papers, there is some subjectivity when using it to score student work. Therefore, it is important to accompany rubrics with samples that exemplify each performance level to concretize the criteria. These samples are called *anchor papers* (see Glass [2017a] as well as appendix E of this text [page 151] for more information and resources).

Refrain from grading every piece of work students produce throughout the writing process—for instance, outlines, notecards, or drafts of an introduction. These are ways that students hone the craft of narrative writing. You can certainly provide effective feedback—and should—but go lightly on grading. Alfie Kohn (2006, as cited in Hattie, 2012) says, "Never mark students while they are still learning" (p. 152). To this, John Hattie (2012) adds:

Students see the mark, so often, as the "end" of the learning. . . . The comments can provide justification for the grade, but there is little evidence that the comments lead to changes in student learning behaviours, or greater effort, or more deliberate practice—mainly because students see the "work" as finished. (p. 152)

Use the rubric to score students' narrative writing. You can attach it to their work and circle or highlight descriptors on the rubric that signify their performance level. Since you've diligently taught the stages of the writing process and lessons around narrative writing skills, it is unlikely that students will turn in a poorly developed paper. However, if they do, consider offering students the opportunity to revise and resubmit their papers at a later time. Writing teacher and author Penny Kittle (2008) puts this into practice when she announces to her students:

> I have a proposal. I care *most* that you write well, not *when* you write well, so you may continue to revise a piece of writing all semester. There is no last draft until you say so. The final grade for a unit will be on your best draft, even if it is months after our initial deadline. (p. 222)

She tells her students that sometimes when they turn in their written product within the deadline it may not represent their best work, and she wants to grant them time to improve it. However, she communicates to her students that this option is not a procrastination tactic. If students neglect to work hard and to write in the allotted time frame, she relinquishes the offer.

If you need to arrive at a letter grade, translating the rubric score can prove challenging because performance levels and letter grades are different scoring systems. Analytic rubrics provide detailed information about how students perform against specific criteria; hence, they indicate what areas need improvement and reveal what students have mastered. Rubric scores are not meant to translate to grades, but the reality is that sometimes we need to convert them. Susan M. Brookhart (2013) offers direction for how to do this: "If you do need one overall grade . . . and must summarize an assessment with one overall score, use the median *or* mode, *not* the mean, of the scores for each criterion" (p. 114).

Review the narrative rubric (figure 2.6, pages 39–43). Notice the row of percentages (100—95—90, and so forth) and corresponding numbers on a four-point rubric scale on the last page of the figure. After scoring a student's paper, use the rubric scale numbers to determine the mode or median using figure 2.7 (page 43) as a guide. Remember that for weighted categories, input and factor in double the score in your list of numbers. Once you identify the mode or median score, identify the corresponding percentage to issue a grade. You certainly may alter the correspondence between percentages and rubric scores based on your preferred scale of what constitutes an A, A–, B+, and so forth to reflect the meaning of grades in your school context.

Although rubrics make for effective instructional and grading tools, you can also better serve and instruct your students by preassessing their knowledge before your instructional unit begins.

(Re)design a Preassessment

Preassessments are diagnostic; they should determine what students know, understand, believe, or can do before approaching a lesson, unit, or course. I have purposely included this discussion about preassessments after topics concerning the initial stages of backward planning—KUDs, guiding questions, and narrative culminating assessment and scoring criteria. In doing so, you can devise a preassessment based squarely on learning outcomes to target the kind of narrative genre you will teach and the expectations for students.

To get an idea of students' abilities, teachers typically issue a short preassessment and allot minimal time for students to complete it, such as one class period. In writing, asking students to compose a genre of narrative in response to a prompt helps determine their writing strengths and weaknesses. Preassessments can mirror the culminating assessment, although in narrative writing, the former will not be nearly as involved. Specifically, the diagnostic writing can reveal their basic grasp of storytelling elements such as developing a character, incorporating dialogue, or presenting a plot. It can also indicate their comfort level or capacity to incorporate figurative language or literary devices, as well as expose misconceptions that you can address. For example, some students might be confused about the elements of memoir versus those of autobiography or how to properly use the mechanics of inserting dialogue.

Depending on how you write them and your goals for design and administration, preassessments can yield information about not only knowledge and skills but also students' interests and learning styles. In this regard, you can provide choices geared toward their proclivities such as allowing them to compose a personal narrative, autobiography, or memoir; realistic fiction or science fiction; or other genre types. Additionally, preassessments can engage students in the work ahead by piquing their attention and priming them for the new material.

It is important to tell students that you will not grade preassessments. The purpose is to collect information so that you can target instruction more directly. In this way, they are similar to formative assessments because they both are used to gather data. For example, by taking notes or making a spreadsheet, you can identify to what degree students perform in the various skill areas. You then use what you learn to inform your teaching practice.

Record-keeping sheets can be as simple as inputting students' names down the left column and each skill organized by categories across the top row. For example, you could group together grammar and conventions skills—*punctuate and capitalize dialogue correctly, use active voice*—and include a section for narrative-related skills—*write descriptively about a setting, develop a character, sequence the plot logically*. In each cell, you can record a symbol indicating a student's level of understanding with a plus (got it!), check (somewhat understand), or minus (missing or incorrect). You can also score students' preassessment writing samples on a rubric (but remember not to enter grades in a gradebook). The record-keeping sheet, which you can use for each class period, and collected data from their writing guide your instructional moves. For example, you might arrange grouping configurations, abbreviate or extend what you planned on teaching, and so forth. Read about options in the following exercise: (Re)design a Preassessment. You might select and issue one or more for your narrative unit.

Exercise: (Re)design a Preassessment

Now that you have determined the narrative writing prompt and the criteria against which you will score it, consider what kind of preassessment you want to conduct at the outset of the unit. The following are options for this diagnostic step; consider issuing more than one preassessment. You can also use any of these suggestions as a formative assessment during the unit.

- **Respond to an on-demand writing prompt:** Issue the narrative prompt from the Achieve the Core website (visit http://achievethecore.org/page/1311/narrative-writing-on-demand to access the 6–12 prompt and student samples and http://achievethecore.org/page/1287/narrative-writing-on-demand for K–5). For grades 6–12, students read text pertaining to the Dust Bowl and view accompanying photographs as the stimulus for writing. They write a narrative showing how a particular small moment during this experience affected one person. Although I designed this book for students in grades 5–12, you might benefit from using or adapting Achieve the Core's K–5 assessment. In it, students write a realistic or imaginary story based on a painting about three dogs and a cat.

- **Review narrative writing samples to identify purpose and characteristic elements:** Select an exemplary piece of narrative writing and distribute it to each student. Instruct students to individually read the piece, determine the purpose for writing, and identify and mark in the margins any of the elements of writing they can name. You can leave this open ended or provide a list of elements. (Visit **go.SolutionTree.com/literacy** or see appendix E [page 151] for links to sample writing resources.)

- **Compare and contrast narrative writing samples:** Distribute a weak and a strong narrative sample to each student. Ask them to articulate in writing the differences between the two pieces and justify their reasons for what contributes to the stronger piece of writing and what the weaker one lacks. Additionally, you can ask students to focus on and improve one aspect of the ineffective paper (for example, setting or character description). Again, find appropriate student samples from the resources at **go.SolutionTree.com/literacy** or refer to appendix E (page 151).

- **Answer open-ended questions:** Ask students to write responses to questions such as the following: Why do people write memoirs (*autobiographies, fables, myths, realistic fiction*, or other)? What are the elements of this genre? Can you create a graphic organizer to show the structure and relationship among these elements? Have you written a memoir (or other genre) before? If so, what was the topic? What might you have done to improve on the paper you wrote, and what questions do you have about this genre?

- **Organize elements of literature:** Issue the preassessment in figure 2.8 that asks students to review the words and phrases and arrange them into an organizational structure (outline, web, or other structure) that explains how they interrelate. Students will select a word or phrase from the provided list that represents the title of an outline or center of a web. Additionally, it asks them to write a rationale. The graphic organizer they devise along with their explanation can assess the degree of their familiarity with narrative. Figure 2.9 (page 48) shows a completed web that you can use to introduce the unit after students complete the preassessment. Ask students to sketch their graphic organizer in their student notebooks, or provide a copy as a reference.

Make a Web Preassessment

1. On a separate sheet of paper, create an outline, web, or other graphic organizer of your choice that uses the following words and phrases in a way that you think makes sense. If you want to add your own words or phrases to your organizer, please do.

• Third person	• Plot	• Central conflict
• When	• Character	• Introduction
• First person	• Rising action	• Time
• Where	• Theme	• Place
• Point of view	• Falling action	• Elements
• Central message	• Antagonist	• Climax
• Setting	• Resolution	• Protagonist

2. Write a paragraph that explains your graphic organizer.

Figure 2.8: Narrative preassessment.

Visit **go.SolutionTree.com/literacy** *for a free reproducible version of this figure.*

Summary

Present the writing task and criteria early in the unit in an intentional way. This positions students for success as they become keenly aware of expectations and can contribute their own ideas. If teachers merely distribute the criteria and do so late in the unit, students will not have the advantage of realizing key learning outcomes and how their daily work contributes to the final product. Rather, conduct an activity to introduce the checklist and rubric in a way that elicits input from them about the expectations. This exercise helps you check for students' understanding of a narrative's elements and structure, further cements their learning about a particular genre, and gives them a roadmap for the upcoming unit. Then, as long as their ideas contribute to a rigorous and robust written form of narrative,

you can use their feedback to augment the criteria you've prepared.

Preassessments can be powerful tools that serve multifaceted purposes. They set the stage for learning, help you identify previous knowledge or misconceptions, assist with future differentiation experiences, and provide the basis for launching the unit. In narrative writing, asking students to write in the genre you will be teaching or examining and commenting on writing samples as a preassessment can yield important information to help direct your instruction.

Now that the beginning stages of backward design are firmly in place—learning outcomes, evidence of student learning, and success criteria—you are primed to design learning experiences. In the next chapter, I feature the gradual release of responsibility model by detailing a sample lesson to describe how the model looks in action.

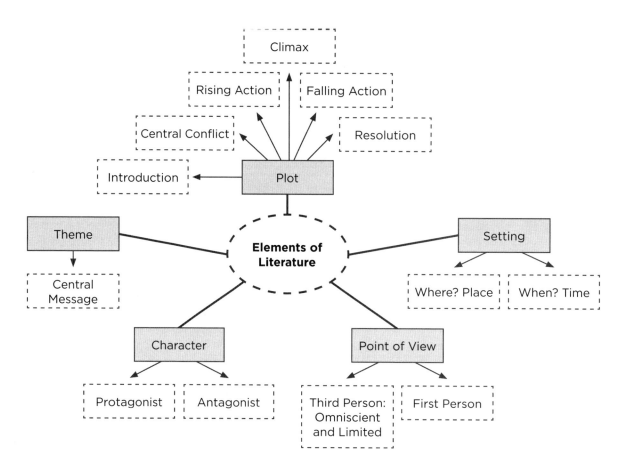

Figure 2.9: Elements of literature web.

*Visit **go.SolutionTree.com/literacy** for a free reproducible version of this figure.*

Using Gradual Release of Responsibility for Lesson Design in Action

In the backward-design approach, educators devise units with a clear focus on learning outcomes before delving into lesson design. The following are the three components of backward planning; the previous chapters cover the first two.

1. Use content-area standards to identify what students should know, understand, and do in a specific unit of study and create guiding questions that emanate from them.

2. Create a culminating assessment so students can show evidence of understanding the learning outcomes. Devise a student checklist and scoring rubric to identify and articulate clear expectations for students.

3. Once in place, these clear intentions and success criteria steer designing lessons, which include other assessments to gauge student learning.

To explicitly teach an unfamiliar skill, strategy, or process in a way that yields success, you can design lessons using gradual release of responsibility (GRR), an instructional framework for new learning (Pearson & Gallagher, 1983). This model has four parts that create a fluid and cohesive instructional sequence. You can implement it when conducting a comprehensive lesson during one class period of varying length (for example, a fifty-minute or block-schedule class), or a series of lessons for more complicated learning topics. Inspired by

P. David Pearson and Margaret C. Gallagher's (1983) model, Douglas Fisher and Nancy Frey (2014) identify these four components in the gradual release of responsibility model.

1. Focused instruction ("I do it.")

2. Guided instruction ("We do it.")

3. Collaborative learning ("You do it together.")

4. Independent learning ("You do it alone.")

For more complete information on this model, consult resources from Fisher and Frey, Pearson, *The Fundamentals of (Re)designing Writing Units* (Glass, 2017a), or others. To illustrate the gradual release of responsibility model in action, this chapter presents a concrete example for a lesson on teaching imagery, specifically for a setting in a narrative. If you plan to teach this comprehensive lesson, notice that it begins with a review of the characteristics of imagery. For activity ideas you can lead prior to teaching it, see the next chapter (page 55). To increase your professional expertise about imagery and figurative language in general, peruse appendix C (page 137), if needed.

This two-part lesson asks that students identify consummate examples of imagery in published work, make a list of words and phrases that they feel are particularly descriptive (Part 1: Identify Examples of Imagery), and practice drafting a descriptive setting that weaves those authors' examples of imagery with their own original creations (Part 2: Draft a Setting). The duration is approximately two fifty-minute class periods.

This featured lesson focuses on learning outcomes within two rows in table 1.2 (chapter 1, pages 11–17)—Setting and Descriptive Words and Figurative Language.

Part 1: Identify Examples of Imagery

As a frame of reference, this lesson is meant to be embedded within a series of other instructional experiences on imagery. Beforehand, orient students to a checklist or rubric to make them aware of the expectations for their narratives, which include imagery. (See figure 2.5 [pages 36–37] for presenting the checklist to students.)

To prepare, find and copy published excerpts of text—in this case, with imagery for setting. You can use what I provide or setting examples from text your students are reading, which can certainly be longer than what I feature.

Focused Instruction—"I Do It"

To initiate the gradual release of responsibility lesson, follow this sequence.

1. **Set the purpose for learning:** Tell students that today they will answer the lesson-guiding question, *What are examples of imagery for setting?* Connect to previous learning by soliciting volunteers to recall the definition of imagery. Use all or some of the following points based on your students' grade level and prior knowledge. Make sure they record the definition in their notebooks if they haven't previously.

    *   Imagery is a type of figurative language that writers use in poetry and prose.

    *   It relies on writing that uses sensory details—words and phrases that appeal to the five senses.

    *   Authors use it to write descriptive sensory details so readers capture vivid mental pictures (or *images*) in their mind's eye of what they read.

    *   In narrative writing, authors can use imagery to describe settings, characters, and events; to depict objects and characters' thoughts or feelings; and for

dialogue tags to add dimension to what a character says.

*   Imagery focuses on *showing* rather than *telling* about a topic.

*   When writers use imagery well, it can arouse an emotional or perhaps physical response.

Point to the section on the checklist about imagery and particular line items that align with the guiding question, such as using imagery for character, setting, or event descriptions. Emphasize during and after this two-part lesson that students should apply what they learn to write descriptively for other parts of their narrative as the checklist and rubric indicate.

2. **Briefly explain the task:** Tell students they will participate in activities that will ultimately prepare them for writing a setting with imagery for their narratives. First, they will identify words and phrases that include imagery—or sensory details—from a published author or authors. Later, they will practice writing with imagery to describe a setting.

3. **Read a text excerpt:** Read an excerpt of imagery for setting from a complex text that students are reading in your class or from the novel *Poppy* by Avi (1995) featured here. (You can also access appendix C or use excerpts from figure 4.1 [pages 57–58] in the next chapter.) Display it on an electronic device that students can see as a class, if available, and distribute a hard copy of it. Avi (1995) writes:

    > It was as if the sun had been stolen. Only thin ribbons of light seeped down through the green and milky air, air syrupy with the scent of pine, huckleberry, and juniper. From the rolling, emerald-carpeted earth, fingers of lacy ferns curled up, above which the massive fir and pine trees stood, pillar-like, to support an invisible sky. Hovering over everything was a silence as deep as the trees were tall. (pp. 83, 85)

4. **Model and use think-aloud to select imagery examples:** Use the think-aloud strategy to show what words and phrases you consider examples of imagery from the excerpt. Here is what you might say to show your thinking:

Think-Aloud Suggestion

My task is to mark words and phrases that are examples of imagery for the setting. First, I'll read the passage all the way through to get a feel for it. I've read it before, so it's familiar text; however, I haven't read it while looking particularly for imagery, so I'm rereading for this purpose now. After I read once, I'll go back to highlight or underline imagery examples.

I'm looking for words and phrases that reveal sensory details—taste, touch, smell, sight, and sound. With this task in mind, I'm going to highlight *(or underline or write on a separate sheet of paper or sticky note if I can't write on the text)* these words and phrases: *thin ribbons of light* and *air syrupy*. I think *thin ribbons of light* is a strong example of imagery because I can visualize this image in my head as I read. It appeals to my sense of sight. *Air syrupy* seems to appeal to both smell and touch. Smell because afterward the author mentions different trees that are fragrant, like pines. Because syrup is thick, this description leaves an effect on me of denseness perhaps from the humidity in the forest, which exaggerates the aroma from the trees. If the author were focusing on taste and the sweetness of syrup, I think he would describe something that is edible.

5. **Check for understanding:** To check for understanding, invite a few volunteers to offer other imagery examples from the paragraph and their rationale. Instruct all students to signal if they agree (thumbs-up), disagree (thumbs-down), or aren't sure (fist) about each suggested imagery example, including the ones you flagged.

Guided Instruction—"We Do It"

After modeling, ask students arranged in homogeneous groups to read another paragraph (or longer passage) and repeat what you showed them: highlight, underline, or write a list of words and phrases that reflect imagery along with the associated sense. Following is a different text excerpt about setting from *Poppy* (Avi, 1995) that you might use, or find your own passage:

The silence was broken by the sound of sharp tapping. Poppy ducked. But nothing happened. From another direction came a yelp. A screech. Poppy shivered. Closer still was the smothered scurry of something slithery and unseen. A tree groaned. A branch snapped. There was the passing scamper of little feet. Poppy's heart raced just as fast. (p. 85)

Scaffold to provide support to students who might need additional assistance. As they work, monitor their learning and provide suggestions to help empower them if they are stuck. For students who flag words and phrases void of imagery, ask them to justify their thinking using textual evidence. You might prompt them to reconsider by saying, "When looking at what you highlighted, does it evoke any of the five senses? Do you get a picture in your head of what the author has written? I'd like you to reread the excerpt and hunt for those words and phrases that are examples of imagery because they help you to visualize something through the use of sensory detail." Perhaps read the text aloud and ask for one sense at a time or model and use think-aloud again to give some students more examples. For more advanced students, extend instruction by sharing more sophisticated text examples.

Like before, to check for understanding, invite volunteers to each share one example and their rationale from this second passage and perhaps signal if they agree (thumbs-up), disagree (thumbs-down), or aren't sure (fist) about each suggestion.

Collaborative Learning— "You Do It Together"

In this part of the lesson, small groups work to identify imagery examples from other text passages for setting that you did not present earlier. Distribute an appropriately challenging excerpt to each group so they can further practice identifying imagery. If students are in literature circles, direct them to preselected pages with imagery excerpts.

Ask students to read the excerpts and discuss their impression of which words and phrases are strong examples of imagery by justifying their reasoning. In their discussions, encourage them to answer these questions: *What is the effect of imagery? Does it enhance the author's work?* After discussion, instruct them to each make a list of their personal favorite examples on a separate sheet of paper. They'll add to their lists during independent learning. Solicit a few volunteers to share examples and highlights of their discussion with the whole class.

Independent Learning— "You Do It Alone"

In the final stage of gradual release of responsibility, students independently apply what they learned. To do so, instruct them to peruse the text on their own, locate passages that contain imagery, use discernment to identify the strongest examples, and add favorite sensory words and phrases to the lists they compiled during the collaborative learning stage. For learners needing extra support, continue to narrow down the text that contains imagery so they are not struggling to manage an overwhelming amount of text.

Part 2: Draft a Setting

Lead this lesson immediately following part 1 either during the same class period, if time allows, or the next day or time you meet with the class.

Focused Instruction—"I Do It"

In this "I do it" stage, use the following to focus instruction.

1. **Set the purpose for learning:** Remind students that earlier they identified examples of imagery that authors use to describe setting in various text excerpts. Plus, they selected and compiled a list of their favorite sensory words and phrases. Now they will use what they recorded to practice writing a descriptive setting. Share these guiding questions with students to set the stage for learning: *How do I write using imagery for setting? What is the effect of imagery?*

2. **Briefly explain the task:** Tell students that they will compose a paragraph about a setting that incorporates selected imagery excerpts from their lists. Their writing can be on any setting or one that complements the text you are reading in class to add or extend an author's setting description. This exercise prepares them to write using imagery for their own narratives for not only setting but also other aspects of their stories in which sensory details enhance the writing.

3. **Model and use the think-aloud strategy to write a descriptive setting:** Using the

think-aloud strategy concurrently with modeling, show students how they can write descriptively using a combination of their own and an author's words. You might begin your think-aloud in this way:

Think-Aloud Suggestion

My assigned task is to look at my list of imagery excerpts I feel are particularly effective and use them along with my own original writing for a setting. Here's the list I compiled from Avi's writing. (Show students figure 3.1.)

When I draft my paragraph or paragraphs, here's what I will specifically keep in mind.

- Choose any setting I want.

- Select items from my list to formulate a setting.

- Add my own sensory words and phrases to the author's so I can be as creative as possible.

- Change the order of the author's words and phrases any way that I wish.

List of Imagery Words and Phrases	
thin ribbons of light	snapped
green and milky air	screech
air syrupy with the scent of pine	smothered scurry of something slithery
rolling, emerald-carpeted earth	scamper
fingers of lacy ferns curled up	seeped
	stolen sun
pine trees stood, pillar-like	silence as deep as the trees were tall
sharp tapping	hovering
yelp	invisible sky
groaned	

Figure 3.1: Imagery words and phrases.

While drafting in front of the class, show students how you struggle with this exercise. Your writing can be halting at times, especially when you first start to compose. Cross out and replace words and phrases to illustrate the iterative process of drafting. Show how the author's work fosters creativity by using what he or she wrote to generate new ideas. If you are uncomfortable with writing, you can use an existing example (such as one of my examples that follows), although I encourage you to try to craft your own piece so students see the authentic struggle writers often experience. If you use a prewritten example, still mimic the arduous task of thinking of ideas so students don't see you copying examples verbatim.

- *The cold was seeping through my thin cotton shirt. The silence was broken as a branch snapped. Instinctively, I ducked my head and faced the invisible sky void of clouds. Through the thin ribbon of light I overheard wings whispering about me. The massive pillar-like eucalyptus shuddered as the creature landed.*

- *Slender fingers of lacy fern wound their way through the tendril-like ribbons of mist. The stolen sun of light began to emerge through the green and milky air. Columns of fir and pine cast elegant shadows over the rolling emerald carpet of moss.*

When thinking aloud while drafting, warn about plagiarism so that you alert students to avoid overusing authors' work. Mention that this exercise is meant to increase their ability to write with imagery by using the authors' selections as a springboard to promote creativity and original thought.

4. **Check for understanding:** Ask students to turn and talk with a neighbor to point to textual evidence of how you incorporated an imagery example or examples from the author, and added your own imagery. Walk around the room to hear their discussions. Solicit a few volunteers to share your original sensory details and the senses they associate with each description.

Guided Instruction—"We Do It"

After modeling, arrange students in homogeneous groups. Ask them to review the items on their lists of sensory details and circle a few words. They share these with each other and practice writing sentences together using their selections.

As always, provide support by offering guidance that enables students to productively struggle. Perhaps suggest settings they might use as the basis for their writing. Some students might need scaffolded instruction in the form of sentence starters. In addition, provide pictures of settings to help them generate original details for writing. After giving them ample time for drafting, return to furnish appropriate feedback.

Check for understanding to ensure students are progressing. They will likely finish their sentences at different times. Therefore, invite volunteers to write sentences on the document camera, chart paper, whiteboard, or interactive whiteboard to share with classmates as everyone works.

Collaborative Learning— "You Do It Together"

Invite students to share their entire lists of favorite imagery examples with small groups. Together, they select a setting and collaboratively write a paragraph incorporating selected authors' words and phrases of imagery along with their own descriptive detail. For an additional challenge, suggest that students include other types of figurative language in their paragraphs, such as simile, metaphor, and so forth. When they finish, invite each group to share their paragraph with another group and respond to this question: What is the impact of imagery on the writing?

Independent Learning— "You Do It Alone"

Allow uninterrupted time for students to work independently to draft a setting using imagery for their own narratives. Remind them they can selectively use authors' words and phrases to inspire them but to not borrow so much that they plagiarize. During this exercise, students can share their paragraphs to solicit feedback from classmates face to face or electronically, or even with a wider audience.

Summary

Gradual release of responsibility provides a sound lesson framework to use for teaching students a new skill, strategy, or process. With the ultimate goal of enabling students to independently and proficiently apply something new, first employ focused instruction to set the purpose for learning and to model—concurrent with the think-aloud strategy—what the targeted learning looks like in action. As the lesson progresses, conduct guided practice with students in homogeneous groups who require similar support. Provide ample scaffolding and, when needed, extension for some students. Then devise collaborative learning opportunities as a precursor to students independently applying the new learning.

Throughout this approach, your role constantly changes. Initially, you operate from a position of high control as you explicitly instruct and model. Gradually, you release this stance, giving students more responsibility so they independently apply the skill, strategy, or process at the center of instruction. Although this approach includes defined elements, there is room for flexibility. For example, you might repeat or switch some components. You decide how to vary the model based on learners' needs, targeted skills for the lesson, previous learning, and so forth.

After implementing the gradual release of responsibility model, continue to provide opportunities for students to use what they learned throughout the year. Reinforce the new learning with feedback and verification to cement the skill, strategy, or process in students' minds so that it rests on solid ground and eventually becomes intuitive.

The next chapter focuses on myriad teaching methods and instructional strategies aligned to key skills for narrative writing. As you read the next chapter, take into account the framework of the gradual release of responsibility model or another research-based direct instruction approach to help you plan sound learning experiences with a higher likelihood of maximizing student achievement.

Designing Lessons

Teachers should design lessons that empower students to master one or more intertwined learning outcomes as shown in the unit map. In Marzano's (2017) *The New Art and Science of Teaching*, he articulates the relationship between lessons and units and their intrinsic links. He emphasizes that lessons are isolated and make sense only within the panoramic framework that a unit can provide:

> A teacher executes a lesson within the context of a set of lessons, oftentimes referred to as a *unit*, that serve a common purpose. . . . I believe it is not effective practice to plan one lesson at a time. Instead, teachers should plan from the perspective of the unit, which should provide an overarching framework for instruction. (Marzano, 2017, p. 107)

To this point, the unit map guides you in ultimately creating, redesigning, or researching to find the necessary lessons to teach a comprehensive unit. Marzano (2017) indicates that, while teaching a unit, "Teachers should be free to adjust daily activities as the unit progresses to take advantage of learning opportunities that might come up or to revise activities based on student feedback" (p. 107). Nevertheless, he makes it clear that teachers should choreograph and thoughtfully design lessons within the context of a sound unit plan; careful planning is imperative.

This chapter focuses on helping you design or redesign lessons to conduct as students move through different stages of the writing process to ultimately produce their narratives. To support you in this endeavor, I provide activities, strategies, and assessments for these topics.

- Imagery and setting (see also chapter 3, page 49)
- Mood
- Character physical description
- Plot elements
- Theme
- Narrative introductions
- Dialogue
- Sentence structure
- Narrative prewriting
- Narrative revision

Consider how and when you would use and adapt what you read in this chapter—as a preassessment, a review, to check for understanding, or to develop into complete lessons. Some material is appropriate for prewriting as you offer explicit instruction before students begin composing their narrative pieces. Other ideas will be prudent for teaching certain skills after students produce their first drafts so they apply and incorporate what they learn in their subsequent versions. Furthermore, it is unlikely that every idea I share will be suitable for what you teach and the level of knowledge of your students. Therefore, choose those ideas that target necessary skills and aptly serve your students. In fact, you might use a specific activity for individuals or a small group of students to differentiate instruction rather than for the whole class.

In addition, in *The Fundamentals of (Re)designing Writing Units* (Glass, 2017a), I include teaching suggestions and tools for all stages of the writing process—prewriting, drafting, revising, editing, publishing, and reflecting. For a brief summary of what you can find in each chapter of the *Fundamentals* book, see the introduction in this text.

As I mention in chapter 3, use the gradual release of responsibility or another explicit teaching model to develop lessons for any skills, procedures, or strategies previously unfamiliar to students. Employing such a model compels you to focus on the learning outcomes and helps ensure that your instruction contributes to achievement. Remember, though, that some topics might be a review; therefore, an entire lesson that adheres to all four stages of the gradual release of responsibility model may not always be necessary.

For KUD and guiding question options that address lesson ideas, refer to table 1.2 (chapter 1, pages 11–17). At the end of this chapter is an exercise that focuses on lesson design. At that time, you can judiciously build lessons using the ideas in this chapter or revise existing ones of your own for targeted topics guided by any of the learning outcomes.

Although comprehensive, I do not include learning suggestions for every facet of all genres of narrative for you to arrive at a totally complete curriculum. Therefore, you can add lessons geared to characteristics for the specific genre you plan to teach. Additionally, you might include learning experiences around general writing skills that contribute to a holistic, sound written product (for example, sentence combining or active versus passive voice).

I begin by offering activity suggestions that provide additional support for imagery that you can use, as necessary, to augment the comprehensive lesson from the previous chapter.

Imagery and Setting

To facilitate learning experiences around imagery, select a combination of the activities in this section. You can also adapt what you read to teach other forms of figurative language, such as metaphor, simile, personification, and hyperbole. What I share focuses on identification and drafting of imagery primarily for setting; when you design your lessons, consider augmenting them with a focus on imagery for other areas of narratives, plus making inferences. To do so, consistently foster discussion around these and other related questions: *What is the impact of the imagery on this passage? What does this passage with imagery mean? What inferences might you make? How does the imagery passage give you a greater sense of the whole piece? If the author does not include imagery, does it give you as much insight as if he or she had?*

To orient you to this topic and where it resides within a comprehensive narrative unit, refer to the Setting and Descriptive Words and Figurative Language rows on table 1.2. Also, review appendix C to add to your knowledge of this topic, if needed, and find text examples for teaching.

Focus on Imagery That Appeals to Sound

When you introduce imagery, consider that some students might benefit from focusing on one sense at a time—in this case *sound*—or a combination of two senses as a stepping-stone to prepare for appealing to all senses in their writing.

1. **Read text and identify imagery that appeals to sound:** Expose students to several passages where authors write strong imagery for sound. (Refer to examples in appendix C, if needed.) As they read text, ask them to find evidence of the following techniques—recommended by George Hillocks (2007)—to highlight a focus on sound. Encourage them to compare and contrast different ways authors depict sound.

   - Indicate the source of the sound.

   - Use words that imitate the sound.

   - Break complicated sounds into parts.

   - Describe the character of the sound (e.g., rhythm, pitch, tone).

   - Use figurative language or analogy to describe the sound, comparing it to something else. (p. 86)

Also introduce Poe's (1843/2002) "The Tell-Tale Heart." After conducting activities in which students examine this complex text thoroughly, return to the following passage, which directly or indirectly refers to sound. This part of the story is when the officers enter the home, and the protagonist places chairs on top of the boards where the corpse lies:

> The officers were satisfied. My manner had convinced them. I was singularly at ease. They sat, and while I answered cheerily, they chatted of familiar things. But, ere long, I felt myself getting pale and wished them gone. My head ached, and I fancied a ringing in my ears; but still they sat and still chatted. The ringing became more distinct: I talked more freely to get rid of the feeling: but it continued and gained definitiveness—until, at length, I found that the noise was not within my ears.
>
> No doubt I now grew very pale; but I talked more fluently, and with a heightened voice. Yet the sound increased—and what could I do? It was a low dull quick sound—much such a sound as a watch makes when enveloped in cotton. I gasped for breath—and yet the officers heard it not. I talked more quickly—more vehemently; but the noise steadily increased. I arose and argued about trifles, in a high key and with violent gesticulations; but the noise steadily increased. (Poe, 1843/2002, pp. 201–202)

2. **Write using a sense of sound:** After examining various texts, invite students to sketch a character or write about a setting or event, paying particular attention to sound. Within their writing, instruct them to invent their own words and phrases guided by Hillocks's techniques described earlier.

Identify Imagery in Complex Text

1. **Identify and discuss imagery:** Distribute a variety of different passages featuring imagery, such as the excerpts in figure 4.1, other ones in this section, those in appendix C (page 137), or some in familiar classroom complex texts. Ask students to read a passage, underline or highlight words and phrases of imagery, and team up with a partner to discuss whether what they flagged constitutes strong examples. Students defend their responses or rethink what they marked, and agree on the words and phrases that evoke imagery. (This part of the exercise is featured in chapter 3 as part of the gradual release of responsibility lesson.)

2. **Use a graphic organizer:** Then instruct them to input imagery words and phrases into the graphic organizer in figure 4.2 (page 59). Invite pairs to share with another partnership to discuss their impressions and interpretations of imagery. As an alternative or in addition to using written text, students can invent imagery from visually appealing artwork and record examples.

Text Excerpts With Imagery
Excerpt from *When the Emperor Was Divine* (Otsuka, 2002):   All through October the days were still warm, like summer, but at night the mercury dropped and in the morning the sagebrush was sometimes covered with frost. Twice in one week there were dust storms. The sky turned suddenly gray and then a hot wind came screaming across the desert, churning up everything in its path. From inside the barracks the boy could not see the sun or the moon or even the next row of barracks on the other side of the gravel path. All he could see was dust. The wind rattled the windows and doors and the dust seeped like smoke through the cracks in the roof and at night he slept with a wet handkerchief over his mouth to keep out the smell. In the morning, when he woke, the wet handkerchief was dry and in his mouth there was the gritty taste of chalk. (p. 77)

Figure 4.1: Text excerpts with imagery.   continued ➤

Excerpt from "The Pedestrian" (Bradbury, 1951):

To enter out into that silence that was the city at eight o'clock of a misty evening in November, to put your feet upon that buckling concrete walk, to step over grassy seams and make your way, hands in pockets, through the silences, that was what Mr. Leonard Mead most dearly loved to do. He would stand upon the corner of an intersection and peer down long moonlit avenues of sidewalk in four directions, deciding which way to go, but it really made no difference; he was alone in this world of A.D. 2053, or as good as alone, and with a final decision made, a path selected, he would stride off, sending patterns of frosty air before him like the smoke of a cigar.

Excerpt from *Johnny Tremain* (Forbes, 1971):

On rocky islands gulls woke. Time to be about their business. Silently they floated in on the town, but when their icy eyes sighted the first dead fish, first bits of garbage about the ships and wharves, they began to scream and quarrel.

The cocks in Boston back yards had long before cried the coming of the day. Now the hens were also awake, scratching, clucking, laying eggs.

Cats in malt houses, granaries, ship holds, mansions and hovels caught a last mouse, settled down to wash their fur and sleep. Cats did not work by day.

In stables horses shook their halters and whinnied.

In barns cows lowed to be milked.

Boston slowly opened its eyes, stretched, and woke. The sun struck in horizontally from the east, flashing upon weathervanes—brass cocks and arrows, here a glass-eyed Indian, there a copper grasshopper—and the bells in the steeples cling-clanged, telling the people it was time to be up and about. (p. 1)

Excerpt from "To Build a Fire" (London, 1908):

Day had broken cold and gray, exceedingly cold and gray, when the man turned aside from the main Yukon trail and climbed the high earth-bank, where a dim and little-traveled trail led eastward through the fat spruce timberland. It was a steep bank, and he paused for breath at the top, excusing the act to himself by looking at his watch. It was nine o'clock. There was no sun nor hint of sun, though there was not a cloud in the sky. It was a clear day, and yet there seemed an intangible pall over the face of things, a subtle gloom that made the day dark, and that was due to the absence of sun. This fact did not worry the man. He was used to the lack of sun. It had been days since he had seen the sun, and he knew that a few more days must pass before that cheerful orb, due south, would just peep above the sky-line and dip immediately from view.

Excerpt from "The Kitten" (Wright, 1967):

It was in this tenement that the personality of my father first came fully into the orbit of my concern. . . . I learned that I could not make noise when he was asleep in the daytime. He was the lawgiver in our family and I never laughed in his presence. I used to lurk timidly in the kitchen doorway and watch his huge body sitting slumped at the table. I stared at him with awe as he gulped his beer from a tin bucket, as he ate long and heavily, sighed, belched, closed his eyes to nod on a stuffed belly. He was quite fat and his bloated stomach always lapped over his belt. He was always a stranger to me, always somehow alien and remote. (p. 141)

Excerpt from *All the Light We Cannot See* (Doerr, 2014):

She has no memories of her mother but imagines her as white, a soundless brilliance. Her father radiates a thousand colors, opal, strawberry red, deep russet, wild green; a smell like oil and metal, the feel of a lock tumbler sliding home, the sound of his key rings chiming as he walks. He is an olive green when he talks to a department head, an escalating series of oranges when he speaks to Mademoiselle Fleury from the greenhouses, a bright red when he tries to cook. He glows sapphire when he sits over his workbench in the evenings, humming almost inaudibly as he works, the tip of his cigarette gleaming a prismatic blue. (p. 45)

Source: Bradbury, 1951; Doerr, 2014; Forbes, 1971; London, 1908; Otsuka, 2002; Wright, 1967.

*Visit **go.SolutionTree.com/literacy** for a free reproducible version of this figure.*

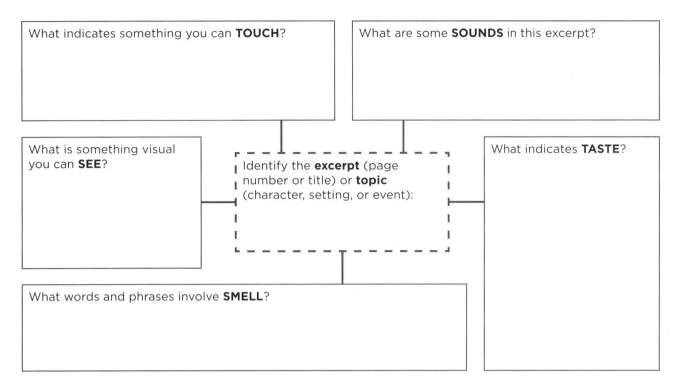

Figure 4.2: Imagery graphic organizer.

*Visit **go.SolutionTree.com/literacy** for a free reproducible version of this figure.*

Write With Specificity

1. **Distinguish between show, not tell:** Ask students to articulate the difference between examples A and B. (A merely *tells* that the park is a disaster whereas B uses imagery to *show* what disaster specifically entails.) Define or review the definition and types of imagery (see appendix C, page 137). Instruct students to cite textual evidence of imagery from example B.

   A. The park is a mess. It is always filthy and disgusting. I hate to come here because it is never clean.

   B. The ancient paint, once a vibrant green, peels off the park benches scratching my exposed thigh. Weeds force their way through the cracked pavement in haphazard patterns. Cigarette butts and beer cans camouflage as toys littering the sandbox, and my rubber soles stick to puddles of day-old soda.

2. **Identify imagery examples:** To prepare for a writing exercise, ask students to articulate and defend which phrases exemplify strong imagery from the following student example.

   ### *The Woman Was Guilty*

   As she rushed out of the room, her eyes rolled around her sockets like the wheels of a bicycle. She quickly yanked a mysterious object out of her pocket and shoved it into her immense purse which was so vast that her life of secrets seemed hidden inside. As she took a step, each one following seemed to become faster and faster until her stroll evolved into a sprint. When made to sit, she was silent and ignored every question that was asked of her. Instead, she crunched her fingers into a tight fist and her blushed face appeared as if she were holding in oxygen. Her foot tapped the wooden floor faster than a heartbeat, her head hung down, and she avoided the ones surrounding her like she was attempting to distract even herself. (Kimmie G., high school senior)

3. **Practice writing with imagery:** Instruct students to write an imagery paragraph modeled after the student sample. Invite them to choose one of the following sentences as the basis for their writing. Explain that they cannot use the actual sentence in their paragraphs. Their goal is to write so descriptively that someone can guess the sentence based on the quality of their work. When finished, student pairs read each other's papers, make an educated guess about the target sentence by citing textual evidence, and confirm the sentence with the writer.

- The amusement park is filled with many rides.
- This is a mild spring.
- Winter here is colder than I remember.
- The house appears dilapidated.
- Her bedroom was filled with posters on the walls.
- The airport lounge had many amenities.
- The kitchen is a disaster.
- School playgrounds have lots of equipment and toys for young children.
- I walked past a bakery.

Write a Setting Collaboratively Using Imagery

Invite students to collectively write a descriptive setting using imagery and perhaps other figurative language. (This activity is like the collaborative learning one in chapter 3 but without borrowing authors' words and phrases.) Before they begin, show them the middle school student samples in figure 4.3 to critique and discuss. Suggest this process for writing their group paragraphs.

1. Each group agrees on a setting—for example, an amusement park, a sports arena, the Alaskan tundra, a sorority house, Monday morning, and so forth.

2. Each group member composes two or more descriptive phrases about the setting to share with one another.

3. Group members provide input on whether or not the writing evokes an image; if not, they collectively revise.

4. Together, they elaborate on the phrases, turn them into sentences, and sequence them accordingly to create a vivid single- or multiple-setting paragraph to share with the class.

Student Samples of Settings
Today is the day! After weeks of waiting, I finally came to the fun-filled amusement park. There is not a single whispering gust of wind and the trees stand still as the ground. The concrete holding my feet is burning from the insufferable heat raging from the flaming sun. Off in the distance, the carousel passes its lively, high-spirited music to the various areas of the park. Where shall I go first? Which ride will first be privileged to provide the most joyous of experiences for me? I look up to see the Big Dipper roller coaster ride, magnifying and lighting the park up with its gleaming magnitude. The blood-curdling screams of small, innocent children tingle my neck with excitement.

It was a dark night. The fog partially covered the moonlight. What was left of the light shone on the marshes. The only sounds were the frogs croaking and the 11:15 train passing by. Seven-year-old Eddie quickly got off the stopped train. He was wearing rags as he silently walked down the gravel path and vaguely heard echoing footsteps in the empty night trailing behind him. Cautiously, he looked back. He saw nothing but heard rattling in the bushes. The thought that someone was watching him sent shivers down his spine. He hoped he would be at his grandmother's soon. As he continued on in the pitch black, again he heard the footsteps, so he forged on speeding his step. He turned quickly into a dark abandoned alley, faced a shadow of a man, and knew he would meet his death. Eddie screamed out, but only the silence called back.

The aromatic breeze wafted through the park on that perfect July morning. The calm buzz of couples courting and children playing and laughing was shattered by the off-beat barking of a stray dog. The dog's cries soon died off as he raced toward the dike at the end of the park. The sounds of the sailboats' splashing echoed off the lake and dominated all sounds for just an instant, before the enthusiastic chit-chat resumed once again.

Figure 4.3: Student samples of settings.

Visit **go.SolutionTree.com/literacy** *for a free reproducible version of this figure.*

Analyze the Impact of Mood on Setting

Teach mood and how it impacts setting so students can apply what they learn to make their narratives more sophisticated.

1. **List various emotions:** Invite students as a class to generate a list of emotions, such as *anxious, gloomy, sentimental, sympathetic,* and so forth, to display on chart paper or an easel. To help them compile the list, show pictures of people or drawings that clearly reflect emotions. Use YouTube videos, such as "Tone and Mood Words" (Hammond, 2008), to facilitate instruction. Additionally, prepare and play a musical collage comprising snippets of various artists representing different genres (for example, country, classical, pop, rock, rap, and alternative). After each musical clip, stop and solicit more words for emotions to add to the student-generated list. Ask students to categorize the list of words so they become familiar with the words.

2. **Define mood:** Share a definition for mood—the reader's attitude toward the text (including artwork and music) and the overall sense she or he gets while reading, such as upbeat, unhappy, or mellow. Authors of narrative carefully choose words and phrases to describe the setting, characters, and events that create a desired effect on readers from which they ascertain a mood. See appendix C (page 137) for more information about this literary device.

3. **Cite textual evidence that supports mood:** Instruct students to read passages from a classroom complex text or the ones in figure 4.4 (page 62) to identify a mood, and pinpoint words and phrases that support it. As students read, foster discussion by posing these questions: *What is the general mood of this passage? What words or phrases support the mood you have identified?* As they continue to read a longer work at the center of instruction, ask them to discuss the mood at strategic points using these and other questions: *Does the mood change throughout the story? If so, what contributes to this change?*

4. **Draft setting that evokes mood:** Allow time for students to draft a setting that includes mood to elicit emotional responses in readers. Encourage them to get feedback from peers or others to gauge their reactions. The goal is to determine if their writing syncs with the mood they intend to convey.

Mood Excerpts Associated With Setting
Excerpts from "The Monkey's Paw" by W. W. Jacobs (1997):
Without, the night was cold and wet; but in the small parlor of Laburnam Villa the blinds were drawn and the fire burned brightly.
<< • >>
"That's the worst of living so far out," bawled Mrs. White, with sudden and unlooked-for violence; "of all the beastly, slushy, out-of-the-way places to live in, this is the worst. Pathway's a bog, and the road's a torrent. I don't know what people are thinking about. I suppose because only two houses in the road are let, they think it doesn't matter."
<< • >>
In the huge new cemetery, some two miles distant, the old people buried their dead, and came back to a house steeped in shadow and silence.
Excerpt from "All Summer in a Day" by Ray Bradbury (n.d.):
It rained.
It had been raining for seven years; thousands upon thousands of days compounded and filled from one end to the other with rain, with the drum and gush of water, with the sweet crystal fall of showers and the concussion of storms so heavy they were tidal waves come over the islands. A thousand forests had been crushed under the rain and grown up a thousand times to be crushed again. And this was the way life was forever on the planet Venus, and this was the schoolroom of the children of the rocket men and women who had come to a raining world to set up civilization and live out their lives.
Excerpt from "The Treasure of Lemon Brown" by Walter Dean Myers (1997):
It was beginning to cool. Gusts of wind made bits of paper dance between the parked cars. There was a flash of nearby lightning, and soon large drops of rain splashed onto his jeans. . . . Down the block there was an old tenement building that had been abandoned for some months. . . .
The inside of the building was dark except for the dim light that filtered through the dirty windows from the street lamps. There was a room a few feet from the door, and from where he stood at the entrance, Greg could see a squarish path of light on the floor. He entered the room, frowning at the musty smell. It was a large room that might have been someone's parlor at one time. Squinting, Greg could see an old table on its side against one wall, what looked like a pile of rags or a torn mattress in the corner, and a couch, with one side broken, in front of the window. (pp. T94, T95)

Source: Bradbury, n.d.; Jacobs, 1997; Myers, 1997.

Figure 4.4: Mood excerpts associated with setting.

*Visit **go.SolutionTree.com/literacy** for a free reproducible version of this figure.*

Use Objects to Promote Imagery Writing

Fill several bags with different objects that appeal to a range of senses, such as a lemon, cinnamon stick, Rubik's Cube, puzzle piece, cotton ball, sandpaper, fabric swatch, carpet piece, nail file, coffee bean, and so forth. Distribute a bag to a small group of students, and ask them to create sentences or a cohesive paragraph of imagery using the objects as the basis for their writing. Once finished, each group passes their bag and paragraph to another group, which uses the objects in the bag to write their own imagery piece. When done, groups compare their writing and discuss the strength of imagery between the two.

Character Physical Description

When readers study methods of characterization to collect evidence and make inferences, they uncover important information that can enliven characters' personalities and complexities and make them more believable. Characterization plays a pivotal role in a narrative as it can contribute to the direction of the plotline and influence other elements of literature. (See appendix C, page 137, for more information about characterization.)

The following activities can prepare students for drafting their own detailed physical descriptions of important characters. Augment any to focus on the other methods of characterization; in fact, the final activity reflects one way to synthesize all of the methods to infer personality traits. As a prerequisite, teach or review imagery and other types of figurative language so students can apply what they have learned when writing about characters.

To provide a focus for this topic, consider options for learning outcomes and guiding questions on table 1.2 (pages 11–17) for Character and Characterization and Descriptive Words and Figurative Language.

Collect Descriptive Words and Phrases About Characters

1. **Collect descriptions:** Arrange students into pairs and distribute a character description card from a published author (see figure 4.5) to each of them. Explain that their goal is to collect and eventually record the most descriptive words and phrases from several excerpts. First, pairs read their card, then discuss and highlight descriptive text. Next, they find another pair of students and together share their impressions of the most vivid words and phrases from their respective cards. During their discussion, instruct them to arrive at a consensus about the most detailed phrases and justify their reasoning. Afterward, students switch cards to examine new paragraphs and repeat the activity several times to experience many rich examples.

2. **Record descriptions:** Lastly, students individually record in their notebooks any words and phrases that impress them to use later in their own writing. (Instead of recording their favorite descriptions after sharing several cards with classmates, you might have them write throughout the exercise.)

Physical Appearance Excerpts
Excerpt from *The Zookeeper's Wife* (Ackerman, 2007):   Balding, with a crown of dark brown hair, Jan needed a hat to fight burn in summer and chill in winter, which is why in outdoor photographs he's usually wearing a fedora, giving him an air of sober purpose. Some indoor photographs capture him at his desk or in a radio studio, jaw tight in concentration, looking like a man easily piqued. Even when he was clean-shaven, a five o'clock shadow stipples his face, especially on the philtrum between nose and mouth. A full, neatly edged upper lip displayed the perfect peaks women create with lip liner, a "Cupid's bow" mouth; it was his only feminine feature. (p. 18)
Excerpts from *Matilda* (Dahl, 1988):   Miss Trunchbull possessed none of these qualities and how she ever got her present job was a mystery. She was above all a most formidable female. She had once been a famous athlete and even now the muscles were still clearly in evidence. You could see them in the bull-neck, in the big shoulders, in the thick arms, in the sinewy wrists and in the powerful legs. Looking at her, you got the feeling that this was someone who could bend iron bars and tear telephone directories in half. Her face, I'm afraid, was neither a thing of beauty nor a joy for ever. She had an obstinate chin, a cruel mouth and small arrogant eyes. (pp. 82–83)   << • >>

Figure 4.5: Physical appearance excerpts.

continued ➤

As for her clothes . . . they were, to say the least, extremely odd. She always had on a brown cotton smock which was pinched in around the waist with a wide leather belt. The belt was fastened in front with an enormous silver buckle. The massive thighs which emerged from out of the smock were encased in a pair of extraordinary breeches, bottle-green in colour and made of coarse twill. These breeches reached to just below the knees and from there on down she sported green stockings with turn-up tops, which displayed her calf muscles to perfection. On her feet she wore flat-heeled brown brogues with leather flaps. She looked, in short, more like a rather eccentric and bloodthirsty follower of the stag-hounds than the headmistress of a nice school for children. (p. 83)

Excerpt from *Sir Gawain and the Loathly Lady* (Hastings, 1987):

She was the ugliest living thing he had ever set eyes on, a freak, a monster, a truly loathly lady. Her nose was like a pig's snout; from a misshapen mouth stuck out two yellowing rows of horse's teeth; her cheeks were covered in sores; she had only one eye, rheumy and red-rimmed, and from a naked scalp hung a few lank strands of hair. Her whole body was swollen and bent out of shape, and her fingers, on which were several fine rings, were as gnarled and twisted as the roots of an old oak. (p. 12)

Excerpt from *All the Light We Cannot See* (Doerr, 2014):

The warrant officer in charge of field exercises is the commandant, an overzealous schoolmaster named Bastian with an expansive walk and a round belly and a coat quivering with war medals. His face is scarred from smallpox, and his shoulders look as though they've been hewn from soft clay. He wears hob-nailed jackboots every second of every day, and the cadets joke that he kicked his way out of the womb with them. (p. 168)

Excerpt from *A Fine Balance* (Mistry, 1995):

A picture begins to form, and Dina let it develop for two days, adding depth and detail, colour and texture. Om's wife, standing in the front door. Her head demurely lowered. Her eyes sparkling when she looks up, her mouth smiling shyly, lips covered with her fingers. The days pass. Sometimes the young woman sits alone at the window, and remembers forsaken places. Dina sits beside her and encourages her to talk, to tell her things about the life left behind. And Om's wife begins at last to speak. More pictures, more stories. (p. 463)

Excerpt from *Esperanza Rising* (Ryan, 2000):

Esperanza's grandmother, whom everyone called Abuelita, lived with them and was a smaller, older, more wrinkled version of Mama. She looked very distinguished, wearing a respectable black dress, the same gold loops she wore in her ears every day, and her white hair pulled back into a bun at the nape of her neck. . . . Although some things were always the same with Abuelita—a lace-edged handkerchief peeking out from beneath the sleeve of her dress—others were surprising: a flower in her hair, a beautiful stone in her pocket, or a philosophical saying salted into her conversation. (p. 13)

Excerpt from *Hoot* (Hiaasen, 2002):

The boy was straw-blond and wiry, and his skin was nut-brown from the sun. The expression on his face was intent and serious. He wore a faded Miami Heat basketball jersey and dirty khaki shorts, and here was the odd part: no shoes. The soles of his bare feet looked as black as barbecue coals. (p. 1)

Excerpt from *Poppy* (Avi, 1995):

He was a large, bony orange cat, with the pinched body of advanced age. One ear was bent. He walked slowly, limping slightly, glancing up at the sun as if to measure its warmth. But by keeping his tail high, he maintained a stately dignity. (p. 128)

Excerpts from *Danny, the Champion of the World* (Dahl, 1975):

The place was absolutely alive with them. There must have been at least two hundred huge birds strutting around among the tree stumps. . . . It was a fantastic sight, a sort of poacher's dream come true. And how close they were! Some of them were not ten paces from where we knelt. The hens were plump and creamy-brown. They were so fat their breast feathers almost brushed the ground as they walked. The cocks were slim and elegant, with long tails and brilliant red patches around the eyes, like scarlet spectacles. (pp. 132–133)

<< • >>

My father once told me that Doc Spencer had been looking after the people of our district for nearly forty-five years. He was over seventy now and could have retired long ago. . . . He was a tiny man with tiny hands and feet and a tiny round face. The face was as brown and wrinkled as a shriveled apple. He was some sort of an elf, I used to think to myself each time I saw him, a very ancient sort of an elf with wispy white hair and steel-rimmed spectacles; a quick, clever little elf with a swift eye and a flashing smile and a fast way of talking. Nobody feared him. Many people loved him, and he was especially gentle with children. (p. 76)

Excerpt from *Kaffir Boy* (Mathabane, 1986):

It was again late afternoon when we were ushered into the same office of a month ago by the same black policeman with the gun. As my mother and I nervously entered the small room, I looked up and had the most terrifying experience of my seven-year-old life. Seated on a reclining easy chair by a small open window and wearing a khaki safari suit, a holstered gun slung loosely about his fat waist; stockinged feet clad in shiny brown boots and placed leisurely and obliquely on a long mahogany table; his big, red, soft and hairy hands twirling a golden pen; his red neck hairy and thick; his spectacles resting lazily upon the ridge of a bulbous freckled nose with flaring, hairy nostrils; his face broad and red and freckled and topped by a bang of carroty hair; and his thick red lips curled around a thick brown and burning cigar, was the white man. (p. 114)

Excerpt from *Harry Potter and the Sorcerer's Stone* (Rowling, 1997):

Perhaps it had something to do with living in a dark cupboard, but Harry had always been small and skinny for his age. He looked even smaller and skinnier than he really was because all he had to wear were old clothes of Dudley's, and Dudley was about four times bigger than he was. Harry had a thin face, knobby knees, black hair, and bright green eyes. He wore round glasses held together with a lot of Scotch tape because of all the times Dudley had punched him on the nose. The only thing Harry liked about his own appearance was a very thin scar on his forehead that was shaped like a bolt of lightning. (p. 20)

Excerpt from *Team of Rivals: The Political Genius of Abraham Lincoln* (Goodwin, 2005):

Lincoln's shock of black hair, brown furrowed face, and deep-set eyes made him look older than his fifty-one years. He was a familiar figure to almost everyone in Springfield, as was his singular way of walking, which gave the impression that his long, gaunt frame needed oiling. He plodded forward in an awkward manner, hands hanging at his sides or folded behind his back. . . . His features, even support-ers conceded, were not such "as belong to a handsome man." In repose, his face was "so overspread with sadness," the reporter Horace White noted. . . . Yet when Lincoln began to speak, White observed, "this expression of sorrow dropped from him instantly. His face lighted up with a winning smile, and where I had a moment before seen only leaden sorrow I now beheld keen intelligence, genuine kindness of heart, and the promise of true friendship." (p. 6)

Excerpt from *To Kill a Mockingbird* (Lee, 1960):

He had been leaning against the wall when I came into the room, his arms folded across his chest. As I pointed he brought his arms down and pressed the palms of his hands against the wall. They were white hands, sickly white hands that had never seen the sun, so white they stood out garishly against the dull cream wall in the dim light of Jem's room.
I looked from his hands to his sand-stained khaki pants; my eyes traveled up his thin frame to his torn denim shirt. His face was as white as his hands, but for a shadow on his jutting chin. His cheeks were thin to hollowness; his mouth was wide; there were shallow, almost delicate indentations at his temples, and his gray eyes were so colorless I thought he was blind. His hair was dead and thin, almost feathery on top of his head. (p. 362)

Excerpt from *David Copperfield* (Dickens, 2016):

When the pony-chaise stopped at the door, and my eyes were intent upon the house, I saw a cadaver-ous face appear at a small window on the ground floor . . . and quickly disappear. The low arched door then opened, and the face came out. It was quite as cadaverous as it had looked in the window, though in the grain of it there was that tinge of red which is sometimes to be observed in the skins of red-haired people. It belonged to a red-haired person—a youth of fifteen, as I take it now, but looking much older—whose hair was cropped as close as the closest stubble; who had hardly any eyebrows, and no eyelashes, and eyes of a red-brown; so unsheltered and unshaded, that I remember wondering how he went to sleep. He was high-shouldered and bony; dressed in decent black, with a white wisp of a neckcloth; but-toned up to the throat; and had a long, lank, skeleton hand, which particularly attracted my attention, as he stood at the pony's head, rubbing his chin with it, and looking up at us in the chaise. (pp. 325–326)

continued ➤

Excerpt from "The Treasure of Lemon Brown" (Myers, 1997):

The person who called himself Lemon Brown peered forward, and Greg could see him clearly. He was an old man. His black, heavily wrinkled face was surrounded by a halo of crinkly white hair and whiskers that seemed to separate his head from the layers of dirty coats piled on his smallish frame. His pants were bagged to the knee, where they were met with rags that went down to the old shoes. The rags were held on with strings, and there was a rope around his middle. Greg relaxed. He had seen the man before, picking through the trash on the corner and pulling clothes out of a Salvation Army box. (p. T97)

Excerpt from "A Christmas Memory" (Capote, 1967):

A woman with shorn white hair is standing at the kitchen window. She is wearing tennis shoes and a shapeless gray sweater over a summery calico dress. She is small and sprightly, like a bantam hen; but, due to a long youthful illness, her shoulders are pitifully hunched. Her face is remarkable—not unlike Lincoln's, craggy like that, and tinted by sun and wind; but it is delicate too, finely boned, and her eyes are sherry-colored and timid. (p. 130)

Source: Ackerman, 2007; Avi, 1995; Dahl, 1975, 1988; Dickens, 2016; Doerr, 2014; Goodwin, 2005; Hastings, 1987; Hiaasen, 2002; Lee, 1960; Mathabane, 1986; Mistry, 1995; Myers, 1997; Rowling, 1997; Ryan, 2000.

*Visit **go.SolutionTree.com/literacy** for a free reproducible version of this figure.*

Critique Adjectives

1. **Review adjectives:** Explain to students that adjectives, which modify nouns, can be an effective way to paint descriptions. They can come before or after the noun or proper noun they modify, such as *Lucy is a <u>remarkable</u> volleyball player. <u>Remarkable</u> Lucy performed a feat on the court that stunned the crowd.* For those needing a construct, any word that fits grammatically in this blank is an adjective: *the very _____ man.* The only adjectives that are an exception to this rule are numbers.

2. **Practice finding adjectives:** Instruct student pairs to underline adjectives in an excerpt card from the previous activity (figure 4.5). Before they begin this task, you might feature the following example for Miss Trunchbull, a character in Roald Dahl's (1988) book *Matilda*, on a document camera, interactive whiteboard, or other projection device. Together with students' input, identify the adjectives (see the bold, underlined words).

   *Miss Trunchbull possessed none of these qualities and how she ever got her **<u>present</u>** job was a mystery. She was above all a most **<u>formidable</u>** female. She had once been a **<u>famous</u>** athlete and even now the muscles were still clearly in evidence. You could see them in the bull-neck, in the **<u>big</u>** shoulders, in the **<u>thick</u>** arms, in the **<u>sinewy</u>** wrists and in the **<u>powerful</u>** legs. Looking at her, you got the feeling that this was someone who could bend **<u>iron</u>** bars and tear **<u>telephone</u>** directories in half. Her face, I'm afraid, was neither a thing of beauty nor a joy for ever. She had an **<u>obstinate</u>** chin, a **<u>cruel</u>** mouth and **<u>small arrogant</u>** eyes. (Dahl, 1988, pp. 82–83)*

3. **Discern between types of adjectives:** After underlining adjectives, students share their words to create a class-generated list. Next, partners critique the comprehensive list and divide words into two groups based on their impressions—extraordinary and common adjectives. Make the point that a combination of different types of adjectives can be an effective tool to create a very clear picture based on how authors use them. Return to the Miss Trunchbull description and discuss how some adjectives that appear rudimentary might be necessary to describe her. Encourage students to defend their opinions on using certain adjectives based on Dahl (1988) and other published authors' works. Allow time for individuals to record adjectives in their notebooks that they want to remember to use.

4. **Find figurative language examples:** Students return to the passages and underline examples of figurative language—simile, metaphor, imagery, personification, and hyperbole—which also contribute to specific detail. They can record their favorites in their student notebooks. Following are some examples:

*The warrant officer in charge of field exercises is the commandant, an overzealous schoolmaster named Bastian with an expansive walk and a round belly and a coat quivering with war medals. His face is scarred from smallpox, and his **shoulders look as though they've been hewn from soft clay**. He **wears hobnailed jackboots every second of every day**, and the cadets joke that he kicked his way out of the womb with them. (Doerr, 2014, p. 168)*

<< • >>

*She was the ugliest living thing he had ever set eyes on, a freak, a monster, a truly loathly lady. Her **nose was like a pig's snout**; from a misshapen mouth stuck out two yellowing rows of horse's teeth; her cheeks were covered in sores; she had only one eye, rheumy and red-rimmed, and from a naked scalp hung a few lank strands of hair. Her whole body was swollen and bent out of shape, and **her fingers, on which were several fine rings, were as gnarled and twisted as the roots of an old oak**. (Hastings, 1987, p. 12)*

Revise an Author's Character Description

Find a passage from a familiar complex text weak in details about a character and ask students to add imagery to it. Tell them that their revision must demonstrate what they know about the character. In this way, it also serves to check for understanding of the content. Additionally, invite them to create a drawing of this character based on what they write. You might devise an assignment sheet like the one in figure 4.6.

How Do Authors Use Details to Describe Characters?
Directions: Read the author's excerpt. Then revise it to include more imagery so that the character description is more vivid and complete. Draw a detailed picture based on your revision. Highlight words and phrases that help you to draw your picture. "Alfonso, Hortensia's husband, was el jefe, the boss, of all the field-workers and Papa's compañero, his close friend and companion. He had the same dark skin and small stature as Hortensia, and Esperanza thought his round eyes, long eyelids, and droopy mustache made him look like a forlorn puppy." (Ryan, 2000, p. 16)
Write a revision of the author's character description to give readers a total picture in their minds of what Alfonso looks like. You can include any part of the author's words and phrases within your revision.

Figure 4.6: Character sketch assignment sheet.

continued ➤

Draw a picture of the character to match your description.

Visit *go.SolutionTree.com/literacy* for a free reproducible version of this figure.

Write a Character Sketch Using Imagery

For this exercise, students use imagery to write in such detailed terms about a character from a print or digital resource that others can match what they visualize to the picture.

1. **Explain and prepare for the task:** Tell students that they will work in pairs to browse through pictures of characters from magazines or online sources, select a picture of a character, and use it as the basis for descriptive writing. Alternatively, you might collect and let them choose a small object—for example, a Disney, Pokémon, or dinosaur figurine—as the basis for their writing. Explain that their goal is to rely on imagery and other figurative language to make their writing so realistic and vivid that others can guess their picture or object from what they compose. For this reason, tell students to keep their pictures or figurines hidden from others while writing. To prepare, ask students to read, critique, and discuss the student work samples in figure 4.7, and then instruct them to begin the task.

2. **Evaluate quality of imagery:** When finished writing, each pair reads their physical descriptions and allows time for classmates to visualize what the picture or object looks like. Then pairs reveal the picture or object and the audience votes to gauge to what level the writing matches the students' visualization impressions. To vote, each student casts a zero if the writing does not resemble the character at all (fold arms), one vote to signify somewhat of a match (raise one hand), or two votes to reflect a total connection to what he or she visualized based on the writing (stand up). This can generate a friendly competition; however, let students know in advance if you are going to institute voting.

3. **Pair descriptions with writing (alternative):** Another option is to line up all the pictures or objects on a table in the front of the room. Collect the papers and read them one at a time, allowing students time to match the description with each character or object. Allow students time to revise if they so choose.

Student Samples of Physical Descriptions
You could see the ocean in her eyes, deep and mysterious. Each swirled like whirlpools, leading to the unknown. They were slightly squinted in an alluring way. A chocolate eye shadow poised her eyes to give a seductive look. Above her eyes were full chestnut eyebrows, curved in passion. Her nose was delicate and petite. Her lips were colored by a touch of pink. They were full and luscious, slightly opened seductively. Her face was slender and crafted like a porcelain doll. Her complexion was peachy overflowing with lust. Chestnut was her hair, parted loosely on her side, yet it did not disturb her face. Instead it was pulled back behind her ears. Each ear was decorated with a magenta flower that clung to her, but seemed to caress her face. (By Ramona)

The baby's glassy sea blue eyes stare at you so innocently that you want to hold her tightly and shield her from all the evil in the world. Her skin looks as soft as a baby rabbit's tail. The bubbles floating from her tender face look as if they were a waterfall cascading down her sweet, pure, and gentle forehead. Her nose is as pudgy as a Cabbage Patch doll's sweet little nose that you just want to tweak it and say, "I got your nose." (By Christina)

The night of glamour was over for that evening, but by her devilish smile and alive pale green eyes, I could tell that the excitement was still in her. A thick sparkling diamond necklace was snug around her neck and dangled down her chest. Her short dirty blonde hair was moussed back with body. Her slender light brown eyebrows curved on top of her dark outlined eyes. Her lips were touched with red, still looking wet. Her arms, covered with long silk black gloves, rested on top of the back of her pink striped chair. (By Kristy)

The uncontrollable young boy looked like he was one and a half or two years old. By the slight squint in his eyes and his partial smile, the boy looked like he was up to no good. His perfect blonde hair was slightly curled at the tips, and his longer bangs swirled down his forehead like a gigantic wave ready to crash on the shore. He squatted resting his plump little body on his hands and knees and appeared ready to jump up and pounce like a cat. (By Kristy R.)

Figure 4.7: Grade 8 student samples of physical descriptions.

*Visit **go.SolutionTree.com/literacy** for a free reproducible version of this figure.*

Make Inferences Using Methods of Characterization

1. **Find evidence of methods of characterization:** Target a complex text at the center of instruction. Ask students to hunt for evidence to support methods of characterization that the author uses and record pertinent excerpts into figure 4.8 (page 70). For example, students can record part or all of this excerpt from Sandra Cisneros's (1991a) "Eleven" in the quadrant "What does the character do?":

   But when the sick feeling goes away and I open my eyes, the red sweater's still sitting there like a big red mountain. I move the red sweater to the corner of my desk with my ruler. I move my pencil and books and eraser as far from it as possible. I even move my chair a little to the right. (p. 2)

2. **Make inferences:** Ask students to share their impressions of these characterization excerpts and use them to infer personality traits. You might first review that traits can be expressed as adjectives, such as *caring, responsible, conceited, rude,* or *loyal,* and have students generate character traits using the roundtable strategy. This is when students in small groups pass around one piece of paper in a circle and each adds an item to make a group list. After the paper circulates numerous times and students exhaust ideas, each group then shares with the whole class to create a comprehensive list. Figure 4.9 (pages 70–71) shows some possible traits.

3. **Show changes in characters:** Characters, like people, can change throughout time and in different situations to exhibit a range of personality traits. Therefore, students can use the graphic organizer in figure 4.8 repeatedly to show characters' development. They can also complete it to juxtapose an antagonist with a protagonist or focus on other characters. After this exercise, ask students to complete the organizer to brainstorm characters for their narratives as a prewriting tool and use it to subsequently draft sketches.

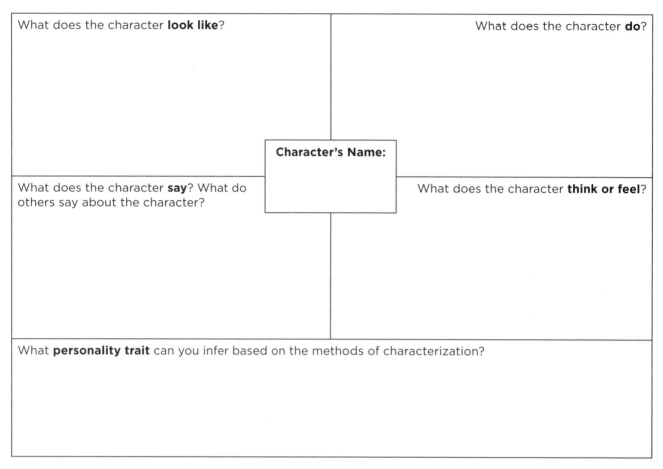

Figure 4.8: Characterization graphic organizer.

Visit go.SolutionTree.com/literacy for a free reproducible version of this figure.

Character Traits			
Adventurous	Envious	Knowledgeable	Secretive
Aggressive	Exuberant	Loving	Self-conscious
Aloof	Foolish	Loyal	Sentimental
Ambitious	Fragile	Mercurial	Serene
Anxious	Grim	Methodical	Sincere
Apathetic	Gullible	Meticulous	Skillful
Awkward	Harsh	Mischievous	Snobbish
Benign	Heroic	Modest	Sociable
Boisterous	Hideous	Morbid	Solemn
Bossy	Hopeful	Nonchalant	Stubborn
Brave	Humane	Opinionated	Suspicious
Capable	Humble	Optimistic	Sympathetic
Careful	Humorous	Overbearing	Tearful
Careless	Imaginative	Passive	Timid
Cheerful	Impatient	Pessimistic	Tough

Clever	Impetuous	Poised	Treacherous
Clumsy	Incompetent	Practical	Trustworthy
Confident	Indolent	Radiant	Unfaithful
Confused	Indulgent	Realistic	Unhappy
Courageous	Ingenious	Reasonable	Unruly
Cowardly	Innocent	Rebellious	Unwise
Cruel	Insincere	Reckless	Vain
Daring	Intelligent	Reflective	Villainous
Defiant	Inventive	Reluctant	Vivacious
Distrustful	Irresistible	Resilient	Wise
Energetic	Joyful	Sarcastic	Witty

Figure 4.9: Character traits.

*Visit **go.SolutionTree.com/literacy** for a free reproducible version of this figure.*

Plot Elements

In this section, I provide a variety of ideas to teach plot elements so students can apply this fundamental structural aspect of storytelling. See appendix B on page 131 for a more comprehensive discussion of plot along with the other elements of literature. Also review any of the rows pertaining to plot in table 1.2 (pages 11–17) to see options for learning outcomes.

Identify Plot Elements

Ask students to read a short story and identify the elements of plot—central conflict, (parts of the) rising action, climax, falling action, and resolution—by writing them in the margins or on sticky notes. Alternatively, they can complete a graphic organizer in print or electronically based on the plot and even other story elements. See the following list of downloadable and printable organizers as well as the figures in this chapter's Narrative Prewriting section. For differentiation purposes, individuals or groups can read stories based on interest or readability levels and even complete different graphic organizers.

Graphic Organizers

- BrainPOP Educators (https://educators.brainpop.com/printable/?printable-type=Graphic+Organizers)
- edHelper.com (www.edhelper.com/teachers/graphic_organizers.htm)
- Education Oasis (http://educationoasis.com/curriculum/graphic_organizers.htm)
- EverythingESL (www.everythingesl.net/inservices/graphic_organizers.php)
- Freeology (http://freeology.com/graphicorgs)
- Houghton Mifflin Harcourt Education Place (www.eduplace.com/graphicorganizer/)
- Teacher Files (www.teacherfiles.com/resources_organizers.htm)
- TeacherVision (www.teachervision.com/graphic-organizers/printable/6293.html)
- TeAchnology (www.teach-nology.com/web_tools/graphic_org)

Sequence Plot Elements

1. **Sequence events:** Using a complex text students have read and discussed, prepare and distribute sets of sentence strips that highlight different plot events to small groups. Ask them to arrange the strips in chronological order according to the time of events in the story. You can use mine from the following stories if they are appropriately challenging for your students.

   - "Breaker's Bridge" by Laurence Yep (n.d.) (figure 4.10) is a retelling of a Chinese folktale about an unforgiving emperor who commands a clumsy but clever boy nicknamed Breaker to build a bridge across a deep river gorge or die. It provides insight into Chinese culture and philosophy. Access the story at http://arvindguptatoys.com/arvindgupta/breakers-bridge.pdf or from *The Rainbow People* by Laurence Yep (1989).

   - "Rain, Rain, Go Away" by Isaac Asimov (1959) (figure 4.11) is a science fiction story with a surprising twist at the end. Students can review the text for foreshadowing that provides hints to the resolution. Access the story at www.scribd.com/document/103382368/Rain-Rain-Go-Away.

2. **Use a plot diagram:** Introduce the inverted check plot diagram (see figure B.1 on page 133 in appendix B) along with the names for plot elements. Then ask students to position the strips in the shape of this diagram that represents how the plot unfolds. They can configure the strips differently from the inverted check and provide a rationale for their design and where they placed the plot elements on it.

3. **Share and discuss:** Each group shares its diagram shape and sequencing with the class. Together they discuss and agree on the order of the story strips. Then they discuss which strips constitute a particular plot element, such as central conflict and climax. Students might differ in their opinions about a sentence strip representing an element. Encourage them to defend their positions by using evidence from the text, such as, "I think the sentence that begins with _____ represents the climax because _____." There can be more than one correct answer, so if students can provide strong justification for a part of the story aligning with a particular element, acknowledge this insight.

"Breaker's Bridge" Sequencing Strips
There was once a boy who people called Breaker because he was always breaking things, but he proved to be quite clever.
The emperor asked Breaker to build a bridge. In return, he would have his weight in gold; however, if he failed, the emperor would have him beheaded.
Breaker traveled to the river and noticed it was mighty. The water flowed fast and splashed fiercely against rocks.
The river was too wide to build a simple bridge, so Breaker would have to construct two piers in the middle of the river.
Breaker encountered many problems and had to change teams of workers frequently.
When he finally was ready to set the stones on top of the logs, the river fought back, crushing the stones and destroying the logs.
Breaker and his workers tried again and again, but each time the river defeated him.
Finally his men built a dam to hold back the river so the largest and sturdiest piers could be constructed.
An official came from the emperor to check on his progress.

The mighty river broke the dam, causing the two piers already built to collapse.
The official gave Breaker a letter from the emperor who wrote that if a bridge wasn't built in one month, he would have Breaker's head.
Breaker tried hard to find a new scheme since the dam was his last resort.
Breaker saw a crooked old man sitting by the roadside and offered to make him a new crutch since his was broken. Breaker had a hard time making the crutch.
Breaker gave the old man his crutch, but the man strongly grabbed him and kept repeating, "We are all bound together and by the same laws."
Breaker was afraid the old man was some mountain spirit. He gave Breaker two pellets and told him where to place them.
Breaker put a pellet where one pier should be, and miraculously a stone pier was constructed.
Breaker rowed quickly to drop a pellet for the other pier, but his clumsy fingers crushed part of it so that only part of the pier was erected.
The workers helped to finish building the second pier; it was not as solid as the first one.
The emperor used the bridge and rewarded Breaker. When winter came, the second pier needed repair, which angered the emperor.
The old man suddenly appeared and told the emperor he didn't say how long the bridge was supposed to last. Everyone kneeled to the crooked old man.
Then Breaker learned that the old man was a saint and a powerful magician.
The emperor spared Breaker's life and sent him to build other projects throughout China.
Every year, the bridge had to be rebuilt, which meant that things change but yet really do not change.

Figure 4.10: "Breaker's Bridge" sequencing strips.

Visit go.SolutionTree.com/literacy for a free reproducible version of this figure.

"Rain, Rain, Go Away" Sequencing Strips
The Sakkaros move in next door to the Wrights and the Wrights often talk about their neighbors' strange habits.
Mrs. Sakkaro won't let her son play outside with the Wright boy because she is afraid it will rain.
When Mrs. Wright visits the Sakkaros' home, she is surprised that the house is so clean and immaculate. Mrs. Sakkaro doesn't even allow water to touch the sink when she gets a drink for Mrs. Wright.
At Murphy's Park, the Sakkaros eat nothing but cotton candy and M&Ms. Mrs. Wright offers Mrs. Sakkaro an orange drink but she refuses.
The Sakkaros are unusually concerned about weather conditions. They listen to the radio on their way home from the park.
Once the Sakkaros get out of the car from the park, they get very nervous and run quickly to their house.
Unfortunately, the Sakkaros get wet and begin to melt and the Wrights finally discover the mystery of the Sakkaros—they are made of sugar.

Figure 4.11: "Rain, Rain, Go Away" sequencing strips.

Visit go.SolutionTree.com/literacy for a free reproducible version of this figure.

Create and Sequence Student-Generated Plot Events

Instead of you preparing sentence strips as in the previous suggestion, lead a two-part activity in which students do so. First, assign each group a different short story to read, ask them to write sentence strips representing elements in the plot, place them in an envelope, and pass the strips to another group. Next, students who receive the strips read the new story together, place the sentence strips they've been given sequentially, and arrange them in the configuration of the basic plot diagram (figure B.1, page 133) or one they create. At the end of this exercise, each group will have read two stories—one for which they have made the sentence strips and another one from a group that prepared the sentence strips.

Create a Plot From Pictures

Many books contain rich and even sophisticated pictures with few or even no words at all. Such books present the opportunity for students to create a plotline or more developed story around them. To name a few, consider *Tuesday* by David Wiesner (1991) or *Free Fall* (1988) by the same author, *The Cinder-Eyed Cats* by Eric Rohmann (1997), or *The Mysteries of Harris Burdick* by Chris Van Allsburg (1984). For example, *Tuesday* contains primarily pictures with just occasional pages that indicate a random day and time.

What follows are just some of the many options for students to practice building a partial or complete storyline using high-quality picture books. Consider how you might differentiate, such as allowing students to choose their books and pictures, or to work individually, in pairs, or in trios. Logistically, choose and feature selected pictures on a document camera or other projection device; consider purchasing a few copies of different books for students to use; or, cut out selected pictures, laminate them, and provide a set of pictures to each student pair or small group.

- **Oral story:** Using the pictures as a stimulus, students orally tell a story using the round-robin strategy. They can use what they invent as a springboard for drafting and developing their own narratives.

- **Storyboard:** Distribute a set of pictures and instruct students to put them in a sequence of their choice. Then, ask them to write captions for each picture that reflect a plot progression.

- **Historical event:** Give each group a set of pictures about a historical event. Instruct them to order the pictures to reflect what actually happened. Students then write predictions, if using this exercise as a preview, or detailed captions to check for understanding about the events in history. If it's a preview, students return to their predictions after studying the historical event and rearrange the pictures and revise their writing accordingly to depict factual events. If it's a review, students work with partners to check and revise their work, as needed.

- **Graphic organizer:** Partners select a picture and discuss options for a central conflict and resolution for a story that this picture might tell. After coming to an agreement, together they complete a plot graphic organizer for an invented story. (See Identify Plot Elements on page 71 for links.)

- **Story draft:** Students choose a series of pictures and create a story around them. If there are some words on the page, students can overlook them to focus on the pictures only. Tell them they have the creative license to use the illustrations in any order and not solely how the author features them. Later, they can compare their version to the author's. Or students can select a picture and create part of a story like the following example that a fifth-grader wrote based on a picture in *Tuesday* (Wiesner, 1991). It is of a man eating a sandwich while incredulously eyeing frogs on lily pads flying through the sky in his peripheral vision. Students can share their paragraphs with others and together formulate a complete story.

Outside frogs were flying on lily pads and the man smiled and said, "Ah, come my friends." As each one entered the door, it evolved into a human. Somehow, they were all different but the same. One would have brown hair and green eyes and the one attached to it had green hair and brown eyes. And it went on like that—each person joined like Siamese twins. It was a horribly amazing sight. Then the frogs began to speak in an odd language and my mind stopped. I stood up too fast so I began to be dizzy. My mind launched into different thoughts about the situation until I was disturbed by a man who suddenly materialized. He was smoky and weird. He said to me that the reason I was having these visions and thoughts is because I no longer exist. I didn't understand him, but he was gone and I never saw him again. (Kendra, Grade 5)

Practice Inventing a Story

1. **Prepare cards:** Cut out each card in figure 4.12 of possible settings, characters, personality traits, and central conflicts. Place each face down in a pile along with the title for each stack—*setting*, *character*, and so forth. Arrange students into small groups.

2. **Students choose cards:** Each student takes a turn and chooses one card from each pile and invents a storyline based on the information. After the first turn, decide how the game can go; following are options.

   - Another student has a turn and chooses four cards and repeats the exercise.

   - The next student has the option to select one to four new cards and use them to add to the previous student's storyline.

   - Students volunteer to embellish the original student's story by adding details to the story without selecting new cards.

At some point, return the cards to the decks, shuffle, and begin again.

Story Cards			
Setting	Character	Personality Trait	Central Conflict
Pool or ocean	Teenager	Adventurous	Lost somewhere
Movie theater	Animal	Ruthless	Worrisome stranger nearby
Airplane	Doctor	Compassionate	Gave bad advice
Driverless car	Religious man or woman	Hyperactive	Caught between two loved ones
Moonlit night	Athlete	Sincere	Lost his or her voice
Silicon Valley	Elderly man or woman	Inquisitive	Won the lottery
Ranch in Dallas, Texas	Lawyer	Resourceful	Defeated in a game
Foreign country	Toddler	Creative	Someone just died
Desert	Teacher	Manipulative	Was not prepared
Top of a mountain	Mother	Gregarious	Doesn't understand the situation
Hiking trail	Military person	Humorous	Help was supposed to come but didn't
Gym	Newly engaged man or woman	Docile	Fell
Cave	Mechanic	Humble	Something broke
Office building	Truck driver	Generous	No heat or air conditioning

Figure 4.12: Story cards.

*Visit **go.SolutionTree.com/literacy** for a free reproducible version of this figure.*

Theme

When writers set out to compose a piece of writing, they must know their assignment and consider the purpose and audience in accordance with the task at hand. Furthermore, identifying the theme they wish to impart supports them in crafting a focused narrative. For example, a biographer might consider the theme of *achieving success despite inordinate odds* and build his or her work around this focus. A writer of historical fiction with the backdrop of a Japanese internment camp in World War II might highlight this theme: *people abuse and ignore justice in the face of fear.* To help students master identifying themes in a complex text, consider conducting one or more of the activities I describe here. Afterward, assist students in translating what they learn to pinpoint a theme for the narratives they will write. To share more information with students about themes within a lesson, review appendix B, page 131. Consider KUDs and guiding questions for Theme in table 1.2 (chapter 1, page 14).

Cite Evidence to Support a Theme in Literature

For this activity, prepare a list of themes associated with a complex text students have read and examined in class. If they align to the text students are reading, use the themes in figure 4.13 or create your own. Then lead this three-step activity, which I recommend conducting after students are familiar with the definition and function of this element of literature.

1. **Cite evidence for a theme:** Ask a volunteer to review the definition of theme. Explain that students will participate in an activity to answer this question about a familiar text: *What evidence does the author provide to support the theme?* Distribute a different theme to each student from figure 4.13 or those you prepare. Instruct students to circulate around the room and initiate a discussion with a classmate about their theme by citing textual evidence as support. Here is what you might say: "You each have a theme card. Read it to yourself and take a minute to think about evidence to support it, such as characters' actions, beliefs, or interactions with another; a pivotal event or a series of situations; and so forth. Then, find a classmate and read your theme, share your impressions of textual evidence, and ask for additional evidence. If your partner disagrees, solicit concerns from him or her and ask for more insight or arrive at one together. Swap roles to repeat the exercise." (Instead of individuals, student pairs can focus on one theme card together. Also, you might intentionally assign themes to students based on readiness levels so you distribute an appropriately challenging one to each student or pair.)

2. **Examine a new theme:** Collect and redistribute the theme cards so each student investigates evidence for a new theme, shares it with another partner, and learns about other classmates' themes and how they support them.

3. **Complete a written assignment:** For individual accountability, students complete figure 4.14 (page 78), answering the question, *What evidence does the author provide to support themes?* They will turn this in as a formative assessment. For this assignment, they can input any themes tied to complex text.

Theme Cards
1. Where people live can affect them.
2. Isolationism might be vital to a community's survival.
3. Isolationism leads to loneliness and stagnation.
4. Lack of knowledge and worldliness leads to ignorance.
5. An ignorant, uneducated society can be easily controlled.
6. Ignorance and lack of a frame for comparison lead to mediocrity.
7. Individual rights are secondary to the protection or well-being of the entire community.
8. Lack of competition controls jealousy and envy.
9. Individual differences lead to inequality.
10. People grant individuals with power and prestige more rights and leeway than others.
11. Individuals with power control information.
12. The human heart yearns for connection.
13. Secrecy leads to suspicion and doubt.
14. Lack of choice or empowerment leads to apathy.
15. Power may be used or abused.
16. Relationships change over time.
17. All relationships serve a particular purpose whether for good or bad.
18. Nuclear families do not always guarantee enduring relationships.
19. Intolerance leads to unspeakable actions.
20. Friendships can be tried and tested.
21. Individual needs can be in conflict with the needs of a community.
22. Vocational choice should be based on individual talents and skills.
23. Arranged marriages create harmony in a community.
24. Euthanasia is an acceptable and humane practice.
25. Human beings give themselves permission to change the environment for their benefit.
26. Through exploration, people confront the unknown and broaden their perspective.
27. People mature and change as a result of a significant life experience.
28. Utopia creates a sense of security.
29. The goal of utopia is to erase societal problems.
30. Individuality comes at a cost.
31. Judgments based on little evidence lead to hurtful or damaging consequences.
32. Diversity can be celebrated and valued.
33. Well-intentioned actions can sometimes lead to negative consequences.
34. Through positive thoughts and earnest attempts, the impossible can sometimes happen.
35. People who have a passion will do almost anything to feed it.

Figure 4.13: Theme cards.

Visit **go.SolutionTree.com/literacy** *for a free reproducible version of this figure.*

What Evidence Does the Author Provide to Support Themes?		
Themes	Textual Evidence	Connections With Other Texts

Figure 4.14: Theme evidence.

Visit **go.SolutionTree.com/literacy** *for a free reproducible version of this figure.*

Determine Evidence of Theme in Other Works

Students can use other works beyond published narrative text to identify evidence to support a theme. Arrange them in pairs, trios, or small groups of four to engage in any of these activities.

- **Songs:** Play a song by a popular artist and distribute the lyrics to it. Or ask students to bring in their own songs and accompanying lyrics. Instruct them to share their impressions about the theme using the lyrics as supporting evidence. You can also give students a theme and ask them to locate songs that represent it. When they play the songs they find, ask them to identify lines in the lyrics that show evidence of the theme. Also discuss how genres of music share common themes, like country tells stories of the downtrodden.

- **Poetry or artwork:** This exercise allows students to discover that seemingly disparate works can share common themes. Collect various poems or artwork with the same or similar themes, and distribute one to each student group. Instruct them to read the poem or study the piece of art and identify the theme along with supporting evidence. Rotate poems or artwork so each group has a different one to examine, and repeat the exercise. As a class, lead a discussion using these questions: *Is there a common theme that these poems or paintings share? How so?* (If using artwork, the online resource www.artchive.com features extensive collections from all periods and genres. If using poetry, access either of these online resources: www.poetryfoundation.org or www.poetry.org.)

- **Student samples:** Review and select a range of student samples from the genre of writing that students will ultimately write. (See appendix E on page 151 or visit **go.SolutionTree.com /literacy** for links to student samples.) Distribute a different student sample to each group. Ask students to silently read the paper, and then discuss answers to these questions: *What is the theme? What evidence supports it? Could the evidence have been stronger? How so?*

Write About the Theme and Supporting Evidence

Students choose a type of complex text—such as a national news program, realistic fiction, or play—as the basis for writing about the theme and evidence to support it. Issue the theme assignment in figure 4.15, or adapt it as needed, for students to demonstrate understanding of this skill.

Theme Assignment
Part 1: Review these complex text options and place an X next to your choice.   _____ Watch a television show or national news program.   _____ Ask a parent or guardian to discuss a book he or she is listening to or reading.   _____ Think about a book you have read. It can be from any genre, such as mystery, fantasy, realistic fiction, and so forth.   _____ Select a print or online article and read it.   _____ Find a movie or play review and read it.   _____ Select another type of complex text; approve it with your teacher.
Part 2: Complete the following with your selection.   Write a single- or multiple-paragraph paper that includes the theme of the complex text you have chosen as the basis for this assignment. Support the theme by explicitly citing certain scenes in the television show or parts of the news report, book, article, or review that relate to it. Elaborate on these pieces of textual evidence that show why you chose to include them and how this evidence links to the theme.

Figure 4.15: Theme assignment.

Visit go.SolutionTree.com/literacy for a free reproducible version of this figure.

Narrative Introductions

When ready, students will amass their brainstorming tools and begin the first draft. Draw their attention to the expectations on the checklist or rubric for an introduction. As well, lead exercises for them to thoroughly examine and analyze myriad introduction models to put them in good stead for writing their own beginnings. The options in this section can help you lead learning experiences on this topic so they can launch their narrative project on the right footing.

Suggested KUDs and guiding questions for teaching students how to start their narratives can be found on the Narrative Introduction row (page 14) of the unit map on table 1.2.

Critique and Draft Narrative Introductions

To prepare for this activity, find and gather at least four introductions from various narrative complex texts that share the same genre, or use the historical fiction introductions in figure 4.16 (pages 80–82). Additionally, copy and distribute the discussion questions in figure 4.17 (page 82) or post the questions on a whiteboard or electronically and arrange students in groups of four.

1. **Set the stage for learning:** State this guiding question to frame the activity: "How can I write an engaging introduction for my narrative?" Tell students they will read and critique introductions to various stories. Feature your checklist (or rubric) to remind students about the expectations for a story beginning. Depending on the genre in which they are writing, the criteria might include the following.

- I engage the reader by writing an exciting and attention-getting narrative beginning.

- I describe my main character and setting.

- I include a central conflict.

Distribute or feature the questions in figure 4.17 and tell students that they will critique story introductions using these prompts. (Revise them, as needed, to appeal to the genre your students are writing.)

2. **Discuss and critique introductions:** Give each pair in a foursome the same story introduction and orchestrate a think-pair-share activity. Ask students to individually read their introduction and think about how they will address the discussion questions. Pairs confer with each other. Then they engage in a group discussion among the four of them to share their ideas. (Alternatively, you can bypass the pair interaction and move from individual introspection to small-group sharing.)

3. **Participate in class discussion:** Initiate a class discussion in which students share highlights of their group discussions and any impression of the introduction they feel is most compelling and effective. Have them use evidence from the excerpts to articulate what makes a particular introduction engaging. Also discuss a weaker excerpt and what made it so. Throughout the discussion, make these points.

- Some questions readers might have after reading an introduction can arouse productive curiosity that compels them to keep going. However, too many unanswered questions in an introduction might frustrate them. Therefore, authors must maintain a fine balance to achieve momentum.

- Some authors draw out the introduction way too long. Remind students to be succinct in stating the context without going into great detail that bores readers and makes them anxious for you to get to the storyline.

- Introductions from different narrative genres can vary. Discuss examples, such as the difference between the opening for a memoir versus a mystery.

4. **Draft an introduction:** When students are well versed in strategies and components for an introduction, they draft one for their own narratives.

Historical Fiction Introductions

Excerpt from *All the Light We Cannot See* (Doerr, 2014):

Leaflets

At dusk they pour from the sky. They blow across the ramparts, turn cartwheels over rooftops, flutter into the ravines between houses. Entire streets swirl with them, flashing white against the cobbles. *Urgent message to the inhabitants of this town*, they say. *Depart immediately to open country.*

The tide climbs. The moon hangs small and yellow and gibbous. On the rooftops of beachfront hotels to the east, and in the gardens behind them, a half-dozen American artillery units drop incendiary rounds into the mouths of mortars. (p. 3)

Excerpt from *Fever 1793* (Anderson, 2000):

August 16th, 1793

The city of Philadelphia is perhaps one of the wonders of the world.

—Lord Adam Gordon
Journal entry, 1765

I woke to the sound of a mosquito whining in my left ear and my mother screeching in the right. "Rouse yourself this instant!"

Mother snapped open the shutters and heat poured into our bedchamber. The room above our coffee-house was not large. Two beds, a washstand, and a wooden trunk with frayed leather straps nearly filled it. It seemed even smaller with Mother storming around.

"Get out of bed, Matilda," she continued. "You're sleeping the day away." She shook my shoulder. "Polly's late and there's work to be done."

The noisy mosquito darted between us. I started to sweat under the thin blanket. It was going to be another hot August day. Another long, hot August day. Another long, hot, boring, wretched August day.

"I can't tell you who is lazier, Polly or you," Mother muttered as she stalked out of the room. "When I was a girl, we were up before the sun . . ." Her voice droned on and on as she clattered down the stairs.

I groaned. Mother had been a perfect girl. Her family was wealthy then, but that didn't stop her from stitching entire quilts before breakfast, or spinning miles of wool before tea. It was the War, she liked to remind me. Children did what was asked of them. And she never complained. Oh, no, never. Good children were seen and not heard. How utterly unlike me. (pp. 1–2)

Excerpt from *A Night Divided* (Nielsen, 2015):

Chapter One

When I want the west to scream, I squeeze on Berlin.

—Nikita Khrushchev, Soviet Union premier, 1958–1964

There was no warning the night the wall went up.

I awoke to sirens screaming throughout my city of East Berlin. Instantly, I flew out of bed. Something must be terribly wrong. Why were there so many?

Although it was a warm morning, that wasn't the reason for my sweaty palms or flushed face. My first thought was that it must be an air raid—my parents had described them to me from the Second World War. I pulled my curtains apart, expecting the worst. But when I looked out, my heart slammed into my throat. Not even the darkest part of my imagination could have prepared me for this.

It was Sunday, August 13, 1961, a day I would remember for the rest of my life. When a prison had been built around us as we slept. (p. 1)

Excerpt from *The Book Thief* (Zusak, 2005):

Death and Chocolate

First the colors.

Then the humans.

That's usually how I see things.

Or at least, how I try.

HERE IS A SMALL FACT

You are going to die.

I am in all truthfulness attempting to be cheerful about this whole topic, though most people find themselves hindered in believing me, no matter my protestations. Please, trust me. I most definitely can be cheerful. I can be amiable. Agreeable. Affable. And that's just the A's. Just don't ask me to be nice. Nice has nothing to do with me. (p. 3)

Figure 4.16: Historical fiction introductions.

continued ➤

Excerpt from *When the Emperor Was Divine* (Otsuka, 2002):

Evacuation Order No. 19

The sign had appeared overnight. On billboards and trees and the backs of the bus-stop benches. It hung in the window of Woolworth's. It hung by the entrance to the YMCA. It was stapled to the door of the municipal court and nailed, at eye level, to every telephone pole along University Avenue. The woman was returning a book to the library when she saw the sign in a post office window. It was a sunny day in Berkeley in the spring of 1942 and she was wearing new glasses and could see everything clearly for the first time in weeks. She no longer had to squint but she squinted out of habit anyway. She read the sign from top to bottom and then, still squinting, she took out a pen and read the sign from top to bottom again. The print was small and dark. Some of it was tiny. She wrote down a few words on the back of a bank receipt, then turned around and went home and began to pack.

When the overdue notice from the library arrived in the mail nine days later she still had not finished packing. The children had just left for school and boxes and suitcases were scattered across the floor of the house. She tossed the envelope into the nearest suitcase and walked out the door. (pp. 3–4)

Source: Anderson, 2000; Doerr, 2014; Nielsen, 2015; Otsuka, 2002; Zusak, 2005.

*Visit **go.SolutionTree.com/literacy** for a free reproducible version of this figure.*

Discussion Questions for a Narrative Introduction

Directions: Critique the story beginnings by discussing answers to these questions in your groups.

1. How does the author introduce one or more characters in an engaging way? What could be improved?

2. How does the author introduce the setting in an engaging way? What could be improved?

3. What is the central conflict? If it is unclear, what do you recommend for revision?

4. Is there something missing in the introduction?

5. Is there an effective title or would you recommend another one?

6. Does the beginning attract your attention? What strategy does the author use that motivates you to keep reading? For example, are there sensory details about a setting, an action that describes what a character is doing, dialogue between characters, an internal monologue, a reaction of the narrator or character to a situation, or some other strategy?

Figure 4.17: Introduction discussion questions.

*Visit **go.SolutionTree.com/literacy** for a free reproducible version of this figure.*

Dialogue

Before students can write dialogue, they need to identify its purpose and how it functions in a narrative so they are sure to incorporate conversations that are salient rather than rambling and erroneous. Learning about dialect and how it adds dimension to characters and other elements presents another valuable skill to teach if it is age appropriate. Additionally, students will benefit from learning about options for speaker or dialogue tags—for example, considering alternatives to *he said* or *she questioned* and adding phrases or clauses to indicate gestures or tone. As well, focusing on the mechanics of dialogue is critical so students incorporate it appropriately. Appendix C (page 137) includes many excerpts as examples to use for teaching these skills.

The KUDs and guiding questions that align to the suggestions in this section are on the Dialogue and Dialect and Dialogue Punctuation rows (page 15) on table 1.2.

Determine the Purpose for Dialogue

Point to a passage in the complex text that contains dialogue. Ask students to read it and answer the questions, Why does the author use the dialogue in this section? What purpose does it serve?

After discussion, read aloud another section in the text but this time purposely omit the dialogue that the author includes. Ask, "What is going on? What is missing that prevents understanding?" Ask students to invent dialogue the author might write. Then read the text to compare students' versions with the author's.

Generate Verbs for Dialogue Tags

1. **Compile verbs used in dialogue:** Ask student groups to generate a list of verbs that authors use in dialogue tags by perusing their literature textbooks, an independent reading book, or a class text. (Remind them that although they may see verbs in the actual dialogue, they should focus on verbs in the tags only.)

2. **Categorize the list:** Groups share their verbs so you can record a class-generated, comprehensive list. Ask students to categorize the compiled list, such as words the authors use instead of *said*, *questioned*, *exclaimed*, and so forth. This exercise is more interactive than simply distributing a prepared list of alternatives to *said* or *replied*. Keep the list up for students to use later when they write dialogue for their stories, or ask them to record verbs in their writing notebooks.

Infer Meaning From Dialect

Read a story with dialect that is challenging to decipher and ask students to rewrite it in their own words. Discuss how it adds to the story and its purpose, using these and other questions: What do readers learn from the dialect passage? How does it enhance an aspect of the story, such as a character, a setting, or an event? What inferences can you make from this dialogue passage? How does it compare to another author's use of dialect? Consider asking students to compare and contrast dialect within the same story, such as Eudora Welty's (n.d.) "Petrified Man," or from different texts.

Punctuate Dialogue

For teaching this skill, use the highly effective concept-attainment strategy, which is one of my favorites. It supports self-discovery as you carefully guide students to arrive at their own learning. To start, I list the steps involved in concept attainment. Next, I demonstrate how to implement this strategy specifically for teaching dialogue punctuation. Consider that students can complete each of the following steps in pairs, trios, or small groups of four.

Concept Attainment

Concept attainment envisions a situation in which students productively struggle to learn a skill or concept, rather than one in which teachers directly furnish a definition or example. It is versatile and applicable for teaching innumerable skills in all content areas, such as recognizing and using parallel structure, distinguishing formal from informal style, identifying art concepts, determining distinctive traits of a leader, defining features of an ecosystem, and the list goes on. These six steps can guide you in implementing this strategy.

1. **Examine and group a set of items according to their commonalities:** You can design this sorting exercise in two different ways.

   A. Students sort all items into a particular category, such as various words by part of speech, pictures indicating a particular artistic style, historical artifacts from different eras, sentences by structure, or paragraphs or essays by their purpose.

   B. Students sort by a *yes* or *no* construct, identifying those items that belong together (examples) and those that do not (nonexamples). The nonexamples are a combination of random items. Your directions to students might be, "Group together those items that share common elements. Put the others to the side."

2. **Identify the specific attributes of this grouped set:** Instruct students to make a list of the common attributes—or distinguishing characteristics—and verify with the class what they are. Ask them to state the name of the like items if they know it (similes, narrative elements, or subordinating conjunctions); otherwise, provide the name. Tell students that the targeted group with similar attributes becomes the focus going forward. If they grouped all items into separate categories (like the preceding option A), then identify which one will receive attention first. Later, you can focus on another group of like items.

3. **Provide a definition:** Ask students to define the term that is the focus for this activity and represents examples from the grouped set. Students share their definition with the class to arrive at a consensus. Ask them to record the attributes and definition in their notebooks.

4. **Create another example:** Students review the items in the grouped set, the list of attributes of these items, and the definition to help them construct new examples. For instance, if the grouped set has similes, students invent their own similes. If the set includes sentences that begin with dependent clauses, students construct similar sentences. (You can switch this step and number 5.)

5. **Find and critique examples:** Direct students to an appropriate source, such as a textbook, print or digital article, website, video, or picture (if applicable), and find examples of this skill that published authors, artists, or professionals in the field have used. Instruct them to discuss and analyze these examples with others and then share their interpretations or observations with the class.

6. **Apply the skill:** Have students practice the skill independently by applying it, for example, to a piece of writing, an artwork, a dance performance, or a science experiment.

Punctuate Dialogue Using Concept Attainment

In this activity to teach the mechanics of dialogue, I feature sentences from "The Lottery" by Shirley Jackson (1949/2010). You can, however, use a text from your classroom that contains a fair amount of dialogue, or use the excerpts from Jackson's story if appropriate for your students. Familiarize students with whatever complex text you choose before this lesson so you do not launch into learning about dialogue punctuation in a vacuum without students experiencing the richness of the literary work's content. This activity can serve either diagnostically as a preassessment to gauge students' level of proficiency with dialogue mechanics, or formatively to check for understanding, so use it as you see fit.

To prepare, make sentence strips of a combination of dialogue excerpts in figure 4.18 for each student pair or trio. (The subheadings with the type of tag—*beginning*, *middle*, and so forth—reveal the answers, so no need to share them with students.) Additionally, copy a class set of the dialogue mechanics rules

Dialogue Excerpts From "The Lottery" by Shirley Jackson (1949/2010)
Beginning Tags
Then he asked, "Watson boy drawing this year?"
A girl whispered, "I hope it's not Nancy."
Old Man Warner said clearly, "People ain't the way they used to be."
Middle Tags
"Well, now," Mr. Summers said soberly, "guess we better get started, get this over with, so's we can go back to work. Anybody ain't here?"
"Well," Mr. Summers said, "guess that's everyone."
"They do say," Mr. Adams said to Old Man Warner, who stood next to him, "that over in the north village they're talking of giving up the lottery."
"Well, everyone," Mr. Summers said, "that was done pretty fast, and now we've got to be hurrying a little more to get done in time."
End Tags
"All ready?" he called.
"There goes my old man," Mrs. Delacroix said.
"I wish they'd hurry," Mrs. Dunbar said to her older son.
"Clean forgot what day it was," she said to Mrs. Delacroix, who stood next to her, and they both laughed softly.
Combination of Tags
"Daughters draw with their husbands' families, Tessie," Mr. Summers said gently. "You know that as well as anyone else."
"Clyde Dunbar," he said. "That's right. He's broke his leg, hasn't he? Who's drawing for him?"
"Horace's not but sixteen yet," Mrs. Dunbar said regretfully. "Guess I gotta fill in for the old man this year."
Mr. Graves nodded and held up the slips of paper. "Put them back in the box, then," Mr. Summers directed. "Take Bill's and put it in."

Source: Jackson, 1949/2010.

Figure 4.18: Dialogue sentence strips.

*Visit **go.SolutionTree.com/literacy** for a free reproducible version of this figure.*

(figure 4.19 on page 87) and the poem "freddy the rat perishes" by Don Marquis (n.d.; www.donmarquis .org/freddy.htm) or make them available electronically. Follow these seven steps.

1. **Set the stage:**

    *   Explain that authors use speaker or dialogue tags to reveal who is speaking and sometimes as an indication of how characters talk. One or more characters can exchange dialogue. When just two are exchanging words, dialogue tags might appear only at the beginning of the conversation between these characters. It is then incumbent upon the reader to keep track of which one is speaking as the conversation continues.

    *   Tell students the following: "Authors position dialogue tags in different places in relation to the dialogue, and each adheres to different mechanics rules. The focus for today is to answer these guiding questions: *What are different types of dialogue tags? What are proper dialogue*

mechanics for each type? You'll use what you learn to properly treat dialogue in your own stories."

2. **Examine and group a set of items according to their commonalities:** Distribute a set of dialogue strips to a pair or trio. You can differentiate by preparing sets from the same or different texts with varying degrees of challenge. Provide these instructions: "I'll distribute an envelope to each pair or trio. In it are various excerpts from _____ (*identify the text*). Focus on the mechanics of the dialogue, specifically punctuation marks and capitalization. Sort the strips into groups that each contain sentences that show the author treating the dialogue mechanics in the same way. Be prepared to defend your rationale for sorting."

3. **Identify the specific attributes of this grouped set:** Ask each pair or trio to share how they sorted the sentences to answer the question, *What is similar about the items in this group?* While they articulate the common attributes of each group, feature the sentence strips on a document camera or other projection device. Students might say something like, "These sentences all have a dialogue tag at the beginning of the sentence, so we put them all in one group."

4. **Provide a definition by stating the rules:** Ask students to specifically state the rules for dialogue in each grouped set, such as, "After a dialogue tag at the beginning of a sentence, there is a comma and then a quotation mark. . . ." Record these rules that students share. Next, distribute figure 4.19, Conventions Rules for Dialogue, and instruct students to compare and discuss their class-generated list of rules with those on the sheet. (Rule 5 focuses on multiple paragraphs of dialogue, which is not part of the card sort, so discuss this rule separately.)

5. **Find examples:** Instruct students to participate in a scavenger hunt to find examples of each type of tag in their literature textbook, independent book, or class text. When they find an example, ask them to record the page numbers in figure 4.19. (Visit **go.SolutionTree.com/literacy** to download a reproducible version.)

6. **Create another example:** Tell students to create their own examples of each type of dialogue (except for rule 5 perhaps) on a separate paper or electronically. They are to indicate the number of each associated rule with their original passages. You can collect this sheet to check for understanding. When they receive it back with your comments, ask them to place this rule sheet in their notebooks for future reference when writing dialogue.

7. **Apply the skill and debrief:**

   - Students practice dialogue mechanics by rewriting Don Marquis's (n.d.) narrative poem "freddy the rat perishes" into prose with dialogue. In it, the poet tells the story from the point of view of Archy, a cockroach. Three other characters are involved and engage in dialogue—(1) a stranger who is a tarantula, (2) a local creature called A Thousand Legs, and (3) Freddy the rat. Marquis (n.d.) narrates it in third-person point of view and sets it in a newspaper office after working hours when all the insects come out of hiding.

   - Access the entire poem at www.donmarquis.org/freddy.htm. Before students convert the poem into prose, read it aloud. Then, have students reread it silently, paying special attention to dialogue treatment. See figure 4.20 (page 88) for how to rewrite the first stanza. I did not concern myself with standard grammatical usage as I wanted to keep the integrity of the content.

   - When they finish, students share their versions with the class. Discuss and compare what they contribute. Collect their work to assess and inform your instruction.

   - They then work on composing dialogue with proper mechanics for their own narratives.

Conventions Rules for Dialogue	
Rules	Examples*
1. Within the dialogue, place the appropriate punctuation mark—question mark, exclamation point, comma, period—inside the second quotation mark. • *Marshall asked, "Where is my burgundy sweater?"* • *"This room is an utter mess!" his mom cried.* • *"You seem unable to fold your clothes and put them away," Marshall's mother stated.* • *The son shrugged and said, "I'll clean it up tomorrow."* • *"Well," his mom continued, "I've surely heard that before."*	
2. When dialogue is interrupted with a tag (*he said, she said*), place a comma and quotation mark before and after the tag. Do not capitalize the second part of the quotation when it's a continuation of a complete sentence. • *"Please," he said in defense, "this room isn't half as cluttered as my friends' rooms."* • *"Who cares," his mom teased, "since this is where you live?"*	
3. Begin a new paragraph each time the speaker changes, even if the dialogue is short. *"Dad, please let me have a pet dog?" whined Kimmie.* *"Well, Kimmie," replied her father, "animals require attention. You'd have to walk him every day."* *"I know."* *"Plus, clean up after a pet."* *"I will."*	
4. Some dialogue sentences do not have tags attached to them. *After Kimmie pleaded for a pet, she approached her mother hoping for a better outcome. Her mom was peacefully sipping coffee and reading the paper, but Kimmie didn't care and interrupted anyway. "I wish Dad would let me have a dog!"* *Startled, Kimmie's mother was annoyed and tired of this repeated conversation begging for a pet. "Your father has made his position perfectly clear." With that, she returned to her coffee and newspaper.*	
5. When an author writes a lot of dialogue that becomes multiple paragraphs, the quotation marks appear only at the beginning of the paragraphs and the end of the last one. *Roger hurriedly recited a fairytale to his daughter, but confused most of the characters. Rocking her gently, he began the somewhat incorrect rendition confusing one tale with another, "Cinderella sadly lived with an evil stepmother because her father met an unfortunate end. She was made to sweep, scrub, wipe, and clean the house from morning until late at night.* *"Eventually the wicked stepmother tired of Cinderella and moved her high up in a tower. She had exceedingly long hair and would toss it through the window for someone to use as a rope.* *"To her rescue, a wolf strolled by and saw the trapped beauty. He found a rope ladder and hoisted a little girl in a red cape up it so she could set Cinderella free.* *"Once she could escape the tower, she ran into little dwarfs who helped her dress in the finest of gowns. The tiny men escorted her to the palace ball where the prince spotted Cinderella and asked for her hand in marriage.* *"The two lived happily ever after."*	

*Find passages with dialogue from a text that follows each rule and cite the page number or numbers.

Figure 4.19: Conventions rules for dialogue.

*Visit **go.SolutionTree.com/literacy** for a free reproducible version of this figure.*

"freddy the rat perishes" (excerpt)	Freddy the Rat Perishes

who are you said a thousand legs
 	
if i bite you once
 	
said the stranger you won t ask
 	
again he he little poison tongue said
 	
the thousand legs who gave you hydrophobia
 	
i got it by biting myself said
 	
the stranger i m bad keep away
 	
from me where i step a weed dies
 	
if i was to walk on your forehead it would
 	
raise measles and if
 	
you give me any lip i ll do it
	To write it in prose with proper conventions, it could look like this.
	
	   "Who are you?" said A Thousand Legs.
	   "If I bite you once," said the stranger, "you won't ask again."
	   "You have a little poison tongue," said A Thousand Legs. "Who gave you that huge scar on your leg?"
	   "I got it by biting myself," said the stranger. "I'm bad. Keep away from me. Where I step, a weed dies. If I was to walk on your forehead, it would raise measles. If you give me any lip, I'll do it."

Source: Marquis, n.d.

Figure 4.20: Excerpt of "freddy the rat perishes."

Practice Writing Dialogue

After students learn to punctuate dialogue and its purpose, ask them to practice writing dialogue in pairs. Each student will assume a different character or a personified object. Provide these suggestions, but tell students to generate their own subjects for the dialogue as they wish: twelve-year-old twins, cosmetic salesperson and customer, new book and reader, dog and cat, two grandmothers, contact lens and eyeball, lost cell phone and the one who finds it, toaster and toast, barista and customer, and so forth. Or find and show pictures of two people or inanimate objects in a print advertisement or piece of artwork and have students assume their roles. Instruct them to do the following activity.

1. **Create a situation:** Students discuss with each other a particular situation that forms the basis for the dialogue among the two subjects.

2. **Write dialogue:** Ask each student to write at least five lines of dialogue assuming the role of his or her assigned subject and use all types of dialogue tags—beginning, middle, end, and no tag. Somewhere in the actual conversation or tag, readers should be able to recognize the identity of the two subjects engaged in the dialogue.

Although each student will write his or her respective dialogue by sharing the paper or electronic device, encourage students to check each other's work and make changes as needed.

Sentence Structure

Intentionally using different sentence beginnings—adjectives, prepositional phrases, dependent clauses, and so forth—contributes to rhythm and cadence from one sentence to the next. It also connects paragraphs so ideas link fluidly to help readers navigate the text. In a narrative, the way sentences start can double as transitions that convey a sequence of events and signal shifts between time and place. Therefore, students will benefit from having a good command of this skill so they can easily write with this awareness.

Proficient writers not only think about sentence beginnings but also consider sentence structures. For example, they might strategically craft a combination of simple, compound, and compound-complex sentences in some parts of their work to promote flow. In other areas of the text, they might purposely write a series of short, simple sentences, for example, to build intensity as the story action climbs to a climax.

When teaching sentence structure, grammar, and conventions, I suggest that you use the classroom complex text as the vehicle for instruction. In this regard, students learn these skills by paying attention to the featured author's work rather than isolated material disconnected from the curriculum. As with other grammar and conventions skills, be sure that students are familiar with the text and its content before launching into lessons of this granular level.

The KUDs and guiding questions you might choose for instruction for this section are in the Sentence Beginnings and Sentence Structure rows on page 16 in table 1.2 (chapter 1).

Vary Sentence Beginnings

This activity serves as a launching pad for introducing ways sentences can begin. Subsequent lessons can focus on each type of sentence beginning that you choose to teach, such as sentences that start with dependent clauses (see appendix D, page 149), prepositional phrases, or adjectives.

To prepare, find sentences from a classroom complex text that begin in a variety of ways or use the excerpts in figure 4.21 (pages 90–91). If you use these strips, cut off the left-hand column that reveals the type of sentence beginning, which is for your edification. Make a class set of figure 4.22 (page 92), Options for Beginning Sentences. Arrange students into small groups of three or four and make sticky notes available to them. Conduct the four steps of this activity as follows.

1. **Set the stage:**

   • Read the following excerpt from *Holes* (Sachar, 1998) aloud and show it on a document camera or other projection device. Alternatively, use a passage from a familiar text from class that has redundant beginnings.

   • Ask, "What do you notice about how the sentences start?" Students will likely say it is repetitive or specifically notice the overabundance of pronouns. Verify their impressions. Avoid devaluing authors who choose to use repetition as an effective rhetorical device; rather, mention that some authors purposely write sentences that begin this way because they might choose to write in the voice of an individual or character, or emphasize a point. Pose this guiding question to set the purpose for this lesson: *How can you begin your sentences in different ways?*

From *Holes* (Sachar, 1998):

> *He had driven straight into a hole.*
> *He lay on the dirt staring at the truck, which stuck lopsided into the ground. He sighed. He couldn't blame his no-good-dirty-pig-stealing-great-great-grandfather this time. This time it was his own fault, one hundred percent. He had probably just done the stupidest thing he had ever done in his short and miserable life.*
> *He managed to get to his feet. He was sore but didn't think he had broken any bones. He glanced back at Mr. Sir, who remained where he was, starting at Stanley.*
> *He ran. His canteen was strapped around his neck. It banged against his chest as he ran, and every time it hit against him, it reminded him that it was empty, empty, empty. (p. 148)*

2. **Assign the task:**

   • Distribute a set of sentence strips with varied sentence beginnings from a classroom complex text or my excerpts from Charles Dickens's (1843) *A Christmas Carol* (figure 4.21, pages 90–91). Students should be familiar with the content of the text you are using for this exercise prior to zeroing in on the skill of varying sentence beginnings. Therefore, if you use my examples, expose students to Dickens's story, if appropriate for your classroom, and conduct activities around it so they appreciate the content fully.

- Instruct students to look at sentences one at a time and group them according to how they begin. Emphasize that they are not sequencing the sentence strips into a logical order—this represents a different skill. They are to read and compare the first several words of each sentence and then group together those that share the same type of beginning.

- Once they sort the strips, tell students to use a sticky note to title each column with a name of a category or identify the common attributes if they don't know a column title. They should be ready to share their rationale for each column.

3. **Identify sentence beginnings:**

- Solicit the names of types of sentence beginnings from each student group and list them on an easel or whiteboard. If needed, provide hints to prompt students on the terms, such as *prepositional phrase* or *proper noun*.

- Distribute figure 4.22 (page 92), which shows different options. Have students compare the class-generated list with this handout. Give groups time to identify sentence strips that fall under any of the categories on the handout, add to the list of examples, and re-sort their strips, if needed. Tell students to store this figure in their notebooks to use as a resource.

4. **Complete exit cards:** The last three to five minutes of class, issue exit cards that you can use as a formative assessment. Ask students to write three sentences that each start differently, plus underline and label how each one starts. You can ask them to generate sentences based on a classroom text to check for understanding. For instance, provide these instructions: "Write three sentences to show your understanding of a character [or setting, character's dilemma, event] in our text. For each sentence, (a) write a different beginning, (b) underline the beginning words, and (c) include the type of sentence beginning in parentheses. Here's an example: <u>Although George constantly talks of the burden of taking care of Lennie</u>, he is clearly devoted to him (dependent clause)." Tell students that the next series of lessons focuses on each of the different ways (if this is indeed your intent).

Excerpts for Sentence Beginning Activity	
Sentence Beginning	**Sentence Excerpts**
Adjective	External heat and cold had little influence on Scrooge.
	Hard and sharp as flint, from which no steel had ever struck out generous fire; secret, and self-contained, and solitary as an oyster.
Dependent Clause	As the words were spoken, they passed through the wall, and stood upon an open country road, with fields on either hand.
	As he threw his head back in the chair, his glance happened to rest upon a bell . . .
	"If these shadows remain unaltered by the Future, none other of my race . . . will find him here"
	Though he looked the phantom through and through, and saw it standing before him . . . he was still incredulous, and fought against his senses.
	Although they had but that moment left the school behind them, they were now in the busy thoroughfares of a city . . .
	"Since you ask me what I wish, gentlemen, that is my answer. . . ."

	When Scrooge awoke, it was so dark, that looking out of bed, he could scarcely distinguish the transparent window from the opaque walls of his chamber.
	When it had said these words, the spectre took its wrapper from the table, and bound it round its head, as before.
Prepositional Phrase	In the main street, at the corner of the court, some labourers were repairing the gas-pipes, and had lighted a great fire in a brazier . . .
	After several turns, he sat down again.
	During the whole of this time, Scrooge had acted like a man out of his wits.
	To his great astonishment the heavy bell went on from six to seven, and from seven to eight . . .
	At the ominous word liberality, Scrooge frowned, and shook his head, and handed the credentials back.
Subject (noun)	The clerk in the Tank involuntarily applauded.
	The apparition walked backward from him; and at every step it took, the window raised itself a little . . .
	The cold within him froze his old features, nipped his pointed nose, shriveled his cheek, stiffened his gait . . .
	Admiration was the universal sentiment, though some objected that the reply to "Is it a bear?" ought to have been "Yes;" . . .
	Holly, mistletoe, red berries, ivy, turkeys, geese, game, poultry, . . . and punch, all vanished instantly.
Subject (proper noun)	Scrooge never painted out Old Marley's name.
	Scrooge had a very small fire, but the clerk's fire was so very much smaller that it looked like one coal.
	Marley's Ghost bothered him exceedingly.
	Master Peter Cratchit plunged a fork into the saucepan of potatoes . . .
Subject (pronoun)	It was the very thing he liked.
	He lived in chambers which had once belonged to his deceased partner.
	". . . We choose this time, because it is a time, of all others, when Want is keenly felt, and Abundance rejoices. . . ."
	They went, the Ghost and Scrooge, across the hall, to a door at the back of the house.
	". . . I don't make merry myself at Christmas and I can't afford to make idle people merry. . . ."
Adverb	Suddenly a man, in foreign garments . . . stood outside the window, with an axe stuck in his belt . . .
	"'Heartily sorry,' he said, 'for your good wife.'"
	Reverently Scrooge disclaimed all intention to offend or any knowledge of having willfully "bonneted" the Spirit at any period of his life.
	Mildly the Spirit gazed upon him.
	. . . [C]onsequently, when the Bell struck One, and no shape appeared, he was taken with a violent fit of trembling.

Source: Adapted from Dickens, 1843.

Figure 4.21: Sentence beginning excerpts.

Visit go.SolutionTree.com/literacy for a free reproducible version of this figure.

Options for Beginning Sentences			
Subjects	**Adverbs**	**Dependent Clauses**	**Prepositional Phrases**
Pronouns You He She It or Its We You They	**How?** Angrily Carefully Haphazardly Joyously Loudly Peacefully Silently Truthfully	**Subordinating Conjunctions** After Although As As if As long as As soon as As though Because Before By the time Even if Even though If If only In case In order that In the event that Once Only Only if Rather than Since So that Though Till Unless Until When Whenever Where Whereas Wherever Whether Whether or not While	**Prepositions** About Above Across After Along Among Around As At Before Behind Below Beneath Beside Between Beyond Down During In Inside Into Near On Outside Over Regarding Since Through To Under Underneath Until With Within Without
Nouns* Cars Desks Mammals Man, woman, or child Rocks Sheet Characterization Diversity Community Immigration *Can begin with an article: *A, An, The*	**When?** Always Early Last Never Now Often Soon Then Tomorrow Usually Yesterday		
Proper Nouns Mr. Smith Dr. Salk Helen Keller President Kennedy Juan Charlene Friday October Wall Street Mt. Rushmore Stanford University Spring Mill School Lake Superior Hearst Castle Indianapolis Ridley Court	**Where?** Everywhere Here Nowhere Outside Somewhere There Underground Upstairs **To What Degree?** Almost Enough Only Too Quite		

Figure 4.22: Options for beginning sentences.

*Visit **go.SolutionTree.com/literacy** for a free reproducible version of this figure.*

Write Complex Sentences

After an introductory activity around sentence beginnings as detailed in the previous lesson idea, you can home in on dependent clauses—a component of complex sentences. For those of you wanting a brief orientation to feel more comfortable teaching this sentence structure, refer to appendix D (page 149).

Students use the card sort from the previous activity (Vary Sentence Beginnings, page 89) to focus on complex sentences that begin with dependent clauses. Prepare a three-column chart with these headings on the board or easel: *Subordinating Conjunctions*, *Subjects*, and *Verbs*. Also, create cards with selected subordinating conjunctions on each one and place them in a box or hat. (You may use the ones in figure 4.22 as a resource.) Divide the class in half and follow these four steps.

1. **Set the stage:** Pose these guiding questions to set the purpose for learning: *How do I write a complex sentence? What is the construction for a dependent clause?*

2. **Identify parts of a dependent clause:**

    - Ask students to focus on the column from their sentence strip sorting that starts with dependent clauses. Point out that these clauses begin with a subordinating conjunction and must have a subject and verb. Refer to the subordinating conjunctions in figure 4.22 with students. They can place this handout in their notebooks for future reference.

    - Tell students to turn and talk with a partner to deconstruct the parts of a dependent clause from the complex and compound-complex sentences in the card sort—subordinating conjunctions, subjects, and verbs. When finished, ask partners to volunteer words from the sentence strips to fill in the prepared three-column chart. If you used *A Christmas Carol* cards, figure 4.23 (page 94) reflects the dependent clause parts with subordinating conjunctions in bold typeface, subjects underlined, and verbs italicized.

3. **Practice creating complex sentences:**

    - Arrange students into two lines facing each other; designate one line of students as line A and the other line B. Alternatively, conduct an inside/outside circle. In this configuration, students stand shoulder to shoulder in a circle facing outward. The other half stands in a circle facing these students. Tell students they will orally create a complex or compound-complex sentence that begins with a dependent clause with the student facing them using a random subordinating conjunction to start each sentence.

    - Take out the prepared subordinating conjunction cards in a hat or box. Ask each student in line A (or the inside circle) to pick a card.

    - Line A students make up a dependent clause using the selected subordinating conjunction; line B students complete the sentence with their invented independent clause or clauses. Some learners might need suggestions for subjects and verbs, so reference the three-column chart for support.

    - The line A student walks to the end of the line. All the other students in line A move one spot up so they face a different partner. (Or, inside circle students rotate clockwise one or two positions.)

    - The new pair of students then generates another complex or compound-complex sentence. Students in line A use the same or a new subordinating conjunction to invent a dependent clause while line B students finish the sentence.

    - Students repeat the task of crafting complex or compound-complex sentences while you walk around the room listening for evidence of proficiency. At some point, ask students to switch roles so that students in line B initiate sentences with a dependent clause. End the exercise when you feel students have mastered this skill. Afterward, invite students to add to the three-column chart based on their newly formulated sentences. You might ask them to complete exit cards with complex and compound-complex sentences.

4. **Connect to future learning:** Explain to students that they will use what they learned about dependent clauses and complex sentences when writing their narratives so they can add variety, fluidity, and interest to their writing. To reinforce, extend, and build on the acquired learning in this activity, focus subsequent lessons on alternative sentence beginnings, such as prepositional phrases or adjectives.

Excerpts From *A Christmas Carol* (Dickens, 1843)
• **As** the <u>words</u> *were spoken*, they passed through the wall, and stood upon an open country road, with fields on either hand.
• **As** <u>he</u> *threw* his head back in the chair, his glance happened to rest upon a bell . . .
• "**If** these <u>shadows</u> *remain* unaltered by the Future, none other of my race . . ."
• **Though** <u>he</u> *looked* the phantom through and through, and saw it standing before him . . . he was still incredulous, and fought against his senses.
• **Although** <u>they</u> *had* but that moment *left* the school behind them, they were now in the busy thoroughfares of a city . . .
• "**Since** <u>you</u> *ask* me what I wish, gentlemen, that is my answer. . . ."
• **When** <u>Scrooge</u> *awoke*, it was so dark, that looking out of bed, he could scarcely distinguish the transparent window from the opaque walls of his chamber.
• **When** <u>it</u> *had said* these words, the spectre took its wrapper from the table, and bound it round its head, as before.

Source: Dickens, 1843.

Figure 4.23: Annotated dependent clause examples.

*Visit **go.SolutionTree.com/literacy** for a free reproducible version of this figure.*

Narrative Prewriting

This section includes tools and strategies for the prewriting stage of the writing process as it specifically relates to narrative. You can adapt and embed other lesson ideas, including suggestions for technology, from *The Fundamentals of (Re)designing Writing Units* (Glass, 2017a), as well.

Once aware of their task, purpose, and audience, students begin *prewriting*. This stage, which prepares them for the first draft, can entail a host of options that writers use in combination or alone, such as completing a graphic organizer, making a chart or table, engaging in a free write or word-association exercise, or drawing pictures or diagrams. For a narrative specifically, students can make webs to brainstorm character types and profiles and create a plot diagram. Writers engage in any of these by hand or electronically.

Prewriting also includes research and other planning measures that position students for success along the way to producing a well-developed piece. Although this stage is essential like all other parts of the writing process, specific genres might stipulate certain prewriting exercises. For example, biographers must interview and conduct research for their subjects, and those writing historical fiction must also research a time period to gather and use accurate details regarding characters, events, and setting. Since the writing process is iterative, students might revisit this stage well into their writing projects to conduct more research or refine ideas, as necessary.

Brainstorm Ideas for a Memoir

In the memoir genre, you can direct students to "look for small self-contained incidents that are still vivid in your memory. If you still remember them it's because they contain a universal truth that your readers will recognize from their own life" (Zinsser, 2006). To learn from their targeted recollections and foster connections with readers, students need to amass multiple reminiscences that they can later think about and select as the basis for their writing.

Figure 4.24 features a memoir brainstorming sheet as a prewriting tool for this genre. To prime students to use it optimally, consider the following activity.

1. **Generate a list of emotions:** Tell students you will distribute a memoir brainstorming sheet but that first you'll prepare them so they can use it most effectively. To do so, solicit students to help generate a list of emotions someone might feel associated with a memory. Explain that there can be a continuum of emotions because they might first feel one way and then their thoughts and reactions evolve. Post the class-generated list of words and invite students to add to it as they continue throughout the unit. Offer some examples to get them started, such as *melancholy, fearless, frightened, timid, assured, responsible, carefree, lonesome, alienated,* and *humiliated*. Tell students that when they work on their brainstorming sheets, they might first land on an emotion that they experienced and then work backward to pinpoint the place or circumstances surrounding it.

2. **Model:** Distribute figure 4.24 and preview the different categories. Then model how to complete it so students witness how you struggle with retrieving information or generating ideas. Let them know that they do not have to automatically share their brainstorming with others. In fact, they might elect to discuss only selective parts of what they sketched with peers, or not share at all.

3. **Expect overlap:** Explain that as they complete this prewriting organizer, they should expect overlap. For example, students might combine two entries by jotting down a memory involving an individual in a public place like Shea Stadium or Yosemite National Park.

4. **Stimulate recollections:** Emphasize that students are merely generating ideas, so there is no need to fill in each line item comprehensively at this point. The exercise should stimulate thoughts that students record.

5. **Elaborate:** After students complete the brainstorming sheet, they review their entries and isolate a few to develop further. On a clean sheet of paper or an electronic device, they elaborate on these targeted memories in any one of the following ways: engaging in free writing, completing a graphic organizer, creating a timeline, or using another idea they want to pursue.

Memoir Brainstorming Sheet
Directions: Use this brainstorming sheet to help trigger your memories about a time, event, situation, or experience. You can check as many items as you want. Then brainstorm memories in the space provided by answering these and other questions to help you. • What kind of memory is it? • What feelings or emotions does it evoke? You can write about a span of feelings and emotions before, during, and after the incident (for example, *content, courageous, carefree, lonesome, alienated, humiliated, emotional*). • Who was there? How were they involved?

Figure 4.24: Memoir brainstorming sheet.

continued ➤

At School

❏ Preschool   ❏ Elementary School   ❏ Middle School   ❏ High School
❏ Other School (for example, a religious school or another specialized school)

At a Place

❏ Your Home   ❏ Someone Else's Home   ❏ Vacation Spot (city, state, country)
❏ Public Place (mall, park, beach, resort, sporting venue, and so on)   ❏ Camp
❏ Vehicle (bus, car, bike, boat, jet ski, and so on)   ❏ Other

With Someone or an Animal

❏ Sibling   ❏ Parent   ❏ Friend   ❏ Teacher   ❏ Babysitter   ❏ Coach
❏ Counselor (camp, college, peer)   ❏ Stranger   ❏ Animal   ❏ Other

During an Event

❏ Graduation   ❏ Birthday   ❏ Wedding   ❏ Party
❏ Religious Ceremony (communion, bar mitzvah, catechism)   ❏ Other
When brainstorming, indicate if the memory involves your event or someone else's.

Involving a Favorite

❏ Toy   ❏ Object   ❏ Hobby   ❏ Vehicle   ❏ Electronic Device   ❏ Other

Brainstorm Ideas for a Memoir or Personal Narrative

George Hillocks (2007) provides an excellent prewriting technique for his students when writing about themselves. Here is a summary of a sequence he recommends to foster ideas.

1. **Listen to story ideas:** Hillocks (2007) features eight ideas for writing about himself that he reads to students; I've shared two of his here. Fairly brief, they contain enough details to compel listeners or readers to ask for more information. Create your own short or long examples to share with your students.

   - In the first grade I was whistling one day and was sent to the principal's office to explain. (p. 38)

   - In elementary school, the biggest bully was a boy named Mars (the god of war). He had failed a few times, and we thought he was about fifteen even though he was in the sixth grade. He would follow me home and punch me for no reason. I tried to hide from him. One day he took our stuff at recess and would not give it back. I ended up in a fight with him and was beaten in no uncertain terms. I felt terrible. (p. 38)

2. **Vote on the most compelling ideas:** After hearing the writing ideas, students vote on those they find most compelling. Discuss the top two or three choices briefly—just long enough to arouse students' curiosity and allow them to see that everyone has a story to tell.

3. **Generate story ideas:** Ask students to generate and record their own story ideas using the following questions and others you devise. If they have trouble getting started, invite a few volunteers to answer some of these questions. Collect students' story ideas or ask them to store them in a writing folder.

   - "What experiences have made you feel really happy or very sad?"

   - "What experiences have been very alarming or really frightening?"

   - "What experiences have made you feel proud of yourself?"

   - "What experiences have been the most difficult tasks you have had to undertake?"

   - "What contests or games have you tried hard to win?"

   - "What experiences have made you feel ashamed of yourself?"

   - "What experiences have made you realize that you truly care about someone?"

   - "What experiences have made you laugh a lot?" (p. 39)

4. **Ask questions:** Return to the teacher-generated ideas and recall the voting results of the top choices. Reread one, ask students what they would want to know more about, and furnish some details about the story. Ask for more questions, which likely center on elements of a story, such as, *Who said . . . ? Where were you . . . ? When did . . . finally realize . . . ?* Review the questions they ask and explain that these should be addressed in their writing about something that happened to them. Then distribute and review a brainstorming sheet you have prepared that includes the structure and elements of personal narrative or memoir and questions for each. For example, one for personal narrative has *setting* (Where does the narrative take place? How important is this place?), *characters* (Who is involved and in what way? What is important to know about the characters?), *central conflict* (What happens to set the story in motion?), and so forth.

5. **Answer questions:** Students review the story ideas they generated earlier and share two with classmates in small groups. When sharing, encourage peers to ask questions of their own. Students then determine one idea they will develop and individually complete the prepared brainstorming sheet to make the prewriting stage tangible.

Brainstorm Ideas for Historical Fiction

If you teach a core subject or a course in the humanities that comprises language arts and social studies, consider assigning historical fiction. To prepare them to write, conduct a brainstorming session in which students record what they know about the period in history that is the basis for their writing. Here is how you might conduct this activity in four steps.

1. **Complete a brainstorming sheet:** Distribute a sheet with different categories on it, such as clothing, food, types of people, pastime activities, living quarters, cities, events, family life, or words people used in that era. Or include headings relegated to aspects of culture, such as government, religion, art, architecture, politics, economy, society, and so forth. Individually, students brainstorm items that they associate with each category based on the period in history.

2. **Confer with peers:** After students complete their sheets, they form groups of four and cross-reference their lists, making sure to agree on all items.

3. **Record items:** Prepare different pieces of butcher paper that are each titled with one of the categories on the brainstorming sheet. Distribute one butcher paper piece to each group. Members then record items onto it. For example, for the category of clothing, a group might record these items from the Western European Renaissance period: beret, corset, doublet (man's bodice), funnel sleeves, tunic, and so forth. Call "time," and then ask students to pass the butcher paper to another group that then reviews the existing items and adds, deletes, or edits, as group members see fit.

4. **Use lists as a resource:** As a class, review all the contributions on the butcher paper sheets to categorize, edit, and delete as necessary. Tell students that while they write their historical fiction stories, they can refer to these items. To support them, consider collecting all the entries on one typed sheet and distributing it to students. Or give them time to review all the sheets of butcher paper and record selected items that they will want to use for their own stories.

Use a Graphic Organizer to Prewrite

Graphic organizers serve multiple purposes, such as to make sense of content, teach the structure and elements of a genre, and brainstorm as a prewriting technique. (Review the section Plot Elements in this chapter or appendix E on page 158 for a list of graphic organizer websites.)

Mystery: See figure 4.25 for an example of how students can focus on characteristic elements of a genre as a brainstorming tool and also to record examples from a student or published mystery model. If you use it for the latter purpose, change the subheading Ideas for Your Mystery to Evidence From the Text. Students then read a mystery and complete the graphic organizer to pinpoint areas that are present. They may leave cells blank to reveal any missing elements. To modify the task, you can adapt this graphic organizer and eliminate some lines.

Generic narrative: See figures 4.26 (page 100), 4.27 (page 101), and 4.28 (page 102) for examples of narrative organizers that students can use to generate ideas that they can later develop. Older and more proficient writers may deviate from the simplistic organizer to include multiple plotlines, flashbacks, or a series of conflicts during the rising action before approaching the climax. Alternatively, students can create their own graphic organizer that frames the story they will write. Students can also complete a graphic organizer based on narrative models they read to examine how authors develop (or underdevelop) story elements.

Mystery Elements and Structure		
Introduction and Central Conflict		
Element	Description	Ideas for Your Mystery
Setting	Time and place of the story	
Characters		
Detective	Someone who investigates a crime; an investigator looking for and gathering clues	
Victim	The person who has been wronged; may also be the person reporting the crime	
Crime	An action that breaks the law	
Motive	A reason that a person does something—can include anger, hatred, love, or greed	
Rising Action		
Characters		
Suspect	A person who appears to have a motive to commit the crime	
Witness	A person who has knowledge about a crime	
Clue	A fact or object that appears to give information toward solving the crime	
Hunch	A guess or feeling that a detective has that is not based on facts; includes a suspect with a motive and words such as *maybe*, *possibly*, *what if*, and *probably*	
Alibi	An excuse that a suspect uses to show that he or she was not at the scene of the crime	
Red Herring	A false lead or clue that throws the investigator off track	
Distraction	Clues, suspects, witnesses, or anything that leads an investigator astray in solving the crime	
Climax, Falling Action, and Resolution		
Evidence	Something (for example, an item or a statement) that helps to prove who committed the crime	
Breakthrough	A discovery that helps solve the crime	
Deduction	Collecting the facts and drawing a possible conclusion; solving the mystery	

Source: Adapted from MysteryNet.com, n.d.; ReadWriteThink, n.d.

Figure 4.25: Mystery elements and structure.

*Visit **go.SolutionTree.com/literacy** for a free reproducible version of this figure.*

Story Graphic Organizer		
Author: _____		Title: _____
Introduction	Setting	
	Characters	
Central Conflict	Sets the story in motion	
Rising Action	Series of events that builds tension and leads to the climax	
Climax	Highest moment of tension in the story	
Falling Action	Wraps up loose ends and leads to closure	
Resolution	Conflict resolved or settled	

Figure 4.26: Story graphic organizer 1.

*Visit **go.SolutionTree.com/literacy** for a free reproducible version of this figure.*

Climax (High Point of Story):

Event 4:

Event 3:

Resolution (Central Conflict Is Resolved):

Event 2:

Event 1:

Central Conflict	
Setting	
Characters	

Figure 4.27: Story graphic organizer 2.

*Visit **go.SolutionTree.com/literacy** for a free reproducible version of this figure.*

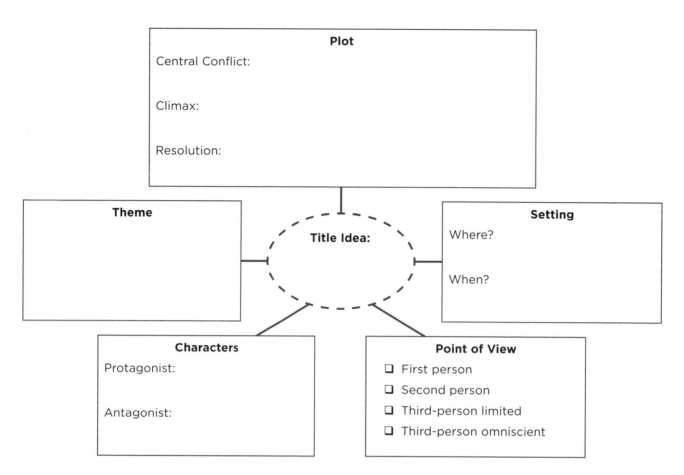

Figure 4.28: Story graphic organizer 3.

*Visit **go.SolutionTree.com/literacy** for a free reproducible version of this figure.*

Narrative Revision

To aide students in revision, they need proper direction, strategies, and tools so they can make informed decisions about how to improve their writing. Orchestrating situations in which students self-assess and collect feedback from others can supply them with the necessary support to isolate weak areas so they can focus their energies there.

Self-assessment is a substantial contributor to achievement. Hattie (2012) states:

> All students should be educated in ways that develop their capability to assess their own learning. . . . When students participate in the assessment of their own learning, they learn to recognize and understand main ideas, and to apply new learning in different ways and situations. (pp. 141–142)

As well, feedback from peers, invested others, and teachers can move learning forward as students collect input, evaluate its worth, and determine what revisions are necessary to refine their writing. When students offer feedback to others, they also benefit because studying another's paper to identify what input they might give helps them become stronger writers.

A genre-specific revision sheet, like the one I feature in figure 4.29 (pages 103–105) for realistic fiction, enables students to critically examine their own writing, helping them glean the information they need to direct their revision. It also provides a framework for reviewers to offer targeted input to writers. This assessment tool yields concrete data for improvement. Students can use it in the following ways.

- **Self-assessment:** After the first draft, students self-assess using the prompts on the revision sheet, which aligns to the writing checklist and rubric. These prompts guide them in providing evidence of the extent to which they have satisfied the criteria. They then use their self-assessment input on the revision sheet to create another draft.

- **Peer review:** After students self-assess and have time to revise their work, they solicit one or more peers to supply feedback using a fresh copy of the revision sheet. Writers use this input to create their next draft.
- **School-home connection:** Make a copy of the revision sheet for someone at home to use. Consider attaching a paragraph indicating that reviewers are to only mark on the revision sheet and not make comments or changes on the student's actual paper. This way, parents or guardians can provide valuable feedback without intruding by being too heavy-handed in editing or rewriting the student's paper (which some might be inclined to do).

Realistic Fiction Revision Sheet		
General Descriptors	**Circle**	
	Yes	**or No**
The writing genre is a **realistic short story**.	Yes	No
There are **no grammar or conventions errors**; the paper is properly **formatted**.	Yes	No
Paragraphs are used where they should be and are indented properly.	Yes	No
There is an original or creative **title**.	Yes	No
The paper maintains a consistent and appropriate **point of view** or is written from multiple viewpoints that readers can easily follow.	Yes	No

Descriptors	Story Elements
An engaging **beginning** draws in readers.	Write a sentence that draws in readers.
A **setting** and **characters** are established and provide context.	Who are the characters?
	What is the setting?
The beginning includes a **central conflict** to set the story in motion.	Briefly identify the central conflict.
The rising action creates **suspense**.	Include three major events that build suspense toward the climax. 1.
	2.
	3.

Figure 4.29: Narrative revision sheet.

Descriptors	Story Elements
The **story's climax** presents the highest point of tension.	Identify the moment of climax in the story.
The **resolution** addresses the central conflict.	What satisfying ending resolves the central conflict?

Descriptors	Literary Devices
Literary devices involving the **plot** create interest, but do not distract or confuse readers.	Which device does the student use, such as flashback, flash forward, multiple plotlines, and suspense?
	Provide proof (evidence) of its effectiveness.
Meaningful and intentional **dialogue** enhances the storyline.	Write an important dialogue exchange showing plot movement or character interaction. (Or indicate this section on the actual paper.)
Dialect reflects characters' geographical region, social status, era, bias, or other.	Write two excerpts of dialogue in which the student effectively uses dialect. 1.
	2.

Descriptors	Description
Vocabulary and **figurative language** enhance setting, characters, or events.	Provide two examples of figurative language—simile, metaphor, personification, hyperbole, or imagery. Underline precise words. 1.
	2.

The writing elicits emotion through **mood**.	Write two phrases that show mood. Indicate the emotion in parentheses. 1.
	2.
Strong verbs in the dialogue tags accentuate a character's words.	List at least four strong verbs used in dialogue tags.
Descriptors	**Sentence Structure and Transitions**
Sentences **begin in different ways**.	Write two sentences that each begin in a different way. 1.
	2.
Sentence structures vary.	Write two sentences that each have a different sentence structure. 1.
	2.
The writing includes **parallel** construction.	Write two sentences that use parallelism. 1.
	2.
Appropriate **transitions** show event sequence and a shift in time and place.	Write two examples of transitional usage. 1.
	2.

Source: Adapted from Glass, 2012.

*Visit **go.SolutionTree.com/literacy** for a free reproducible version of this figure.*

Before students self-assess or review a peer's work using the revision sheet in figure 4.29, model how to complete it using a student sample. First direct their attention to the top, which includes *yes* or *no* responses. Explain that they should mostly focus on the more revisionary prompts from the rest of the sheet by responding in one of three ways. Model which of these options is suitable.

1. **Strong:** If the writer or reviewer can state with conviction that an aspect of the paper is present and done well, he or she enters evidence from the paper along with an asterisk denoting it is strong and fine as is.

2. **Average or weak:** The writer or reviewer recognizes an element is included, but ascertains that it is average or rather weak. If this is the case, he or she writes down the evidence and places parentheses around it to indicate that it needs attention for improvement when the writer revises for the next draft.

3. **Nonexistent:** The writer or reviewer realizes that the element is missing; therefore, the cell remains blank or has a dash to acknowledge its absence.

Besides using a revision sheet, students collect and offer feedback by conferencing with peers one on one, in a small-group setting, or in an online community.

They determine in advance of peer review what part of the paper they would like feedback on so they can focus on targeted input. To do so, they can highlight portions of the checklist or rubric for reviewers to use as a guide or use figure 4.30, the Narrative Feedback Sheet. It includes a list of questions from which writers can choose to flag for reviewers to use in giving input.

If writers do not meet with reviewers face to face, tell them to type or record an introduction to accompany the marked feedback sheet stating the help they need in preparation for their next draft. If they are soliciting input from online community members, instruct them to type a note that includes direction, such as, "Here is a realistic fiction story I've drafted. I'm asking for comments specifically about suspense and whether you feel I've built sufficient tension. Your input will give me direction in writing a new draft. Thank you in advance. Please respond by [date]."

For feedback to be useful, you must teach students how to share accurate, sufficient input based on the established criteria, and to do so in a way the recipient welcomes. Also, those receiving the feedback may accept or deny what they receive because it is, after all, their paper. Aside from using a narrative writing checklist and rubric (chapter 2, page 33) plus figures 4.29 and 4.30 in this chapter, access the tools and resources in *The Fundamentals of (Re)designing Writing Units* (Glass, 2017a).

Narrative Feedback Sheet			
Writer Directions: Highlight or place a check next to the questions you want a reviewer to concentrate on when reading and providing you with input. Enter any additional questions in the blank spaces at the end of this sheet, if necessary.			
Writer: _____ Reviewer: _____			

Questions to Guide Revision	**Check Appropriate Column:**			**Comments**
	Yes	Some-what	No	
Is my **introduction** compelling enough to engage you?				
Is the **central conflict** intriguing?				
Do I build enough **suspense**?				
Is the story **sequenced** and **well paced** to facilitate reading and avoid confusion?				

Does the **climax** create tension and put you on the edge of your seat?				
Is the **resolution** satisfying and does it answer any questions you might have?				
Are the **characters** realistic? Do I provide enough information about them?				
Is the **dialogue** important to the story, and does it represent characters well?				
Are there areas that are **too wordy** or **long**? If so, what can I delete?				
Is there a section of the story that I need to **develop** more?				
Are there **confusing parts** that interfere with following the story?				
Do I include enough **figurative language** and strong **vocabulary** to provide vivid **descriptions about characters**, **setting**, or **events**?				

Figure 4.30: Narrative feedback sheet.

*Visit **go.SolutionTree.com/literacy** for a free reproducible version of this figure.*

Exercise: (Re)design Lessons

Redesign or craft formal lessons for your narrative unit using your unit map as a guide, and collaborate on this undertaking with colleagues if you can. You may have conducted some lessons before, found them online, or received them from colleagues and chosen to modify them. Other lessons will be originals you create from scratch. You can elect to use the suggestions I present in chapter 3 (page 49) with the focus on imagery geared to setting, or any from this chapter.

Building lessons throughout the stages of the writing process—prewriting, drafting, revising, editing, publishing, and reflecting—is an art that incorporates many features. To guide you in lesson design, include the components of gradual release of responsibility (see chapter 3, page 49) or another direct instruction approach to teach something unfamiliar to students. Consider how you might adjust the model if the focus is a review of previously learned content. Be sure to select appropriate instructional strategies and embed formative assessments.

You might also access *The Fundamentals of (Re)designing Writing Units* (Glass, 2017a) for other lesson ideas related to the writing process stages. Chapter 2 of that text includes extensive information, strategies, and suggestions for each stage with an emphasis on ways peers and teachers can provide feedback. It also provides general resources for digital communities and technology that students can use throughout each stage. Additionally, chapter 3 features a gradual release of responsibility lesson about developing a character as well as a section on differentiation.

Instructional Strategies

Notice that I employ a variety of instructional strategies across all lesson ideas. When you craft or revise your own lesson, use and adjust the strategies I present as you see fit. In doing so, proactively select those that are appropriate for students' characteristics and the learning goals you are targeting. Keep this salient point in mind as you consider which strategies to use when writing and subsequently conducting your lesson:

> Our attention . . . should be on the effect that we have on student learning—and sometimes we need multiple strategies, and more often, some students need different teaching strategies from those that they have been getting. A strong message from the findings in *Visible Learning* (Hattie, 2009) is that, more often than not, when students do not learn, they do not need "more"; rather, they need "different." (Hattie, 2012, p. 93)

You surely have an arsenal of strategies at your disposal, and I include many in this book. The message is to choose wisely so that the strategies you select align to learning outcomes and move students forward in their proficiencies.

Formative Assessments

I discuss preassessments and culminating assessments in chapter 2 (page 29), but it's imperative that you incorporate formative assessments into your lessons, as well. Even when you orchestrate activities using engaging strategies, students do not necessarily learn what you intend to teach, so collect evidence throughout the unit to inform your instruction:

> Formative assessment, if used properly, can become a powerful contributor to a teacher's instructional decision making. But formative assessment is *not* the same thing as instruction. *Instruction* refers to the set of teacher-determined activities carried out in an effort to get students to accomplish a curricular outcome. Using this definition, instruction is the *means* by which a teacher's students attain a curriculum *end*. Therefore, formative assessment can be regarded accurately as a process intended to make a teacher's instructional means more effective. (Popham, 2008, p. 50)

Integrate both unobtrusive and obtrusive (Marzano, 2017) assessments to show what students are learning. For example, you can listen to and observe students participating in a group discussion, literature or nonfiction circle, simulation, sequencing activity, or game. These unobtrusive assessments do not interrupt the flow of a classroom activity and yield useful information. Therefore, track students' progress on a record-keeping sheet that lets you stay abreast of their growth. In obtrusive assessments—which interrupt an activity—you can collect something tangible that students produce (for example, exit cards, entries in their notebook, drafts, notes from literature circles, graphic organizers, or blog entries) as further evidence of their progression toward learning. When you critically examine this work and use it to determine your next instructional moves—reteach, move on, modify, enrich, or scaffold—the assessments become formative. That is to say, you are checking for understanding, often called assessment *for* learning.

Questions to Guide Lesson Design

Address these areas of curriculum and instruction, using the following questions to prompt you.

- ❑ **KUDs:** Is my lesson standards based? Does it target what I want students to know and understand? Does it target one or more explicit skills? Can I direct students to the skill on the checklist or rubric?

- ❑ **Assessments:** What observable evidence do I have that students are progressing and learning during each part of the lesson? Do I include appropriate self- and formative assessments? What are my plans for assessing data? Do I ensure that students independently apply the new learning in a novel situation?

- ❑ **Differentiation:** How can I plan to differentiate content, process, product, or the learning environment based on interest, readiness, or learning style, as appropriate?

- ❑ **Guiding question:** What guiding question or questions set a purpose for learning?

- ❑ **Resources:** What print, digital, artifact (object, illustration), human (librarian, technology specialist), or other resources do I need to conduct this lesson? Do I incorporate complex text within this or other lessons, as appropriate? Where can I find the necessary differentiated resources or direct students to them? What student and published narrative samples can I use in this lesson, and how will I use them to target specific skills?

- ❑ **Technology:** Are there differentiated electronic tools or apps that would enhance this lesson? What preparation or support might I need to incorporate this technology tool into the lesson?

- ❑ **Instructional strategies:** Do I include differentiated strategies that match the lesson goals and take into account students' characteristics? Do I vary my instructional strategies to facilitate engagement?

- ❑ **Grouping:** During the learning experience, do I account for varied grouping (individual, pair, small group, whole class) based on the task and learning goal? Do I incorporate collaboration so students can learn together and capitalize on each other's expertise and thinking?

- ❑ **Lesson plan model:** Do I use the gradual release of responsibility or another direct instruction model to teach a new skill, procedure, or strategy? Do I change the order of the parts or conscientiously alter it based on my student population and learning outcomes?

Additionally, be sure to peruse the extensive resource list in appendix E (page 151) to increase your professional learning, find what you might embed within lessons, share with students for complex text, and more. I have divided up what I offer for easy access. For example, if you are curious about available online units and want to borrow or adapt some lessons, then look in the Unit and Lesson Examples section. To find student and published texts that show a range of proficiencies and skill examples and nonexamples, check out the links I include in the Sources for Complex Text section. When students have published their work, invite them to submit their narratives to the organizations listed in Essay Contests and Submissions. There are undoubtedly more resources than I could possibly catalog, but I trust I have given you a substantial start to your journey.

Summary

As students move through the writing process, conduct differentiated lessons that provide them with the tools necessary to successfully craft a well-developed narrative. You may teach some lessons early in the writing process to frontload students with skills they can use for drafting their papers. Other times, orchestrate lessons during the first revision so they can make changes to incorporate into another draft with a new skill they have just learned.

A well-choreographed and complete series of lessons within a unit produces far better results for students to advance in their learning than one that you have haphazardly designed. Therefore, use your unit map as a guide to create lessons or workshops, and judiciously select strategies and incorporate them into a gradual release of responsibility or another direct instruction model, especially when teaching new skills, strategies, and processes.

Within each lesson, use formative assessments to gauge where students need your help, whether scaffolding instruction more definitively or extending a skill they have mastered with relative ease. Do not feel it is necessary to grade everything that students generate. Consider that each time an athlete practices, it doesn't reflect the score of the game. Similarly, realize that the exercises you conduct and the assessments you observe and collect are all practice runs before students arrive at the end product of their narratives:

> Grading everything students do discourages the very kind of grappling that is fundamental to complex thought and genuine understanding. . . . Young people routinely engage in strenuous practice to get better at basketball, soccer, playing a musical instrument . . . They literally "see" that the practice moves them forward. They don't expect or want a grade for every segment of practice because it is clear to them that the practice makes them more skilled when a "grading moment" (game, swim meet, recital . . .) occurs. (Tomlinson & Moon, 2013, p. 130)

Remember to include self-assessments within your lessons to encourage and empower students to monitor their own learning and work toward achievable goals. Certainly, providing feedback on progress or how they might redirect or approach the work differently proves essential. Comment? Yes. Grade each piece? Not necessarily.

In the next chapter, you will find exercises you can conduct for delving into a text so students can study an author's craft. This can support them in composing their own writing products.

Examining Text to Appreciate Content

Reading and writing are complementary forms of literacy that interconnect, and students require exposure to many narratives within your writing unit. Teachers understand the efficacy of creating experiences designed for students to study authors' works so they can translate what they learn to their own writing—a repeated refrain in this book. Steve Graham and Dolores Perin (2007) cite these opportunities as one recommendation in their report *Writing Next: Effective Strategies to Improve Writing of Adolescents in Middle and High Schools*. They state that "students are encouraged to analyze these examples and to emulate the critical elements, patterns, and forms embodied in the models in their own writing" (p. 20). (In *The Fundamentals of (Re)designing Writing Units* (Glass, 2017a), you can read about the other recommendations from this report in more detail, or you can access the report yourself.)

Aside from examining aspects of a writer's style, students also need to analyze and demonstrate understanding of the content of complex text at the center of instruction. Although some suggestions in the previous two chapters clearly require students to examine texts, the primary focus is to steer writing instruction with comprehension as a byproduct. In this chapter, I focus squarely on presenting myriad ways students can glean insight from content. Conducting reading and writing lessons caters to the intrinsically linked nature of these strands of literacy.

Small-Group Text Analysis

Throughout a literary unit, you will conduct a series of lessons designed for students to examine and analyze elements of literature, specific literary devices, and types of figurative language for express purposes. In the following small-group activity, students work together and collectively leverage one another's expertise and insights through the lens of the targeted focus to gain deeper meaning from content.

1. **Identify a purpose for reading:** During each reading segment—one chapter, a collection of chapters, or a section of text—each group will track the progress of a particular emphasis you assign to them, such as plot, theme, tone, allusion, imagery, the interplay among literary elements or figures of speech, and so forth. For example, one group might address this guiding question and textual evidence to support it: *How does setting influence characters' beliefs and the decisions they make?* Another group will tackle this: *How does the narrator impact readers' impression?* Base this focus on the work of literature and what you have articulated on your unit map.

2. **Prepare a presentation of key insights:** During the week, ask each group to prepare a presentation for the class centered on their assigned emphasis incorporating textual evidence and pictures or symbols. This can take many forms—a PowerPoint or Keynote

presentation, a poster to display on a bulletin board, a game, or another way. In their presentations, students must go beyond the factual, surface information and reveal insight and depth.

3. **Present to peers:** On Friday of each week or every other week, groups share what they create to broaden and deepen classmates' understanding. During these presentations, encourage audience members to ask questions and note the key points.

4. **Show understanding:** To stimulate individual accountability, ask students to respond to a prompt you devise based on group presentations, or write a summary of what they learned.

As students work together to glean meaning, they overtly focus on the content to further their understanding that they then share with others. In the process, they also experience the way an author crafts his or her work to help them stimulate ideas for their own narratives.

Reading for Meaning

As students read, have them complete figure 5.1 individually or in pairs, or they can work on figure 5.2, Making Meaning. If you assign the latter, which has nine squares, students can complete three cells like tic-tac-toe, such as three across or three down. Alternatively, cut out each prompt in the figure to make cards. Students can sit in small groups with the cards face down and randomly choose one at a time to base their discussion on for that passage. Repeat the exercise so students choose another card and focus on the same passage or move to another one. Afterward, they write and submit individual responses based on significant insights from the discussion.

Read for Meaning	
Text title, chapter, or page number:	
Clarify	**Illustrate**
I was confused by: But then I figured out that:	Draw a picture of a quote or concept: Write the quote or concept:
Pose Questions	**Connect**
Write two questions that begin with *who, what, where,* or *when*. 1. 2.	Explain how this quote or concept connects with another text or the world.

Write two questions that begin with *how* or *why*. 3. 4.	Predict what you think will happen next in the reading or predict the impact of this topic or concept on the world.

Figure 5.1: Read for meaning.

Visit **go.SolutionTree.com/literacy** *for a free reproducible version of this figure.*

Making Meaning		
Clarify What were you confused by in the reading? How did you figure it out?	**Understand Concepts** Find a meaningful quote or concept from the text. Then draw a symbol or picture of it.	**Connect** Explain how a quote or concept you select connects with your life, other historical time periods, or the world today.
Pose Questions Pose questions that begin with *who*, *what*, *where*, *when*, *why*, and *how*. Answer any of them that you can.	**Compare and Contrast** Compare and contrast aspects of the text, such as different characters' or individuals' beliefs or actions, settings, or writers' styles.	**Predict** Predict the impact of a topic, theme, or concept from the text on the world today. Or predict what will happen next.
Answer Questions Select and respond to a guiding question. Incorporate textual evidence in your response.	**React** Choose and react to some part of the text. Consider what made you angry, think differently, disagree, agree, hope, rejoice, or react in another way.	**Summarize** Provide a three-sentence summary of what you learned in a selected reading passage.

Figure 5.2: Making meaning.

Visit **go.SolutionTree.com/literacy** *for a free reproducible version of this figure.*

Graphic Organizers

As I discussed in the previous chapter, students commonly rely on graphic organizers for prewriting. They also serve as effective tools to make sense of content and demonstrate understanding. To further support students in deriving deeper meaning from texts, read about ways to use the organizers in this and the subsequent section.

A diamanté poem, in which the lines are organized in a diamond shape, focuses on words associated with two opposites like the example in figure 5.3 (page 114) of Cinderella and her stepmother. Students can use it to juxtapose other aspects of a text besides characters, such as two different settings, moods, perspectives, vocabulary words, historical individuals, or events. Figure 5.4 (pages 114–115) instructs students to summarize a fictional work in the form of a pyramid that homes in on the key features of the text. In this way, students must know the text well to target their entries.

Template

Formula
Line 1: Enter a topic.
Line 2: Write two adjectives describing the entry in line 1.
Line 3: Write three participles (verb form ending with –ed or –ing) for line 1.
Line 4: Write four nouns; the first two nouns relate to line 1; the last two nouns relate to line 7.
Line 5: Write three participles for line 7.
Line 6: Write two adjectives describing the entry in line 7.
Line 7: Enter a topic opposite from line 1.

Example
Cinderella (line 1)
Compassionate, altruistic (line 2)
Toiling, forgiving, weeping (line 3)
Princess, chambermaid—witch, devil-woman (line 4)
Demanding, overbearing, favoring (line 5)
Devilish, sinister (line 6)
Stepmother (line 7)

Figure 5.3: Diamante poem.

*Visit **go.SolutionTree.com/literacy** for a free reproducible version of this figure.*

Template

Formula
Line 1: Write the character or individual.
Line 2: Write two words describing the character or individual.
Line 3: Write three words describing the setting.
Line 4: Write four words stating the central conflict.*

Line 5: Write five words associated with one event in the narrative.*

Line 6: Write six words associated with a second event.*

Line 7: Write seven words associated with a third event.*

Line 8: Write eight words associated with the solution to the central conflict or the theme.*

*Or a _____-word sentence—for example, "Write a six-word sentence describing a second event."

Figure 5.4: Story elements.

Visit go.SolutionTree.com/literacy for a free reproducible version of this figure.

Collective Interpretations

This exercise allows students to study quotes from a complex text independently and then share their interpretations with group members to arrive at a synthesized and collective impression of their thoughts. To prepare, determine three passages from one text and enter each on a separate organizer as I show in the graphic organizer examples (figures 5.5, 5.6 on page 116, and 5.7 on page 116) for passages from *Esperanza Rising* (Ryan, 2000). Replace these excerpts for your own complex text, or use what I present if it is appropriate for your students. Arrange students into trios to conduct this activity.

1. **Read and interpret the first quote:** Give each student a graphic organizer with a different quote. Instruct students to each read his or her assigned quote, enter an interpretation in the quadrant for student 1, and put their name on the provided line.

2. **Rotate quotes and add insights:** Students rotate their papers. They each read the new quote first, then their group member's interpretation. In the quadrant labeled student 2, they record any new insights from student 1's entry along with their name.

3. **Repeat the exercise:** Students rotate their papers again and repeat the exercise by reading the quote and then the two entries already on the organizer. Lastly, they record their name and own impressions in the spot marked student 3.

4. **Arrive at a collective impression:** When the sheets rotate again, each student should have the graphic organizer back that he or she worked on originally. Students discuss the entries on each graphic organizer one at a time. Together, either they determine that one interpretation recorded on each graphic organizer is spot-on and circle it, or they write a new one in the quadrant labeled Collective Interpretation. When they finish their discussions and any revisions on each graphic organizer, groups can share highlights with the class and then submit the organizers for review.

Student 1: _____   Student 2: _____

> Excerpt from *Esperanza Rising* (Ryan, 2000):
>
> "What happened to your finger?" asked Abuelita.
> "A big thorn," said Esperanza.
> ". . . There is no rose without thorns."
> Esperanza smiled, knowing that Abuelita wasn't talking about flowers at all but that there was no life without difficulties. She watched the silver crochet needle dance back and forth in her grandmother's hand. When a strand of hair fell into her lap, Abuelita picked it up and held it against the yarn and stitched it into the blanket. (p. 14)

Student 3: _____   Collective Interpretation

Source: Ryan, 2000.

Figure 5.5: Quote interpretation 1.

Visit go.SolutionTree.com/literacy for a free reproducible version of this figure.

Student 1: _____   Student 2: _____

> **Excerpt from *Esperanza Rising* (Ryan, 2000):**
>
> But now that she was a young woman, she understood that Miguel was the housekeeper's son and she was the ranch owner's daughter and between them ran a deep river. Esperanza stood on one side and Miguel stood on the other and the river could never be crossed. In a moment of self-importance, Esperanza had told all of this to Miguel. Since then, he had spoken only a few words to her. (p. 14)

Student 3: _____   Collective Interpretation

Source: Ryan, 2000.

Figure 5.6: Quote interpretation 2.

*Visit **go.SolutionTree.com/literacy** for a free reproducible version of this figure.*

Student 1: _____   Student 2: _____

> **Excerpt from *Esperanza Rising* (Ryan, 2000):**
>
> "Esperanza, in this way my love and good wishes will be in the blanket forever. Now watch. Ten stitches up to the top of the mountain. Add one stitch. Nine stitches down to the bottom of the valley. Skip one."
>
> Esperanza picked up her own crochet needle . . . her valleys were all bunched up.
>
> Abuelita smiled, reached over, and pulled the yarn, unraveling all of Esperanza's rows. "Do not be afraid to start over," she said. (pp. 14–15)

Student 3: _____   Collective Interpretation

Source: Ryan, 2000.

Figure 5.7: Quote interpretation 3.

*Visit **go.SolutionTree.com/literacy** for a free reproducible version of this figure.*

Games

Invite students to participate in games as a vehicle for examining a text with peers.

Literature Game

Although many are available, here I explain how you might use a generic game board like the one in figure 5.8 that you can download, enlarge, and duplicate for each small group. (Visit **go.SolutionTree.com/literacy** to access a reproducible version.) To accompany it, use the narrative game cards in figure 5.9 (page 118) or create your own. When students use these game cards, determine what text they use as the basis for their responses—a complex text in a literature circle group, a whole-class text, or the original narratives that your students compose.

To play, equip each student with a game piece such as a bean, penny, colored bead, paper clip, or another common object. Tell them which text they use for their responses. Instead of rolling dice, each game card includes a value so students advance according to the difficulty level of a clue. For example, for more challenging questions or prompts, assign three spaces, and for those less complex—like a true/false question—give one space. As students answer, they move up or back the number of spaces indicated on each card. I did not assign values to the literature prompt examples in figure 5.9 (page 118); I leave that to you to determine based on the skill level of your students.

Here are additional elements you can incorporate in the game.

- **Star cards:** Notice in figure 5.8 there are star symbols dispersed throughout the game board. When students land on one, they choose a star card. These cards include messages that allow students to move either forward or backward. Similar to a chance card in the game Monopoly, a player doesn't know if the selected card is a bonus or a setback until he or she reads it. Here are some examples to guide you in creating your own star cards.

- A classmate was absent from class and you offered to help him or her learn material that he or she missed. Move forward two spaces.

- A classmate dropped his or her three-ring binder and all the papers fell everywhere. You helped to collect papers and even reorganize the binder. Move forward two spaces.

- You procrastinated on a long-term project and turned in something that did not show your personal best. Next time budget your time more wisely. Move back three spaces.

- **Rules:** Students can determine in their groups some specific rules of the game such as the following: Should one group member be a judge who decides whether to accept answers that are not exactly as listed on the card? Should the person whose turn it is read his or her own card? Should different people take turns reading the question cards?

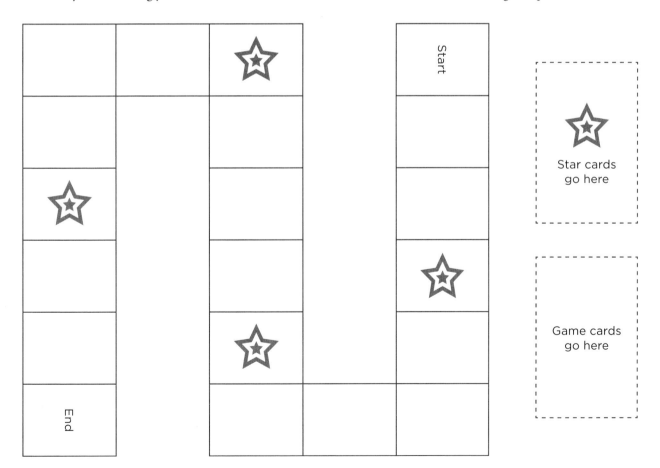

Figure 5.8: Generic game board.

*Visit **go.SolutionTree.com/literacy** for a free reproducible version of this figure.*

Literature Game Cards		
Who is the narrator of the story? How does this narrator impact the text?	Describe a setting in the text. What mood does it evoke? Cite evidence.	What is a personality trait for the protagonist? Cite evidence to support it.
If you could rewrite the narrative in a different point of view, whose perspective would you choose? How would the narrative change?	How does the title relate to the text? How could it be stronger and in what way?	What is a personality trait for the antagonist? Cite evidence to support it.
Juxtapose the motivations or beliefs of two characters using textual evidence.	Name three methods of characterization and an example of one from the text.	What weakness does the writing show? Use textual evidence to support your response.
Identify the relationship between two characters and how it impacts the plot.	What is the story's theme? Cite evidence to support it.	How does the theme connect with another text?
Justify adding dialogue between characters somewhere in the narrative. Who would engage in the conversation and what would they discuss?	What advice would you give a character in a particular situation? Justify your reasoning.	What is the central conflict? Is it internal or external? Explain.
Find a place in the text where the dialogue impacts the story and explain how it achieves this.	Identify a problem other than the central conflict and explain how it is resolved.	Using textual evidence, explain the difference in behaviors or thinking of a round versus flat character or a static versus dynamic character.
What is the tone of the text and evidence to support it?	What archetypal characters, themes, or symbols do you find in the text?	What are any examples of a pattern throughout the text?
Give an example of how the author uses figurative language and interpret its meaning.	What text-to-world connection can you make?	What significant event changed the course of the story? How so?
Identify a particular literary device (symbolism, allusion, dialect, suspense, or other) that the author uses. Explain and show an example.	What indications does the author provide of a certain historical or contemporary setting?	What other plausible ending could the author have invented? Using evidence from the text, explain how your alternate ending is conceivable.

Figure 5.9: Literature game cards.

*Visit **go.SolutionTree.com/literacy** for a free reproducible version of this figure.*

Invite students to make their own handwritten or electronic game cards based on the text. They can write clues related to vocabulary as well as content. In doing so, they cement their own learning as they dive back into the text to determine what information they will base the cards on and how they want to write the clues. To guide them, access figure 5.10 for a checklist and adapt it as appropriate.

Who Am I?

This activity is a popular game in and out of school. You might have even played it at a party. Prepare cards (one for each participant) that state a character, vocabulary word, literary term, or something else associated with the complex text. Each student affixes one card on his or her back without knowing what is written. Students walk around the room and pose questions to others to try to guess what is on the card they are wearing. Students may provide hints as necessary.

Game Card Checklist
Directions: Use this checklist to guide you when making game cards based on a text. You may work with a partner if you choose.
❑ Create at least ten game cards. ❑ Some game cards can be true or false, multiple choice, or fill in the blank. ❑ Other game cards can be open-ended questions or prompts.
❑ Neatly write each game card or use an electronic device to type. ❑ Write the question or prompt on one side. ❑ Write the answer on the other side along with a point value that reflects the difficulty level of the question. Write "1 space" for basic questions, "2 spaces" for moderately challenging questions, and "3 spaces" for difficult questions. ❑ All questions and prompts need to be thoughtful. All answers must be accurate. ❑ Use proper spelling and punctuation.

Figure 5.10: Game card checklist.

*Visit **go.SolutionTree.com/literacy** for a free reproducible version of this figure.*

Literary Discussion: The Café

Conduct an authentic simulation to immerse students in the content of the text that mirrors what adults might do. When we go to the movies or read the same text, we sometimes grab coffee or a meal together and organically discuss the elements of literature and literary devices to probe and extend our thinking through collaborative interaction. Prepare students for this kind of real-life exchange by inviting them to a coffeehouse or café so they can emulate what we do—authentically analyzing literature. Here is how you might conduct such a literary exchange.

1. **Prepare for the activity:**

   - Find a short, engaging, fifteen- or thirty-minute film geared to your students' interests. It should contain material to encourage their thinking and generate conversation and introspection.

   - Prepare and deliver a print or electronic invitation for students to attend a Day at the Movies. Ask them to bring drinks and snacks or other refreshments.

   - If you have enough room, arrange for two gathering areas: (1) chairs in front of the screen, and (2) tables with tablecloths and napkins for small groups in the back of the room. Place drinks and snacks at each table. If you don't have enough room or furniture, then do your best to set up for the movie and discussion to mirror a café.

2. **Explain and prepare for the task:** Tell students that they will watch and then discuss a movie with each other like adults (and even they) might do by focusing on strengths, weaknesses, interpretations, and insights. In their discussions, they should use terms they have learned—specific literary devices, elements of literature, and figurative language.

3. **Show the film and open the café:** After students watch the film, you may break them into groups or let them choose their own. Tell them that the café manager (you) does not allow more than four people at a table.

4. **Promote discussion and offer refreshments:** If necessary, provide a sheet of paper with questions at each table to prompt student discussion. Walk around the room to assess how actively engaged they are to determine if you need to participate in some groups to keep them on track or deepen their thinking with another question. Replenish refreshments as necessary.

Summary

Complex text serves as a vehicle for students to see what their writing can look like as they study the pattern, style, and craft of a writer. When they critique and dissect the text for discrete skills, they can study what might and might not work for their own products. While looking at the text to support them as writers, we often isolate discrete skills. However, students also need to delve deeply into the content to make meaning, which enriches their knowledge and understanding of literature and what each piece can teach them.

In the epilogue that follows, I provide suggestions for meaningfully working with colleagues and how you might effectively use existing resources for building a narrative unit.

Epilogue

Once you finish writing the unit, you may be tempted to teach it and move on to another one. I urge you to make the time while teaching it, and shortly afterward, to participate in the suggestions in this epilogue. You will thank yourself later when the next year rolls around and you teach narrative once again—this time with a stronger version.

Next Steps

As teachers—and professionals in other fields as well—we create, revisit, massage, pilot, rework, learn from results, and try again. It is a constant cycle of implementation, reflection, and revision, though not always major revision. Sometimes we get it right or make minor adjustments and take what we learn to apply to the next unit.

Once you finish your narrative unit, follow the suggestions in *The Fundamentals of (Re)designing Writing Units* (Glass, 2017a) for piloting it, participating in calibration sessions with colleagues to collect anchor papers, and reflecting on your unit using granular-level questioning. In addition, when you initiate the unit, you can engage in a number of tasks.

- Evaluate and make comments by hand or electronically on an ongoing basis as you pilot the unit. Solicit colleagues to join you in this exercise if they teach the same curriculum. If your unit is online, save an original copy and make a version for collecting changes and feedback. Use this later for reflection and unit revision.

- Lead or participate in a calibration session in which you (and colleagues) use your students' narratives as the basis for discussion and assessment against the scoring rubric. Determine which samples will serve as anchor papers. Discuss whether you need to make any changes to the rubric, citing excerpts from student papers as support for any revisions you do recommend. Determine which student samples or excerpts you can use within specific lessons to teach targeted skills to prepare for the next time you teach this unit.

- When scoring student work, accumulate data to determine strengths and weaknesses for your classroom and across the grade. Use this information for what you might revise, such as a particular activity within a lesson or an assessment for the future. However, seize the opportunity now to immediately address any skill areas that students did not yet acquire that you uncovered while scoring their narratives.

- Reflect on the narrative task or prompt and adjust as necessary. Was it clear enough? Did you write it in a way that allowed students to demonstrate what they learned?

These activities will help you focus on what is most important for student improvement as you make revisions to this narrative unit.

Final Thoughts

As I began the challenging project of writing this book, I scoured research pertaining to writing and teaching in general, called on my own experience with teaching writing, tapped colleagues for their expertise, reflected on my own habits and processes as an author, and perused the work of others in this field. I have attempted to harness all this work to present you with research-based practical tools and suggestions for teaching writing—particularly narrative writing and its various genres and characteristics.

My goal with this book is to offer an accessible process to follow, sound pedagogy, and useful resources and tools to create a well-rounded, standards-based narrative writing program. Other print and digital works, plus online and classroom learning and workshops, can augment your professional expertise. Some of this learning and your experience as a teacher may align with what I present to you; some professional resources might have a different approach. I suggest that you determine what works for your students to produce the best writing possible by trying what you learn in this text and elsewhere, challenging yourself to grow, paying careful attention to students' feedback, noting their progression or stagnation as writers through keen observation and examination of data, and planning the appropriate next steps in instruction to meet their needs. Hopefully you have expanded your professional knowledge while reading this text, found satisfying resources, and implemented what you created. You have, I trust, become a more impactful teacher of burgeoning writers as you've propelled them forward in their learning progression and given them the tools and guidance to be more adept. I appreciate you taking this journey with me.

Appendix A

Narrative and Descriptive Text Types

For this section of the book, I offer an overview of narrative and descriptive text types (also called modes or categories), plus an in-depth discussion about narrative genres and subgenres. I intend the explanations and examples in this appendix to help you plan a standards-based narrative unit of instruction. As mentioned in the introduction to this book, if you are familiar with narrative and descriptive text types and all they entail, you might skim this material or forgo reading it altogether.

Since what I present here are expansive topics, sometimes authors and educators disagree on definitions and classifications. For example, are tall tales a legend or fantasy? What constitutes *contemporary* in contemporary realistic fiction? What is the difference between autobiography, personal narrative, and memoir? Therefore, after reading this appendix, you might confer with colleagues in your school or district to agree on the characteristics and elements specific to each genre that you will teach so there is consistency for students.

What Is Genre?

Genre is a term used across artistic endeavors: writing genres, musical genres, and film genres. When different works share commonalities—like a distinctive style, form, or element—they are grouped together in a genre. Text types—narrative, descriptive, expository, and persuasive—house a collection of genres. Each text is aligned to a writer's purpose for crafting the piece,

which in turn dictates other factors like audience, style, and genre. If writing to inform or explain, a writer can create something expository like a technical manual or article. If the purpose is to entertain, the writer might compose a myth or fantasy.

The distinction between genres and formats is often confusing. Sometimes people refer to any particular narrative genre more generically—for example, as a novel or short story. In actuality, these are the *formats* for displaying a particular work of literature. For instance, an author can produce a mystery, autobiography, or science fiction piece and write it in different formats, such as an essay or short story.

Formats of literature can be divided by length in order from shortest to longest: specifically, flash fiction, short story, novella, novel, and epic novel. Flash fiction can be as brief as sixty words. An epic—which means surpassing the usual in size and scope—novel, such as Leo Tolstoy's (2001) *War and Peace*, can be upwards of two hundred thousand words. Epic can also refer to a long, serious narrative poem that often features a hero (for example, *Beowulf*) and even appears as its own genre in some resources. The exact word count among these formats varies, so do not consider one source as definitive.

Table A.1 (page 124) provides some examples of popular genres and subgenres within the narrative (fiction and nonfiction) text. The sections that follow describe each of these genres and subgenres and a discussion about the descriptive text type as well.

Table A.1: Narrative and Descriptive Text Types

Text Types	Genres and Subgenres		

Narrative Fiction	• Folktales
	  • Fairy tales
	  • Myths
	  • Legends
	  • Tall tales
	  • Animal tales
	    • Trickster tales
	    • Fables
	    • Pourquoi (or etiological) tales
		• Fantasy
		  • High and low fantasy
		  • Science fiction
			• Realism
			  • Realistic fiction
			  • Contemporary realistic fiction
			  • Historical fiction
			  • Mystery

Narrative Nonfiction	• Biography • Autobiography • Memoir • Personal narrative		
Descriptive	Various genres incorporate descriptive writing for different purposes.		

Narrative Fiction

Genres of fictional narrative, and some nonfiction narrative discussed later (see the end of this appendix and appendix B, page 131), include five elements of literature: (1) character, (2) setting, (3) plot, (4) point of view, and (5) theme. What differentiates one genre and subgenre from another is the treatment of each element along with specific characteristics. There are certainly instances of overlap in which a text can straddle two genres or subgenres; however, the prominent features dictate where it resides. Narrative fiction can break down into three genres—(1) folktales, (2) fantasy, and (3) realism—each with various subgenres as shown in table A.1.

Folktales

Although they each have a different purpose and include distinctive characteristics that differentiate one from another, folktales share the commonality of historically originating in oral tradition somewhere in the world. In time, *folktales* became literature when people actually wrote down and interpreted what they heard. Some published folktales include the byline *Retold by* or *As told by* because the writer acknowledges that the story was handed down from generation to generation, and he

or she did not originally create the story. To note, modern fairy tales that derive from authors, such as Hans Christian Andersen, Jane Yolen, and Lloyd Alexander, rather than oral tradition, belong to the genre of modern fantasy rather than folk literature.

Fairy Tales

A *fairy tale*, an unbelievable and far-fetched story, includes clearly imaginary enchantment or supernatural elements. The pervasive theme among fairy tales—even though they are widely diverse—revolves around a protagonist who begins as timid and desperate in some way. With the support of others, plus a little magic, the oppressed overcomes evil. A fairy tale with the same basic plot and similar characters can be found worldwide across many different cultures.

Fairy tales share the following common characteristics.

- **A special beginning** like "Once upon a time . . ." or "Long ago in a faraway land . . ." or a similar phrase

- **Magical or unreal characters** such as a fairy or talking animal

- **Magical events or objects** like a fairy performing magic, an animal talking, or a magic wand

- **A good character**
- **An evil character**
- **Recurring odd numbers or patterns**, such as three, five, or seven; for example, a character repeats a phrase three times
- **Royal characters** like a princess, king, or queen who lives in a castle
- **A special ending**, such as "And they lived happily ever after" or a similar phrase

Students can invent a fractured fairy tale, a popular assignment, in which they change some aspect of the plot, characters, setting, or point of view to amuse readers. Or they can write fairy tales from different points of view of characters in or inferred from the story to practice this element of literature and demonstrate understanding of perspective. *The True Story of the 3 Little Pigs!* by Jon Scieszka (1989) or *The Three Pigs* by David Wiesner (2001)—two books by renowned authors—can set the stage for a writing exercise connected to the latter example. For either writing idea tied to fairy tales, students should incorporate the unvarying elements in the preceding bulleted list.

Myths

Myths, folktales that storytellers in a culture consider factual and sacred, develop a theory of the origin of natural events, the creation of the world, or an explanation of humanity and why people behave as they do. They are set in a primordial (the beginning of time), distant past when gods lived on the earth and humans had not yet developed an understanding of the arts and customs of life.

The principal characters are ancestral heroes or deities—gods and goddesses—with supernatural powers who often possess mortal attributes and interact with humans. Myths are pervasive and provide a way to better appreciate the history and culture of a society. These include, for example, Greek, Roman, and Native American myths.

There are many different types of myths, some of which I mention here. Creation (or origin) myths provide an explanation for the genesis of things like how the world began or how the sky or people came to be. Nature myths focus on explanations about how seasons change, how the Earth formed, or certain characteristics animals possess. Hero myths feature a hero or heroine accepting treacherous assignments and either achieving success or facing death amid a final quest. Greek myths involve myriad tales of gods' conflicts, jealousy, struggles for power with humans, creation, and more. They feature Greek mythological deities (such as Zeus, Prometheus, Aphrodite, or Hercules) and mythical creatures (for example, centaurs, cyclops, Pegasus, and the Minotaur). These myths are the subject of many allusions in literary text and artwork like sculptures and paintings. For those who teach about civilizations, asking students to write a myth or legend can be an effective method to demonstrate understanding of a particular culture.

Legends

Legends are folktales that a storyteller presents as fact and presumably believes. This applies to myths, which is why sometimes these two genres are combined. Unlike a remote, mythical setting, legends reside in a historic time and place in a recognizable world. The nature of the tale—either sacred or secular—is often focused on changes in creation, transformation of humans and animals, or heroic deeds. Humans, animals who act like humans, and supernatural creatures represent main characters. A legend will often state a natural or historical fact, and then proceed to prove it through drawing erroneous conclusions. People in legends concern themselves with results of a conflict of natural phenomena.

Tall Tales

Tall tales, closely related to legends or sometimes considered a legend (Fountas & Pinnell, 2012, p. 97), center on characters with a unique and exaggerated personality or physical trait, which constitutes their key feature. These characters possess larger-than-life attributes or perform feats beyond what is possible, such as the biggest, fastest, or strongest. Throughout the world, people tell tall tales about real or invented figures in history who perhaps began life as ordinary and accomplished or achieved the extraordinary, such as the American legendary heroes Paul Bunyan, Pecos Bill, Davy Crockett, and Johnny Chapman (Johnny Appleseed).

The line between folk and literary origin appears somewhat nebulous with regard to tall tales, making it difficult to definitively classify this genre. In other words, to qualify as folklore, the telling of the story must originate in the oral tradition from word of mouth. However, some legendary heroes were invented through print. For example, people learned about Paul Bunyan through the literary versions of the early 1900s, plus "innumerable journalistic accounts and children's books" (Leach & Fried, 1972, p. 847). Additionally, Davy Crockett became popular via print: "Beginning with a pseudo-biography in 1833, followed by his own autobiography in 1834 . . ., a plethora of Davy Crockett books and almanacs appeared over the next two decades" (Foner & Garraty, 1991). Since it's unknown whether some heroes became the source of entertainment via print or oral renditions, it makes it unclear whether to place them in folklore or perhaps in fantasy. Nevertheless, the combination of fact with enhanced fiction makes tales about these subjects engaging and captivating.

Animal Tales

Animal tales, one of the oldest forms of folk literature, center on animals who act like people. These stories teach about life, usually offering lessons about personal traits and cooperation with others, and are divided among three main categories: (1) trickster tales, (2) fables, and (3) pourquoi (or etiological) tales.

Trickster tales include one central character in animal shape who is both a creator and clown. "Characteristically the trickster is greedy, erotic, imitative, stupid, pretentious, deceitful; he attempts trickery himself in many forms, but is more often tricked than otherwise" (Leach & Fried, 1972, p. 1124).

Brief and direct, the element of trickery is essential to the plot of this form of animal tale. The tales typically rely on one action—a trick or joke—as the solution to a problem. The climax involves something unusual that requires impressive mental prowess, and the resolution has a surprising and clever element that engages or amuses readers. Specific animal heroes appear around the world in various cultural groups, such as the tanuki in Japan and Anansi the spider in West Africa. Important in both North and South American Indian tribes, the trickster can be a coyote (most popular in North American tribal cultures), raven, turtle, or other animal.

Fables are short animal stories with a specific lesson, generally stated at the beginning or the end in the form of a moral. Often, one animal depicts positive traits while another displays evil in some way. Unnamed animals, such as a frog, toad, or tortoise, are often developed beyond the single purpose of the tale. Although rather brief and to the point, fables tend to be simplistic on the surface, but carry profound insight and levels of meaning revealing general truths about human nature. Two major collections of fables include the ancient Jātaka tales from Eastern culture and Aesop's fables from Western culture (Greece).

Pourquoi—French for "why?"—*tales* explain the origin of certain animal characteristics, and storytellers share them to entertain. They explain why an animal looks or acts a certain way, such as how the leopard got his spots or why mosquitoes buzz in people's ears. Authors of invented stories, such as Rudyard Kipling (1993) in his famous *Just So* stories, often emulate the pourquoi form. His titles indicate the subjects for his stories—for example, "How the Camel Got His Hump" and "How the Rhinoceros Got His Skin." In contrast to myths and legends, readers and tellers of pourquoi tales do not consider them true.

Fantasy

The hallmark of fantasy is that readers encounter unique characters and settings where magic, the supernatural, suspension of disbelief, unclear reality, and the unexpected and unexplained run free. Characters might be animals, people, or creatures with magical or supernatural powers, or others created for the benefit of a fantasy. Although there are very specific subgenres that splice fantasy even further, such as vampire fantasy, sword and sorcery fantasy, superhero fantasy, and so forth, I will focus on the more common high and low fantasy and science fiction. Subgenres of folklore share elements of fantasy and perhaps spawned modern fantasy.

High and Low Fantasy

Settings for high fantasy are altogether unreal and alternative—an invented world often resembling medieval Europe. They possess a magical, strange, or otherworldly quality invented by the imagination. Low fantasy stories involve the real world or an imaginary place that appears familiar albeit fictional. Since it centers in a recognizable fictitious or believably realistic world, some intriguing ambiguity exists between what constitutes realism and fantasy.

In *high fantasy*, the protagonist—typically a hero fighting for what is morally just—must prevail against evil. Although it is a tale of good versus evil, it often focuses on coming of age, as well, since the protagonist matures in experience and skill as he or she learns to combat evil. Oftentimes, he or she has a mentor who serves as a mystical, sage guide. The antagonist, evil personified, possesses supernatural or magical powers. Other typical characters run the gamut of imagination, such as goblins, elves, dragons, giants, wizards, sorcerers, or ogres. *The Lord of the Rings* and other works of J. R. R. Tolkien (2004) and *A Clash of Kings* by George R. R. Martin (1999) fall under this category.

Low fantasy includes characters who possess magical or supernatural powers involved in nonrational events that are unexplained and surreal. In this subgenre, characters with magical, supernatural, or superhuman powers can interact with mortals; however, this species keeps its secret hidden from humans. Whereas the magical qualities characters exhibit in low fantasy are regarded as strange, in high fantasy they are accepted as natural and normal behavior. Examples of this subgenre of fantasy include books in the *Harry Potter* and *The Dark Is Rising* series.

Science Fiction

As the name denotes, this is fiction that has a basis in scientific principles or altered scientific elements and scenarios. Authors known for their work in this genre include Ray Bradbury, Isaac Asimov, H. G. Wells, Kurt Vonnegut, Arthur C. Clarke, and Orson Scott Card. These writers employ manipulation of time and place. For example, they can set stories in a future time period and on another planet somewhere in outer space. Additionally, they can creatively shape the sequence of events and develop characters who time travel into a futuristic society or through space or dimensional portals. It could be a story based on Earth with alien life forms from other planets interacting with humans or earthlings, or incorporate technological characters, such as intelligent robots. As part of the plot, writers invent and speculate about science, technology, inventions, space, and discoveries. Some compose a science fiction piece as a cautionary tale to readers about what will happen to society in years to come if people do not heed the warnings of current situations such as climate change, environmental abuse, or technological misuse.

As a teaching aid, consider watching the YouTube video "What If—Why Educators Should Teach Science Fiction" (Theed of Naboo, 2011) and even showing it to students for inspirational purposes. The premise is that science fiction challenges people to ask, *What if . . . ?* which can uncover a bold examination of future possibilities in science, technology, and other areas like diversity that can release the imagination in endless ways. Quoted in the video (Theed of Naboo, 2011) is this statement by Isaac Asimov:

> Science fiction is the only form of literature that consistently considers the nature

of changes that face us, the possible consequences, and the possible solutions.

Realism

Writers of realism create characters (people or animals) in believable settings that participate in events that could plausibly happen. The story centers on real life in the current world in either the present or the recent past. The characters represent people who confront conceivable problems, and the events leading to the solution, as well as the solution itself, could truly occur. The setting or settings are not fantastical but rather actual places or ones that could exist.

Realistic Fiction and Contemporary Realistic Fiction

In both realistic and contemporary realistic fiction, writers can develop humorous characters who participate in whimsical situations, or center their work on serious and profound themes. They might entertain readers through a lighthearted story about finding love or mistaken identity. Or perhaps characters tackle a somewhat challenging issue in contemporary society like finding a job or beginning college. The story could even focus on a more sensitive or desperate situation like a character encountering the death of a loved one, illness, gender identity, or drug abuse. In short, characters mirror authentic people living in our current world who face and tackle realistic issues.

If a text does not reflect current society as you know it, consider referring to it as *realistic fiction*. For example, stories about authentic issues facing individuals and coming of age in society may very well be contemporary concerns, but if the writer includes outdated technology or conveniences like pay phones, cars with manual door locks and windows, chalkboards, or Blockbuster video stores, then it is likely realistic fiction. What constitutes *contemporary realistic fiction* comprises works that mirror current-day society and all that it entails—slang, technology, social and political climate, and so forth. *The Hate U Give* (Thomas, 2017), *The Fault in Our Stars* (Green, 2012), *Wonder* (Palacio, 2012), and *Fangirl* (Rowell, 2013) are contemporary realistic fiction examples. These books represent mature themes, so be sure to vet them thoroughly before using them in your classroom or recommending them to students. Powerful storyline *The Hate U Give* also contains some adult language.

Historical Fiction

Historical fiction involves those stories that contain settings and characters based on historical facts. Authors of historical fiction expose readers to the people and situations from the past by providing them with the ability to envision how life was, experience how characters from an era behaved and responded to their circumstances, understand different perspectives of events that occurred then, and see parallels with other historical time periods or the present. *All the Light We Cannot See* (Doerr, 2014) and *The Book Thief* (Zusak, 2005) both set during WWII, *Fever 1793* (Anderson, 2000) based on the yellow fever epidemic in Philadelphia in the late 1700s, *A Proud Taste for Scarlet and Miniver* (Konigsburg, 1973) centered on Eleanor of Aquitaine and Henry II, and *Johnny Tremain* (Forbes, 1971) featuring individuals and events that led to the American Revolution are just some of the innumerable works of historical fiction.

Since the story is based on fact, writers must conduct research to ensure accuracy of any settings, characters, and events within the pinpointed historical period. Since this genre is under the umbrella of fiction, writers can contribute fictional details to embellish their work and engage readers as long as it is based on what actually happened and makes sense within the time period. This genre works well for students to show what they learned in history in a creative manner, perhaps as a supplement to other assessments based on social studies learning.

Mystery

Plot takes center stage in a mystery, also called a detective story, as it contains suspense and intrigue with various characters assuming roles to help solve (or divert solving) a crime or mystery. The literary device of foreshadowing is often present in this kind of narrative as writers strategically drop hints to suggest what will happen later in the work. When composing their mysteries, writers incorporate or allude to certain types of characters like detectives, victims, suspects, and witnesses, as well as elements (for example, clue, red herring, evidence, and deduction) specific to this genre. To note, some mysteries might also qualify as realistic fiction, such as *Thirteen Reasons Why* (Asher, 2007) and *The Curious Incident of the Dog in the Night-Time* (Haddon, 2003). Beloved writers Arthur Conan Doyle (of Sherlock Holmes fame) and Agatha Christie are names synonymous with mystery.

Narrative Nonfiction

Nonfiction narrative encompasses the genres of biography, autobiography, memoir, and personal narrative—all of which are based on fact rather than predicated on fiction. (Sometimes you might see biography as an overarching genre with the others as subgenres.) Writers of these narratives treat elements of literature (see appendix B on page 131) somewhat differently than they do in fictional narrative genres. Furthermore, each author chooses and employs selected literary devices and figurative language (see appendix C on page 137) to enhance his or her work as all authors are inclined to do.

Biography

Authors write biographies in third-person point of view about a noteworthy person. The subject could be a figure from the past, or someone alive today. He or she could be a famous individual or someone who is publicly unknown but whose circumstances would interest others. For example, maybe the person survived against insurmountable odds in the wilderness, was the victim of misfortune and may or may not have overcome a dire situation, or inspired others through deeds or actions.

Biographers typically cover the subject's entire life or most of it. They can write sequentially to incorporate life's stages (such as birth, childhood, adolescence, and so on) but may not always begin with birth and can start later in the subject's life. Examples of biographies around famous people include *Alexander Hamilton* (Chernow, 2004), *John Adams* (McCullough, 2001), and *Steve Jobs* (Isaacson, 2013). In the biography *Into the Wild* (Krakauer, 1996), the author uncovers the tragic facts of a young man who ventures into the wilderness and four months later turns up dead. *Unbroken: A World War II Story of Survival, Resilience, and Redemption* (Hillenbrand, 2014) chronicles the extraordinary story of a man who survived seemingly intractable odds as a captive during WWII.

Students can write biographies about individuals connected to a content area. When they write, they need to base their work on facts; therefore, they conduct and collect research from reliable sources and then cross-reference and synthesize the information. For example, they amass primary and secondary source material, such as speeches, interviews from a variety of people, personal journals, articles, book quotes, and more. Biographers often incorporate text features in their work such as pertinent maps, artwork, photographs, and perhaps related charts, graphs, and excerpts of historical documents.

Autobiography, Memoir, and Personal Narrative

Autobiographies—stories people write about themselves in first-person point of view—serve to communicate what makes the subject's life particularly remarkable. Sometimes a collaborative writer helps with the project. The autobiography usually covers the person's life chronologically from birth up to the point of the writing, which can cover many decades or most of a life span.

Memoirs are also stories written in first-person point of view—sometimes even poems or dramas—that people convey about themselves. Instead of spanning a lifetime, a memoirist recalls and focuses on one particular experience or event that was significant or life changing. Although all nonfiction narrative genres are based on truths, autobiographies and biographies contain carefully researched facts whereas those included in memoirs are what the author recalls—which should be true. For instance, a memoirist might recollect a conversation or a time when an episode occurred that should be relayed as accurately as possible, so it is factually based but may contain some latitude in exact accuracy.

Autobiographies reveal details about a person's public and private life; memoirs can be intimate and focus on more private content. The purpose of the latter is to conjure up memories and reflections of a significant situation or experience and the feelings and emotions associated with it. Through the memoir, the author engages in introspection, arrives at an insight or personal realization, acquires new knowledge, and learns a beneficial lesson. The narrative brings to light the relevance and significance of the chosen event so that the memoirist draws a conclusion and arrives at an emotional truth about what transpired. This reflection or realization does not always have to be uplifting or positive, as some life situations unfortunately result in an unfavorable or unwanted outcome. As a byproduct, readers make a connection and grow personally from the text as they may learn about a life very different from their own or gain insight about a similar personal situation.

Common memoir topics include death, divorce, or a major transition like moving to a new school or area. However, it is important to allow students to explore other potentially meaningful topics and time to develop one or more ideas. For example, they can brainstorm the following types of scenarios and what happened in their aftermath: a time when you lost your temper and felt out of control, a time you knowingly and reluctantly disobeyed your parents or broke a rule, or a disagreement with someone you love or thought you loved that ended well or disappointingly.

Nancie Atwell's (2015) *In the Middle: A Lifetime of Learning About Writing, Reading, and Adolescents* provides this expansive description of the qualities of a memoir:

> Memoirs are how writers consider our pasts. We figure out who we were, who we've become, and why. We gain perspective on experiences and learn from them. We question or confirm decisions. We recognize and explore moments along the way to becoming ourselves. We distill the essence of an event through what we decide to include and exclude. We consider ourselves in relation to the others in our lives—memoirs celebrate people and places no one else has heard of. And memoirs invite writers to tell our own truths, give them shape, and understand what they mean. (p. 415)

A cautionary note about memoirs is to ensure that students do not disclose private matters that would embarrass or even incriminate them. There is a delicate balance between what students share and the risk of revealing too much. An insecurity may very well serve to unite peers who have similar experiences. Conversely, if what they disclose results in humiliation or embarrassment, it could create an unfortunate situation that is best to avoid.

Memoirists structure their work with a beginning, middle, and end and are not wedded to a plotline that includes a rising action fueled by suspense. Or perhaps they relay a series of related episodes that contribute to a common theme that represents the experience and the realization and teachings they derive from it.

Personal narratives, like memoirs, are written in first person and focus on a real-life powerful episode. However, the authors employ a plot structure centered on this specific event or experience that becomes the central conflict or climax, and they also incorporate suspense. (See appendix B on page 131 for a thorough discussion of plot elements.) Like memoir, authors of personal narratives are looser with some of the dialogue or specifics on fact because their memories may be imperfect. They may also take more liberties to embellish in order to compose an engaging story. In the resolution of personal narratives, the authors can demonstrate how the experience facilitated a change in their lives or their outlook.

Descriptive Writing

Prevalent across prose and poetry, detailed description for an extensive array of topics is embedded in all styles of writing: an idea, an image, a place, a person, a character, an animal, an element of nature, the environment, a physical or imaginary object, an event, a situation, and so on.

Writers rely on imagery to elicit what the focus of the description looks, sounds, feels, tastes, and smells like. Well-written descriptions are replete with sensory detail in order to make the reader picture or imagine in his or her mind's eye what the writer intends to describe. This kind of crystallized, vivid writing also contributes to how authors convey tone—their attitude toward their subject. Depending on the purpose and focus, sometimes writers intend for readers to not only view their descriptions mentally but also experience the image in such realistic terms that the writing elicits an emotional sensation and reaction. For example, a memoirist can intentionally write expressively about feelings or emotions associated with a life-changing event to compel readers to viscerally experience his or her pain or joy.

Although descriptive writing is a text type, it is typically without its own dedicated, prescriptive genres. Rather, it can be pervasively applied to almost any genre across text types. Sometimes students are asked to produce a descriptive piece of writing. For example, students write a paragraph to display next to a piece of artwork in a museum, a plaque near a species at a zoo explaining an animal's traits and behaviors, or captions describing the features of various shapes or angles for mathematics. Often, though, students embed descriptive writing across content areas such as these examples.

- In a genre for fictional narrative, writers can compose a character sketch, invent a vibrant setting to elicit a mood, or devise a series of gripping actions in descriptive terms, which can make a story vibrant and engaging.

- Students can write personal narratives or memoirs in history class assuming the point of view of a person who lived during a particular time period. In their work, they can describe actual people, settings, and events of that era and reveal how these historical individuals and situations affected people physically and emotionally. Or, students can write descriptively about the causes leading to an event, such as a war, economic crisis, or protest.

- In an argumentation essay, writers can provide context by relaying an anecdote in descriptive terms to set the stage for a claim. Strategically and wisely using description in the introduction can predispose readers to the writer's position from the start.

- Within a science research report, students can show changes in a process, portray characteristics of an animal and its habitat, or write observational notes about a topic using descriptive words and phrases.

For more insight into descriptive writing, see appendix C (page 137) on figurative language. Imagery as well as metaphor, simile, and other figures of speech are techniques writers use to create vivid descriptions. Teachers can also focus students' attention on how authors use adjectives, verbs, and adverbs to contribute to detailed depictions.

Summary

Of the four text types for writing (narrative, descriptive, expository, and persuasive), this appendix focuses on the former two types. Whereas both fiction and nonfiction narrative include dedicated genres within each category, the descriptive text type does not. Rather, detailed descriptive passages pervade poetry and most writing genres. Genres and subgenres—the terms applied to texts that share recognizable patterns, techniques, styles, or even conventions—are tricky. For example, some writing blends genres; resources define genres slightly differently, making a distinction between them and classification challenging; and new genres and subgenres appear. Once writers become familiar with their task, purpose, and audience, they choose a particular genre of narrative (as is the case with this text), and infuse description as needed. When composing, they engage in the writing process and show awareness and evidence of applying the characteristic elements and structure of the targeted genre.

Appendix B

Elements of Literature

This section details the elements of literature and how they are used in narrative fiction and nonfiction. However, a narrative rarely rests on just these elements alone. When authors compose their work, they enhance these characteristics through a range of literary devices and figurative language—the focus for appendix C. For example, an author might use imagery to create a descriptive setting to elicit a mood. Or, he or she can incorporate flashbacks in a plot to add dimension to his or her work. The purpose, task, audience, genre, and other factors drive these decisions. For activity, assessment, and lesson ideas to teach these elements, see chapters 3 (page 49), 4 (page 55), and 5 (page 111).

Elements of Literature in Fictional Narratives

The elements of literature—or narrative elements—are the heart and soul of fictional narrative. They include *characters*, *setting*, *plot*, *point of view*, and *theme*. Without them, a work of fiction seems incomplete, undeveloped, or inadequate. Most standards include them in their list of reading and writing expectations. (Elements as they pertain to nonfiction narrative appear later in this appendix on page 135.)

All stories include elements of literature; however, the genre dictates which elements to emphasize more than others. For example, in historical fiction the setting is altogether critical to the telling of the story and affects characters, plot, and theme. In myths, the setting might be an ill-defined, amorphous, and remote past, but the principal characters are pronounced and can possess supernatural powers. In mysteries, authors fashion a plotline with a crime that launches the story.

Create instructional experiences that revolve around the specific task and the development of these interconnected elements, guided by content-area standards. Plan learning accordingly and consider these and other types of guiding questions within your instructional program.

- Does the task dictate a specific genre? If so, how does the genre influence the elements of literature?

- How does setting affect the plot? How does setting impact characters' perspectives and motivations?

- How do the setting, characters, and plot support a theme?

- How does the narrator's point of view impact the writing?

- How do characters' interactions develop over the story and advance the plot?

Characters

Within literature, characters can be people, animals, deities, creatures, or even inanimate objects or nature, depending on the genre. The method an author uses to reveal characters to the reader is called *characterization* (see Characterization in appendix C on page 139 for further explanation). Here are key points related to characters.

- A *protagonist* serves as the central, main character. Sometimes teachers portray the protagonist as the good guy or hero, but this is not always the case. Typically, there is one protagonist, but some longer works have more than one.

- The character who is in opposition to the protagonist is the *antagonist*; the central conflict of a story revolves around their struggles. (See the following Plot section for more information.)

- Literary works contain all types of characters: round and flat, dynamic and static, stock, and others. Protagonists and antagonists denote round and dynamic characters. *Round characters* are well developed and possess various and sometimes contradictory personality traits. Additionally, they are typically *dynamic* in that they experience some kind of internal transformation throughout the course of the work—perhaps a shift in personality, values, or perspective.

- Minor characters operate in more supporting roles, and readers do not learn much about them. These types include *flat* (one-dimensional with a distinctive characteristic), *static* (unchanging), *stock* (a typecast character like the shrewd businessman or teacher's pet), and others.

Setting

The setting encompasses the time and place in which the events of a narrative occur and answers the questions, When? and Where? An author may specifically state a setting, such as noon on the Broadmoor Golf Course or Akron, Ohio, in mid-January in 1935. Or he or she can provide a more general description like a small, country road in a Midwestern town. Often the author introduces the primary setting at the very beginning of a work and also suggests and directly states it and perhaps other settings through the use of details scattered throughout the story.

Setting also includes other aspects that inform readers about a time, a place, and its surroundings. It can comprise, but is not limited to, the following.

- **Climate:** The predictable, average weather condition over long periods; for example, an author might write, "Over the insufferable summer . . ." or "During the bleak winter where we anticipated a blanket of white snow. . . ."

- **Weather:** The conditions of the atmosphere over short periods, which affect people's lives and activities, such as temperature, humidity, wind factor, hail, sleet, tornado, thunderstorms, or sunshine; for example, an author might write, "Joel didn't expect the sun to abandon the sky and give way to a sudden downpour, drenching every park bench and ruining his party."

- **Historical events, time periods, dates, and eras:** Writers can express these using a specific date in history or a general period—for example, "When the Japanese bombed Pearl Harbor in 1941 . . .," "In our modern era, we rely on technology to . . .," or "While waiting in the eternal soup lines during the Great Depression. . . ."

- **Geographical features:** Mountains, oceans, lakes, and valleys, for example, fall into this category.

As mentioned previously, sometimes setting can be vital to the narrative and provide a significant backdrop that can affect the plot, reveal a character's motivation or interaction with other characters, or create an atmosphere that drives the story. In other works, the setting can be relatively unimportant—the story could take place almost anywhere or at any time. Awareness of the characteristic elements of a genre will help students determine how prominent the setting needs to be so they can make a decision about how they treat this element.

Plot

The *plot* is a pattern of related events the author carefully constructs to present and resolve some internal or external conflict. The author carefully selects and arranges the incidents in a cause-and-effect relationship and typically, but not always, in chronological order with each incident becoming a necessary link leading to the climax and resolution of the work. Whereas people can disagree on the theme of a piece of literature, the plot is largely indisputable because it represents the concrete events as read, seen, or heard. It is what actually happens in a story; readers can point back to the text or rewind an audio or video to review an event.

Many authors craft narratives in a linear fashion aligned to a simplistic plotline that follows a rise-fall-rise structure. The following list itemizes and explains the key components of a basic plotline, which appear in figure B.1. Stories, however, typically include multiple plotlines, subplots, parallel plots, flashbacks, or flash forwards. In these narratives, the author manipulates, restructures, or even repeats the fundamental plot structure and its elements according to his or her purpose and craft.

- **Introduction:** Most authors include an introduction. If there is one, it usually entails background information about the setting and characters to offer context. Furthermore, in the introduction, readers become aware of the narrator and point of view.

- **Central conflict:** This is the most important conflict (or problem) in the story because it sets the story in motion and compels people to continue reading. Without the central conflict, there would be no story. There are likely other conflicts or problems within the story, but this is the crucial one. (See the types of conflict in table B.1.)

- **Rising action:** The rising action represents a significant portion of the story. It encompasses the many series of events that occur after the author establishes the central conflict, and these events lead to the climax. Successfully designing a plot that is rife with excitement and engagement is determined largely by how an author creates suspense, which involves building tension and uncertainty about what will come next. Suspense is a literary device rather than one of the five elements of literature, although it is closely aligned with rising action. More proficient writers incorporate suspense into their work.

- **Climax:** This is the highest point of intrigue and intensity in the story. It is when readers experience the greatest emotional response to the characters' problems, and the text confronts the central conflict. During the story's climactic moment, the protagonist must finally make a decision or overcome a challenge. A riveting climax will leave the reader on the proverbial edge of his or her seat.

- **Falling action:** Once the climax occurs, the falling action represents those events leading to the resolution (or denouement). The falling action can be relatively brief and follows quickly on the heels of the climax. It ties up loose ends and can begin to provide closure to any unanswered questions.

- **Resolution (denouement):** The central conflict is resolved and the story ends. Readers recall passages in the text, make inferences, and arrive at a satisfying conclusion; in other words, their questions are answered. In fairy tales, the author signifies the resolution with ". . . and they live happily ever after" or a similar ending.

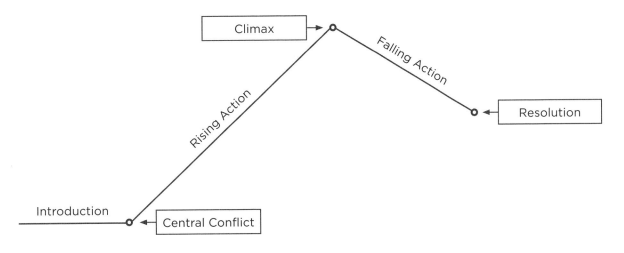

Figure B.1: Basic plot structure.

*Visit **go.SolutionTree.com/literacy** for a free reproducible version of this figure.*

Table B.1: Types of Conflict

Types of Conflict
Some consider conflict one of the five elements of literature, when in actuality it is embedded in the plot. The central conflict is, however, significant and worthy of attention because it forms the basis for the essence of the literary work.
There are four kinds of conflict divided into two categories: internal and external. Stories can contain more than one type of conflict simultaneously. For example, a character's internal struggles revolving around coping with a situation might lead him or her to engage in a precarious situation with nature (an external conflict).

Internal Conflict	External Conflict
This is a situation when the protagonist is experiencing an internal struggle within him- or herself. The antagonist in this case is the self, which can often be a person's own worst enemy. Throughout the course of the work, the protagonist wrestles with internal strife, doubts, or identity issues, and readers experience his or her thinking and actions to overcome them. Sometimes the protagonist succeeds and reaches desired goals; other times, he or she is unsuccessful and succumbs to temptation. A character's internal struggles and the way in which he or she resolves them indicate inner strength or weakness. An example of this type of conflict is Edgar Allan Poe's (1843/2002) short story "The Tell-Tale Heart."	There are three forms of external conflict, although some divide it into even more finite categories. 1. **Protagonist versus another:** This is a fairly typical scenario in which the protagonist is in opposition to an antagonist—a human, an animal, a character, or even technology or a supernatural being. The protagonist must prevail over the antics and efforts of the antagonist, who attempts to prevent or thwart him or her from reaching a goal. 2. **Protagonist versus nature:** In this situation, the protagonist is faced with a challenge of overcoming some force of nature, such as a tornado, a mountain, or the wilderness. This type of story—for example, "To Build a Fire" by Jack London (1908)—can be one of survival in which the protagonist may or may not triumph in the end. These narratives can reveal human insignificance against powerful, indomitable, universal phenomena or show a character's strength or sheer willingness to live amid such forces. 3. **Protagonist versus society or a group:** A protagonist confronts and challenges the norms, customs, or values of a collective society or group that are in opposition to his or her beliefs or ideals, such as those pertaining to bigotry, war, treatment of others, or an injustice of some kind. The society or group disagrees with the protagonist and might threaten or ridicule him or her so that he or she confronts it or takes action. The outcome can vary in that sometimes the antagonistic group eventually aligns with the protagonist's perspective, or the protagonist is unsuccessful in garnering its support to adopt his or her way of thinking or behaving. The story could end with the protagonist dying to protect his or her convictions or even succumbing to the opposition.

*Visit **go.SolutionTree.com/literacy** for a free reproducible version of this table.*

As an interesting data point, after careful analysis of emotional arcs in over 1,700 stories, researchers assert that there are just six core plots in any fictional narrative ever created (Emerging Technology from the arXiv, 2016):

A steady, ongoing rise in emotional valence, as in a rags-to-riches story such as *Alice's Adventures Underground* by Lewis Carroll. A steady ongoing fall in emotional valence, as in a tragedy such as *Romeo and Juliet*. A fall then a rise, such as the man-in-a-hole story, discussed by Vonnegut. A rise then a fall, such as the Greek myth of *Icarus*. Rise-fall-rise, such as *Cinderella*. Fall-rise-fall, such as *Oedipus*.

Point of View

Point of view is the author's choice of narrator and provides the vantage point from which he or she is conveying the story. Is the narrator telling the story from the outside, or is the narrator a character in the story telling it from the inside? Although there are the following points of view, some complex stories bounce around from different points of view to provide readers with different perspectives.

- **First-person (or personal) point of view:** The narrator is a character within the story—often the protagonist—who is telling it and can reveal his or her own thoughts and feelings and what others tell him or her. However, the narrator cannot describe with complete certainty what other characters are thinking and feeling because the author is telling the story only through this narrator's first-person account. You might ask students to write a piece of historical fiction in which they assume the persona of a figure who lived during a certain time period and tell the story from his or her point of view.

- **Second-person point of view:** The second-person pronoun *you* rarely sees use, especially in formal writing. However, it is present in informal letter or journal writing and other informal texts.

- **Third-person point of view:** In this point of view, the narrator uses third-person pronouns to convey the story from the outside. This narrator may be *omniscient* (all-knowing and able to reveal multiple characters' thoughts and feelings) or *limited* (able to reveal the thoughts and feelings of one character). Students can select which type of third-person point of view—as well as other point-of-view decisions—they will use based on the task.

Theme

The *theme* is the central message, significant and unifying idea, or underlying meaning and insight a reader extrapolates from a literary work. Unlike a fable, which explicitly states its moral, most stories only generally imply their themes. Texts can share the same theme but have different plotlines. As well, a text can entail more than one theme. Use the following points to assist students in understanding this element of literature.

- The theme expresses a general truth or abstract concept about life or people. Readers must uncover it through interpretation and inference using textual evidence, such as characters' actions, motivations, thoughts,

and beliefs; their interactions with others; the influence of setting; situations and events; or a motif (a repeated element throughout the story that carries significance like an image, event, phrase, and so forth).

- As readers experience and interpret a text, they can arrive at different impressions of the theme. By engaging in deep discussions about texts and their themes, readers can form new insights based on others' contributing thoughts and ideas.

- Although students in kindergarten to third grade typically express themes in one word (such as *friendship* or *loneliness*), encourage upper elementary and secondary students to articulate them in phrases. To construct a theme, they can first identify the concept word, and then ask, "What about it?" to arrive at a thematic statement, such as the following: *Intolerance* leads to unspeakable actions. *Kindness* prevails over evil. *Maturation* can occur when individuals experience situations and events that provoke introspection and learning. *Greed* and *jealousy* drive people to act immorally. *Friendship* can be tested over time.

Students can address a task in which they write a story based on a particular theme. For example, the class might read and discuss various stories about characters who have succeeded despite adversity. Based on what they learn about narrative techniques and elements of literature, they then craft a work of realistic fiction based on this theme.

Elements of Literature in Nonfiction Narratives

Whereas the five elements of literature are present in fictional narrative, authors of nonfiction narrative include some but are not wedded to them all. The treatment is slightly different based on the specific genre of nonfiction narrative.

1. **Characters:** In narrative nonfiction, the characters are actual people. There are not necessarily protagonists and antagonists. However, real-life situations can mirror the conflicts between literary characters; for

example, this happens if the author is writing about struggles with another person or with society. Or perhaps the internal conflict is the writer's struggle within himself or herself.

2. **Setting:** In narrative nonfiction, authors certainly describe settings that complement and prove critical to the telling of the story. Sometimes prevalent settings serve as the impetus for sharing one's own story or relaying information about another person. For example, if a biographer writes about a president and his time in office, the setting is altogether essential in that it impacts decisions the subject makes and the events of the time. If one is writing a memoir about brutality or genocide that occurred in a particular country, again setting is central to the writing and the author must convey it with care.

3. **Plot:** This element forms the structure of a personal narrative in which the significant life event that is the basis for the story represents either the central conflict or the climax. In other forms of nonfiction narrative, for example, writers are not bound to a rising action or climax. They may, though, elect to weave some plot elements into their pieces.

They do, however, abide by an organizational structure, which might include a beginning, middle, and end.

4. **Point of view:** In autobiographies, personal narratives, and memoirs, the authors tell their own stories, so the point of view is first person. A biographer will write in third-person point of view because the subject is about another individual.

5. **Theme:** The author's purpose for writing aligns with the theme. For example, autobiographers or biographers might illuminate how one might go to great lengths to overcome obstacles and persevere to achieve fame or distinction.

Summary

Elements of literature play a critical role in crafting a narrative work and enabling readers to fully understand and appreciate it. The quality of how an author treats these elements contributes to its popularity. When readers describe their impression of a book—whether it be weak, outstanding, or somewhere in between—they would be hard-pressed to support their assertions without mentioning the interplay of elements.

Appendix C

Literary Devices and Figurative Language

This appendix provides a comprehensive overview of literary devices and figurative language that authors select and employ to suit the purpose for which they are writing and enhance a work of narration. (Some sources include figurative language under the umbrella of literary devices, whereas I choose to give them equal attention.) I share literary examples throughout this appendix; use them for your own professional learning, if needed, or embed them within lessons to share with students. Solicit students to find examples in texts they are reading independently or as part of classroom instruction. Encourage them to or expect that they will invent their own examples in writing they compose. When making decisions about which devices and types of figurative language to teach, defer and be accountable to your grade-level content standards. For activity, assessment, and lesson ideas around some of the material in this appendix, see chapters 3 (page 49) and 4 (page 55).

Literary Devices

Literary devices are techniques that writers intentionally use to enrich and add dimension to their work, such as allusion, analogy, mood, tone, flashback, foreshadowing, dialect, dialogue, irony, and others. The skillful use of appropriate devices compels readers to interpret and analyze them to get more meaning from the narrative. Since there are numerous such devices, teach students specific ones aligned to their writing task, purpose, and intended audience. Certainly, consider grade-level content standards that need addressing. For example, the Common Core expects students to create dialogue across grade spans; the Language strand suggests several literary devices, such as allusion, irony, and euphemism in some secondary grades (NGA & CCSSO, 2010).

When teaching, find reading selections that meet guidelines for text complexity and feature targeted devices to use within your instructional program. This way, students can experience published examples of authors employing the devices as a guide for their own writing. Also, feature student writing samples within instruction that contain examples and nonexamples of these devices as the basis for lessons.

In this section, I highlight some of the many literary devices. For others, refer to your own resources or access the links in appendix E (page 151).

Allusion

When writers employ allusion, they are referencing a noteworthy person, historical event, or piece of literature; the Bible; or even artwork, sports, politics, or classic movies to contextualize their writing and deepen the meaning of the targeted content. Authors commonly use religious, mythological, and classic literary allusions, including Shakespearean works, because these texts are often familiar to readers. Sometimes allusions are direct; other times, they are not explicitly stated. By employing this literary device, authors connect the context of their work to the larger world. In doing so, it deepens the meaning of what they intend to convey because it associates the allusion to their ideas and emotions.

If readers are unaware of the reference, the meaning is lost to them unless they make the effort to research the allusion in order to understand its significance. Here are some examples.

- **Jekyll and Hyde:** This reference is from the novel *The Strange Case of Dr. Jekyll and Mr. Hyde* by Robert Louis Stevenson (1886/1991). It features an exceptionally unpredictable person who possesses the ability to swing from one personality to another, specifically from a respectable doctor (Dr. Jekyll) to a vicious murderer (Mr. Hyde). Writers commonly use it as an allusion to juxtapose good and evil or civilized and depraved within a single character.

- **Scrooge:** A character from Charles Dickens's (1843) *A Christmas Carol*, Scrooge refers to a rancorous and miserly person.

- **Casanova:** Someone who is called a Casanova is noted for his amorous adventures and perhaps considered a womanizer. It is a reference to the Italian adventurer Giacomo Girolamo Casanova (1725–1798) who seemingly was involved romantically with many women and wrote of his trysts.

- **McCarthyism:** This historical allusion refers to Republican Senator Joseph McCarthy (1908–1957) who instigated a modern witch hunt by making false accusations without evidence. As a result, many citizens were accused of being Communist sympathizers, faced discrimination, and were blacklisted.

- **Prodigal son:** This is a biblical reference to a wayward son who leaves home, squanders his inheritance on a reckless lifestyle, and winds up destitute. He finally returns home full of shame and remorse, and discovers his father forgives him. The allusion refers to someone who moves away from home to pursue a reckless lifestyle, but returns home repentant.

- **Achilles's heel:** Achilles, a Greek mythological hero, was a renowned warrior, strong and courageous. His only vulnerability was his heel. (The Achilles tendon takes its name from this myth.) A reference to Achilles's heel is someone's particular area of weakness or susceptibility.

Analogy

Some sources consider *analogy*—making an elaborate and extended connection—as the overarching category to which metaphor, simile, allegory, and parable belong because they each represent different forms of comparison. By studying the relationship between the two concepts or ideas, readers come to a deeper understanding of the content.

Analogies are similar to similes and metaphors (see the Figurative Language section that follows) in that they also serve to draw comparisons between two unlike ideas or objects. In an allegory, nearly every element, like each character and action, has symbolic meaning. A parable is written to reveal a religious principle, moral lesson, or general truth like "The Prodigal Son" or "The Good Samaritan."

Used with words, analogies can include part to whole, cause and effect, synonyms, or antonyms. For example, *light is to feather as heavy is to sandbag; friendship : rift :: society : schism;* and "As smoking is to the lungs, so is resentment to the soul; even one puff is bad for you" (Gilbert, 2016, p. 215). The following literary examples include analogy along with other forms of figurative language:

> A nation wearing atomic armor is like a knight whose armor has grown so heavy he is immobilized; he can hardly walk, hardly sit his horse, hardly think, hardly breathe. The H-bomb is an extremely effective deterrent to war, but it has little virtue as a weapon of war, because it would leave the world uninhabitable. (White, 1999, p. 117)

<< • >>

> Imagine that the universe is a great spinning engine. You want to stay near the core of the thing—right in the hub of the wheel—not out at the edges where all the wild whirling takes place, where you can get frayed and crazy. The hub of calmness—that's your heart. That's where God lives within you. So stop looking for answers in the world. Just keep coming back to that center and you'll always find peace. (Gilbert, 2006, pp. 228-229)

<< • >>

> Falsehood flies, and truth comes limping after it, so that when men come to be undeceived, it is too late; the jest is over,

and the tale hath had its effect: like a man, who hath thought of a good repartee when the discourse is changed, or the company parted; or like a physician, who hath found out an infallible medicine, after the patient is dead. (Swift, 1729)

Analogy, like simile and metaphor, serves to compare dissimilar things. However, analogy is used more for the purpose of explanation. As such, people tend to write more extensively or elaborately about the ideas behind the topics at the center of the comparison.

Characterization

To create and develop characters, authors employ one or more of the following methods of *characterization*. They:

- Describe the character's physical appearance and clothing (what the character looks like)

- Report the character's speech or dialogue (what the character says)

- Display the character's actions and behavior (what the character does)

- Give other characters' opinions and reactions toward a particular character (what others say to and about the character and how they react to the character)

- Reveal the character's thoughts and feelings (what the character thinks and feels)

There are two approaches to characterization based on how the author delivers the information: (1) directly or (2) indirectly. When authors use the direct form, the narrator or protagonist explicitly states information about a character, as in this example from Anthony Doerr's (2014) *All the Light We Cannot See*: "Her great-uncle seems kind, curious, and entirely sane. Stillness: this is what he radiates more than anything else. The stillness of a tree. Of a mouse blinking in the dark" (p. 135).

In indirect or implicit characterization, authors subtly write about subjects and rely on readers to use textual evidence to make inferences and deductions about them. For example, in the following excerpt, Harper Lee (1960) doesn't name a trait explicitly to define Atticus in *To Kill a Mockingbird*. Instead, readers must make an informed decision about his personality:

"First of all," he said, "if you can learn a simple trick, Scout, you'll get along a lot better with all kinds of folks. You never really understand a person until you consider things from his point of view . . . until you climb into his skin and walk around in it." (p. 39)

Readers might deduce from this excerpt that Atticus is insightful and compassionate.

Authors can craft a passage utilizing a method in isolation like this example from Sandra Cisneros (1991) who writes what a character is thinking and feeling in her story "Eleven":

Only today I wish I didn't have only eleven years rattling inside me like pennies in a tin Band-Aid box. Today I wish I was one hundred and two instead of eleven because if I was one hundred and two I'd have known what to say when Mrs. Price put the red sweater on my desk. (p. 1)

More often, authors combine methods as they rarely set out to focus on one at a time, nor do they need to include them all. It's doubtful that authors compose with this kind of internal monologue: "First, I'll describe what a character looks like. Next, I'll write about what other characters say about him. Then, I'll do a section that focuses on what this character is thinking and feeling." That would seem unnatural. Rather, they write a fluid integration of characterization methods to develop and form a whole picture of a character, which contributes to moving the plot forward.

Dialogue and Dialect

Dialogue and dialect are intrinsically related. Dialect, a more sophisticated literary device, adds dimension to characters by the manner and content of their dialogue. However, since dialect is typically a complex skill to master, elementary students have an easier time recognizing its use in a text than they do writing it themselves. At the secondary level, encourage students to analyze the use of dialect in published works and employ this literary device in their narratives.

Dialogue, an integral part of storytelling, can further the plot forward in myriad ways. These verbal exchanges can be either *direct*—indicating the exact words of a speaker, which are always enclosed in quotation marks— or *indirect*. When using indirect dialogue, writers summarize what a speaker says, so they do not use quotation marks to record a conversation verbatim.

Writers need to make several decisions about dialogue so it enhances their work. First, they must strike a fine balance when composing between ample dialogue and overuse. Also, it should be natural and represent words and phrases the characters would realistically utter within the context of the narrative. Lastly, the dialogue needs to have purpose and meaning. It could serve multiple functions—to advance events, develop a conflict, reveal relationships and interactions with other characters, create mood, uncover personality traits, foreshadow an event, or establish a setting. Dialect, which I discuss later, can enrich the dialogue and support these purposes.

Writers can also capitalize on dialogue or speaker tags (such as *Mr. Tuttle groused, the woman shrieked*) to augment what characters say so readers better understand a situation, motive, reaction, setting, or character. However, the dialogue should be strong enough that the tags do not carry the entire meaning and serve as a crutch to insufficient or inadequate conversation between characters, the point being that tags should be used intentionally and for an express purpose, and like dialogue, even sparingly. Here are types of dialogue tags (underlined) and the punctuation protocol for each form. Chapter 4 (page 55) includes a lesson on dialogue mechanics.

- **Beginning dialogue tag:** <u>Marshall exclaimed,</u> "I got a new job!"

- **Middle tag:** "If you are invited to dinner," <u>I tell my children,</u> "remember to call the next day or write a short note of thanks to show your appreciation."

- **End tag:** "Otherwise, the hosts may not be eager to invite you back to their home or treat you for dinner again," <u>I stated.</u>

- **No tag:** "My father has always taught me that behavior that is rewarded is repeated." I try to live by this motto and teach it to my kids. If I notice a good deed, I strive to comment on it to acknowledge that person. Often I'm granted a smile.

Dialect refers to the language characters use, such as particular words, grammar construction, slang or formal language, and so forth, that reveals characters' country or regional origin, era or century, gender, culture, race, and social standing or group. For example, obsolete words like *shantytown, colored people, hippie,* or *I pray thee* can indicate that a story takes place in a previous era. Or authors can use words to reflect a character's bias or crassness that might offend some readers but, within the context of the piece, intentionally illustrate characters' proclivities and mindsets. How characters pronounce words and proper or improper grammatical construction can also give readers insights into characters' education and social standing.

Figure C.1 features examples of different ways to incorporate dialogue into a narrative piece. You can use these excerpts within instruction by asking students to identify what the dialect and tags reveal about characters and the effect on the readers. This exercise would be a precursor to a more developed lesson in which students read an entire literary selection and examine the impact of the use of dialogue, dialect, and tags. Then they apply these skills to enhance their own narratives. For more lesson ideas to teach dialogue, see chapter 4.

Enhancing Dialogue

"The Monkey's Paw"

Tags can work in concert with dialogue to create mounting tension as in this excerpt from W. W. Jacobs's (1997) "The Monkey's Paw." Pay particular attention to the verbs Jacobs intentionally uses for effect.

"Come back," he said tenderly. "You will be cold."

"It is colder for my son," said the old woman, and wept afresh.

The sound of her sobs died away on his ears. The bed was warm, and his eyes heavy with sleep. He dozed fitfully, and then slept until a sudden wild cry from his wife awoke him with a start.

"The paw!" she cried wildly. "The monkey's paw!"

He started up in alarm. "Where? Where is it? What's the matter?"

She came stumbling across the room toward him. "I want it," she said quietly. "You've not destroyed it?"

"It's in the parlour, on the bracket," he replied, marveling. "Why?"

She cried and laughed together, and bending over, kissed his cheek.

"I only just thought of it," she said hysterically. "Why didn't I think of it before? Why didn't you think of it?"

"Think of what?" he questioned.

"The other two wishes," she replied rapidly. "We've only had one."

"Was not that enough?" he demanded fiercely.

"No," she cried, triumphantly; "we'll have one more. Go down and get it quickly, and wish our boy alive again."

The man sat up in bed and flung the bedclothes from his quaking limbs. "Good God, you are mad!" he cried, aghast.

"Get it," she panted; "get it quickly, and wish—Oh, my boy, my boy!"

Her husband struck a match and lit the candle. "Get back to bed," he said, unsteadily. "You don't know what you are saying."

"We had the first wish granted," said the old woman, feverishly; "why not the second?"

"A coincidence," stammered the old man.

"Go and get it and wish," cried the old woman, quivering with excitement. (Jacobs, 1997)

"Young Goodman Brown"

Dialogue tags can also include action and gestures to provide readers with information about what the character is doing while speaking as in this example from Nathaniel Hawthorne's (1835) "Young Goodman Brown," which also shows an excellent sample of dialect.

"Friend," said the other, exchanging his slow pace for a full stop, "having kept covenant by meeting thee here, it is my purpose now to return whence I came. I have scruples touching the matter thou wot'st of."

"Sayest thou so?" replied he of the serpent, smiling apart. "Let us walk on, nevertheless, reasoning as we go; and if I convince thee not thou shalt turn back. We are but a little way in the forest yet."

"Too far! too far!" exclaimed the goodman, unconsciously resuming his walk. (Hawthorne, 1835)

Roll of Thunder, Hear My Cry

Mildred Taylor (1976) writes dialect to authentically reflect how an elderly, disadvantaged southern black woman might speak in this *Roll of Thunder, Hear My Cry* excerpt. Along with the dialect that highlights region and social status, pay attention to the terminology *land sakes* and *old bones*.

The door swung wide then and an elderly woman, frail and toothless, stepped out. Her left arm hung crazily at her side as if it had been broken long ago but had not mended properly, and she walked with a limp; yet she smiled widely, throwing her good arm around Mama and hugging her. "Land sakes, child, ain't you somethin'!" she exclaimed. "Comin' to see bout these old bones. I jus' sez to Sam, I sez, 'Who you reckon comin' to see old folks like us?' These yo' babies, ain't they? Lord a'mighty, ain't they fine! Sho' is!" She hugged each of us and ushered us into the house. (Taylor, 1976, p. 73)

Of Mice and Men

In *Of Mice and Men*, Steinbeck (1968/1994) uses dialect to reveal not only the social status and region of characters George and Lennie, but also Lennie's limitations. Notice that the dialogue also includes ellipses to indicate pausing for effect that reflects a characteristic of the speaker.

Lennie looked timidly over to him. "George?"

"Yeah, what ya want?"

"Where we goin', George?"

The little man jerked down the brim of his hat and scowled over at Lennie. "So you forgot that awready, did you? I gotta tell you again, do I? Jesus Christ, you're a crazy bastard!"

"I forgot," Lennie said softly. "I tried not to forget. Honest to God I did, George."

"O.K.—O.K. I'll tell ya again. I ain't got nothing to do. Might jus' as well spen' all my time tellin' you things and then you forget 'em, and I tell you again."

"Tried and tried," said Lennie, "but it didn't do no good. I remember about the rabbits, George."

"The hell with the rabbits. That's all you ever can remember is them rabbits. O.K.! Now you listen and this time you got to remember so we don't get in no trouble. You remember settin' in that gutter on Howard Street and watchin' that blackboard?"

Lennie's face broke into a delighted smile. "Why sure, George. I remember that . . . but . . . what'd we do then? I remember some girls come by and you says . . . you says . . ."

"The hell with what I says. You remember about us goin' in to Murray and Ready's, and they give us work cards and bus tickets?"

"Oh, sure, George. I remember that now." His hands went quickly into his side coat pockets. He said gently, "George . . . I ain't got mine. I musta lost it." (Steinbeck, 1968/1994)

Figure C.1: Enhancing dialogue.

continued ➤

"Petrified Man"

The drama in Eudora Welty's (n.d.) "Petrified Man" unfolds largely in the dialogue, which is replete with dialect, between the beautician Leota and her customer Mrs. Fletcher.

"Well," Leota answered at last, "you know what I heard in here yestiddy, one of Thelma's ladies was settin' over yonder in Thelma's booth gittin' a machineless, and I don't mean to insist or insinuate or any-thing, Mrs Fletcher, but Thelma's lady just happ'med to throw out—I forgotten what she was talkin' about at the time—that you was p-r-e-g., and lots of times that'll make your hair do awful funny, fall out and God knows what all. It just ain't our fault, is the way I look at it."

There was a pause. The women stared at each other in the mirror.

"Who was it?" demanded Mrs Fletcher.

"Honey, I really couldn't say," said Leota. "Not that you look it."

"Where's Thelma? I'll get it out of her," said Mrs Fletcher.

"Now, honey, I wouldn't go and git mad over a little thing like that," Leota said, combing hastily, as though to hold Mrs Fletcher down by the hair. "I'm sure it was somebody didn't mean no harm in the world. How far gone are you?"

"Just wait," said Mrs Fletcher, and shrieked for Thelma, who came in and took a drag from Leota's cigarette.

"Thelma, honey, throw your mind back to yestiddy if you kin," said Leota, drenching Mrs Fletcher's hair with a thick fluid and catching the overflow in a cold wet towel at her neck.

"Well, I got my lady half wound for a spiral," said Thelma doubtfully.

"This won't take but a minute," said Leota. "Who is it you got in there, old Horse Face? Just cast your mind back and try to remember who your lady was yestiddy who happ'm to mention that my customer was pregnant, that's all. She's dead to know." (Welty, n.d.)

Source: Hawthorne, 1835; Herriot, 1994; Jackson, 1949/2010; Jacobs, 1997; Sloane, 1979; Steinbeck, 1968/1994; Taylor, 1976; Welty, n.d.

Irony

Writers incorporate irony into their work when they contrast the expected outcome with the actual way things turn out. In short, it is a disparity between expectation and reality and divided into three types: (1) verbal, (2) situational, and (3) dramatic irony.

Verbal irony is when a character or speaker literally and intentionally says something but means the opposite. Sometimes people mistakenly think that verbal irony and sarcasm are interchangeable. Sarcasm can be biting and ridiculing; whereas, irony is void of attitude or contempt. People can, however, take irony a step further to include sarcasm if they add a biting remark that has attitude or is hurtful and derisive.

In "A Modest Proposal," Jonathan Swift (1729) uses verbal irony pervasively to address Ireland's social, political, and economic problems. After engaging readers with a false sense of good intentions, he tosses in this example of irony near the end to jolt readers and bring attention to the overpopulation problem:

I have been assured by a very knowing American of my acquaintance in London, that a young healthy child well nursed, is, at a year old, a most delicious nourishing and wholesome food, whether stewed, roasted, baked, or boiled; and I make no doubt that it will equally serve in a fricasie, or a ragout. (Swift, 1729)

Situational irony occurs when an incongruity or discrepancy exists between what readers expect or anticipate will happen and what actually transpires. In literature, this literary device serves to punctuate a situation in which people are often caught in forces beyond what they are able to understand or control. For example, in Edwin Arlington Robinson's (n.d.) iconic poem "Richard Cory," the subject appears confident and others envy his appearance, wealth, and education. The unexpected outcome of suicide takes readers by surprise. (Simon and Garfunkel recorded a song with the same title.) In the following portion of Samuel Taylor Coleridge's (1834) "The Rime of the Ancient Mariner," the ironic element presents itself because the subject desperately craves water. However, he is surrounded by an ocean, and the saltwater content would ultimately dehydrate and kill him rather than quench his thirst:

Water, water, everywhere,
And all the boards did shrink;
Water, water, everywhere,
Yet not a drop to drink.

In *dramatic irony*, the reader or audience has more information than the characters, who are unaware of what is going to happen. The reader anticipates that this unwitting character will fall prey to something surprising, unpleasant, or even frightening because he or she is ignorant of certain information that other characters, the reader, or the audience knows. This creates heightened emotions on the part of the reader as he or she cannot alert the unsuspecting character. It is as if the reader or audience knows a secret—for example, William Shakespeare's (2017) *Othello*. This tragedy depicts dramatic irony because the audience is cognizant of Iago's evil intentions and his manipulations that cause Othello to think Desdemona unfaithful, but the protagonist is unaware of the truth. Consider reviewing and sharing these YouTube resources about irony with your class.

- **General irony:** "Teaching Irony: Help Students Understand Verbal, Situational, and Dramatic Irony" (http://goo.gl/29iS6a; Randazzo, 2015)

- **Situational irony:** "Situational Irony: The Opposite of What You Think" (http://goo.gl /UHyhLs; Warner, 2012)

- **Verbal irony:** "What Is Verbal Irony?" (http://goo.gl/GQm7oh; Warner, 2013b)

- **Dramatic irony:** "In on a Secret? That's Dramatic Irony" (http://goo.gl/i98XJm; Warner, 2013a)

Mood

When viewing artwork or listening to music, certain emotions surface. The same applies to literature. The mood, or emotional atmosphere, is the reader's attitude toward what he or she reads and reflects the overall feeling about the text. For example, literature can make a reader feel cheerful and joyous, angry and irritated, perhaps peaceful, or even gloomy.

Readers can articulate mood by using an emotion to complete this sentence starter: "As I read this passage, I feel _____ [*melancholy, disgusted, energized, anxious*] because _____." For example, "This story makes me feel anxious because I think something

terrible is going to happen to the protagonist." To create mood, authors carefully select words—particularly verbs and modifiers—and craft phrases that describe the setting, characters, and events in a particularly intentional way to evoke the response they desire, either positive or negative. They might use imagery, as well as other forms of figurative language, to create this effect. To assist with teaching mood for setting, see chapter 4 (page 61).

Figurative Language

Authors intentionally enhance setting, character, plot elements, feelings, ideas, and other content with figurative language (also called figures of speech) to make the text vivid, realistic or fantastical, and compelling. In doing so, they offer fresh perspectives and leave an impression on readers.

The term *figurative language* refers to simile, metaphor, imagery, personification, and hyperbole. When writers use any of these forms, they want readers to understand the connotation rather than the literal interpretation of their words. As a result, readers must employ interpretation skills once they recognize and identify instances where the writer uses figurative language.

Some authors and many poets rely heavily on figurative language and it becomes part of their writing style. Others pepper their work with it sparingly. Natalie Babbitt, Charles Dickens, Shakespeare, and countless others compose works that are replete with figures of speech. Caution students, however, to avoid its overuse. Otherwise, the writing can be distracting and confusing for readers.

The following sections examine in more detail the types of as well as the need for authentic figurative language.

Simile and Metaphor

Simile and metaphor make comparisons between two essentially unlike objects, things, or ideas. It is the association between dissimilar items that makes the simile or metaphor effective. They typically link something that appears perhaps commonplace to an unfamiliar idea or concept to extend and deepen understanding. *Similes* make the comparison using these indicator words: *like, as, as if,* or *resembles. Metaphors* offer an implied comparison void of trigger words that provides hints of a connection, without overtly stating it. Sometimes writers use forms of the verb *to be* (*is, are*) to draw the association as in this example from *Fahrenheit 451*: "'Kerosene,' he said, because the silence had lengthened, 'is nothing but perfume to me'" (Bradbury, 1995, p. 4).

The literary excerpts in figure C.2 can help cement students' understanding; use them or excerpts from your class complex text within lessons, as appropriate. For example, you can orchestrate an activity in which you cut out each excerpt and place the set in an envelope for each small group. Then instruct students to read each strip and place it in one of two piles—simile or metaphor. When students write their own examples, emphasize that they should avoid similes that are clichés, such as *fast as a cheetah*, *run like the wind*, *skinny as a rail*, and so forth. These lack originality and suffer from overuse.

Simile and Metaphor Examples in Literature
Simile Examples
• "She always pictured a troupe of burly men with long black moustaches who would tumble her into a blanket and bear her off like a sack of potatoes while she pleaded for mercy" (Babbitt, 1975, p. 31).
• "The next day when I got home from school, I discovered draped on my bedpost a jacket the color of day-old guacamole. I threw my books on the bed and approached the jacket slowly, as if it were a stranger whose hand I had to shake" (Soto, n.d.).
• "This is when I wish I wasn't eleven, because all the years inside of me—ten, nine, eight, seven, six, five, four, three, two, and one—are pushing at the back of my eyes when I put one arm through one sleeve of the sweater that smells like cottage cheese, and then the other arm through the other and stand there with my arms apart like if the sweater hurts me and it does, all itchy and full of germs that aren't even mine" (Cisneros, 1991a, p. 3).
• "Hard and sharp as flint, from which no steel had ever struck out generous fire; secret, and self-contained, and solitary as an oyster" (Dickens, 1843).
• "What the knitting was, I don't know, not being learned in that art; but it looked like a net; and as she worked away with those Chinese chopsticks of knitting-needles, she showed in the firelight like an ill-looking enchantress, baulked as yet by the radiant goodness opposite, but getting ready for a cast of her net by and by" (Dickens, 1850).
• "The giggles hung in the air like melting clouds that were waiting to rain on me" (Angelou, 1997, p. 5).
• "He drank palm-wine from morning till night, and his eyes were red and fierce like the eyes of a rat when it was caught by the tail and dashed against the floor" (Achebe, 1995, p. 55).
Metaphor Examples
• "With the brass nozzle in his fists, with this great python spitting its venomous kerosene upon the world, the blood pounded in his head, and his hands were the hands of some amazing conductor playing all the symphonies of blazing and burning to bring down the tatters and charcoal ruins of history" (Bradbury, 1995, p. 1).
• "My school-days! The silent gliding on of my existence—the unseen, unfelt progress of my life—from childhood up to youth! Let me think, as I look back upon that flowing water, now a dry channel overgrown with leaves, whether there are any marks along" (Dickens, 1850).
• "The fog came pouring in at every chink and keyhole, and was so dense without, that although the court was of the narrowest, the houses opposite were mere phantoms" (Dickens, 1843).
• "If growing up is painful for the Southern Black girl, being aware of her displacement is the rust on the razor that threatens the throat. It is an unnecessary insult" (Angelou, 1997, p. 6).
• "Among the Ibo the art of conversation is regarded very highly, and proverbs are the palm-oil with which words are eaten" (Achebe, 1995, p. 4).

Source: Achebe, 1995; Angelou, 1997; Babbitt, 1975; Bradbury, 1995; Cisneros, 1991a; Dickens, 1843, 1850; Soto, n.d.

Figure C.2: Simile and metaphor examples in literature.

Imagery

Imagery appeals to the five senses, which enable readers or listeners to visualize particular passages in their mind's eye. The familiar saying "Show, don't tell" applies here. Like with other forms of figurative language, writers invent imagery to describe settings, characters, and events, propelling readers to delve deeply into meaning making. They also use it for depicting objects and characters' feelings, or for crafting words and phrases for dialogue tags to add dimension to what a character says. Imagery, when writers use it well, can arouse an emotional or perhaps physical response. Figure C.3 (page 146) features different types of imagery along with sample words writers can use alone or incorporate into descriptive phrases.

See the following examples of published authors employing imagery and those in chapter 4 (page 55), which includes imagery activity options that you can conduct. Additionally, refer to chapter 3 (page 49) for a comprehensive lesson on using imagery to describe a setting:

> The sun came out.
>
> It was the color of flaming bronze and it was very large. And the sky around it was a blazing blue tile color. And the jungle burned with sunlight as the children, released from their spell, rushed out, yelling, into the springtime. . . .
>
> But they were running and turning their faces up to the sky and feeling the sun on their cheeks like a warm iron; they were taking off their jackets and letting the sun burn their arms. (Bradbury, n.d.)

<< • >>

> On rocky islands gulls woke. Time to be about their business. Silently they floated in on the town, but when their icy eyes sighted the first dead fish, first bits of garbage about the ships and wharves, they began to scream and quarrel.
>
> The cocks in Boston back yards had long before cried the coming of the day. Now the hens were also awake, scratching, clucking, laying eggs.
>
> Cats in malt houses, granaries, ship holds, mansions and hovels caught a last mouse, settled down to wash their fur and sleep. Cats did not work by day.

> In stables horses shook their halters and whinnied.
>
> In barns cows lowed to be milked.
>
> Boston slowly opened its eyes, stretched, and woke. The sun struck in horizontally from the east, flashing upon weathervanes—brass cocks and arrows, here a glass-eyed Indian, there a copper grasshopper—and the bells in the steeples cling-clanged, telling the people it was time to be up and about. (Forbes, 1971, p. 1)

Personification

Writers employ personification when they assign human qualities or characteristics to something nonhuman, specifically inanimate objects, ideas, deities, forces of nature, or animals. Usually a noun assumes the personified subject, which the writer couples with a human-like action verb and other words or phrases for effect. Often advertisers rely on personification as a technique to sell their products, such as animated candies conversing, animals as insurance spokespersons, or dancing food items. In the following literary examples, I place the personified subject in bold typeface and underline the words that make it so.

From *Tuck Everlasting* (Babbitt, 1975):

- "So the **road** underline{went humbly} by and made its way, past cottages more and more frequent but less and less forbidding, into the village" (Babbitt, 1975, p. 6).

- ". . . the graceful **arms** of the pines stretched out protectively in every direction" (Babbitt, 1975, p. 47).

- ". . . streaks of **light** swam and danced and wavered like a bright mirage, reflected through the windows from the sunlit surface of the pond" (Babbitt, 1975, p. 52).

From *David Copperfield* (Dickens, 1850):

> I lay down in the old little bed in the stern of the boat, and the **wind** came moaning on across the flat as it had done before. But I could not help fancying, now, that it moaned of those who were gone; and instead of thinking that the **sea** might rise in the night and float the boat away, I thought of the sea that had risen, since I last heard those sounds, and drowned my happy home.

Imagery Types and Excerpts

Senses	Explanation and Sample Words	Passage Excerpts
Sight (Visual)	Visual imagery—the most common type—is when authors describe what they want readers to see, such as a particular place or a character's physical appearance or clothing. To conjure up a visual, authors might use particular words and phrases to describe colors (*colorless, crimson, pitch black, sky blue, vermilion*), shapes (*irregular, oblong, shapeless, triangular*), sizes (*diminutive, massive, wide*), movement (*bolt, meander, saunter, scramble, slide, slither*), or appearances (*disheveled, handsome, muscular, shimmery, transparent*).	"... dim and little-traveled trail led eastward through the fat spruce timberland. It was a steep bank ..." "North and south, as far as his eye could see, it was unbroken white, save for a dark hair-line that curved and twisted from around the spruce-covered island to the south ..."
Sound (Auditory)	Loud or soft sounds and someone's speech are all associated with this type of imagery. For example, authors can describe a dog's bark, the snap of a twig, the sizzle of bacon, a grown man's moaning, a baby's wail, or the hoarseness or register of someone's voice. The author can also include onomatopoeia—a word that imitates its sound—like *bang, beep, buzz, clang,* or *whoosh.* See these words associated with sounds: loud—*bang, bawl, blare, crash, stomp,* or *thunder;* soft—*chime, crackle, gurgle, hiss, hush, rumble, rustle, sigh,* or *snap;* speech—*chatter, drawl, murmur, scream, stammer,* or *whimper.*	"... he spat speculatively. There was a sharp, explosive crackle that startled him. He spat again. And again, in the air, before it could fall to the snow, the spittle crackled." "He had felt the give under his feet and heard the crackle of a snow-hidden ice-skin."
Taste (Gustatory)	Describing what food or something other than food tastes like is another form of imagery that writers use to make a story realistic. Words to define taste include *bitter, bland, burnt, buttery, crisp, fruity, medicinal, savory, sour, spicy, sugary, sweet, tangy,* or *tasteless.*	"He smiled agreeably to himself as he thought of those biscuits, each cut open and sopped in bacon grease, and each enclosing a generous slice of fried bacon."
Touch (Tactile)	When writers provide readers with an experience that involves texture and what someone might feel, they are using another sense that is ripe for imagery. Words for touch might be *bumpy, cool, crisp, feathery, furry, greasy, gritty, hairy, rough, rubbery, scalding, sharp, slippery, sticky, thick, velvety,* or *waxy.*	"Day had broken cold and gray, exceedingly cold and gray ..." "Fifty degrees below zero stood for a bite of frost that hurt and that must be guarded against by the use of mittens, earflaps, warm moccasins, and thick socks." "... and lying against the naked skin." "But rub as he would, the instant he stopped his cheek-bones went numb, and the following instant the end of his nose went numb."
Smell (Olfactory)	Describing nature, foods, or scents can capture the sense of smell. Writers may describe brownies baking in an oven, an athlete's uniform after a game, or freshly blooming jasmine in a garden to conjure up various scents that readers can imagine. Writers might use words like *piney, acrid, rotten, perfumed, fishy, fresh, earthy, salty, rancid, dank, musty, spicy,* or *sweet.*	"Next he brought out his bunch of sulphur matches." "His flesh was burning." "And still later [the dog] crept close to the man and caught the scent of death."

Source: London, 1908.

Figure C.3: Imagery types and excerpts.
Visit go.SolutionTree.com/literacy for a free reproducible version of this figure.

Hyperbole

Authors use hyperbole to offer an extreme exaggeration that illustrates a point and accentuates a quality or feature. Generally the action, desire, or feeling expressed in the hyperbole is impractical or implausible, but the overemphasis helps to convey the meaning and elicit emotion. The popularity of this dramatic technique fosters many clichés, such as the following.

- I'm so hungry I could eat a horse.
- He runs like the speed of light.
- He's older than the hills.
- He's as skinny as a toothpick.
- His brain is the size of a pea.
- Everyone knows that.

You'll notice that some couple as similes and hyperbolic statements. Share these and others with students to point out familiar clichés and encourage them to write original text.

In the following example from "The Tell-Tale Heart," Edgar Allan Poe (1843/2002) asserts that he can hear beyond what is possible, which underscores his warped self-perception and sets the stage for the story that will unfold:

> True!—nervous—very, very dreadfully nervous I had been and am; but why will you say that I am mad? The disease had sharpened my senses—not destroyed—not dulled them. Above all was the sense of hearing acute. I heard all things in the heaven and in the earth. I heard many things in hell. How, then, am I mad? Hearken! And observe how healthily—how calmly I can tell you the whole story. (p. 3)

In this example from *To Kill a Mockingbird*, Harper Lee (1960) uses hyperbole to exaggerate the insulated small town and the familiar behavior of the citizens in it:

> People moved slowly then. They ambled across the square, shuffled in and out of the stores around it, took their time about everything. A day was twenty-four hours long but seemed longer. There was no hurry, for there was nowhere to go, nothing to buy and no money to buy it with, nothing to see outside the boundaries of Maycomb County. (p. 6)

Authentic Figurative Language

Authors do not compartmentalize types of figurative language and set out to have a recipe, such as one simile, two metaphors, an example of personification, and so forth. Instead, they likely write freely and infuse their writing with figures of speech purposefully to elicit a mood, amplify an image, or enhance an element of literature so readers more fully appreciate their work. See these rich examples of a combination of figurative language at play:

> All through October the days were still warm, like summer, but at night the mercury dropped and in the morning the sagebrush was sometimes covered with frost. Twice in one week there were dust storms. The sky turned suddenly gray and then a hot wind came screaming across the desert, churning up everything in its path. From inside the barracks the boy could not see the sun or the moon or even the next row of barracks on the other side of the gravel path. All he could see was dust. The wind rattled the windows and doors and the dust seeped like smoke through the cracks in the roof and at night he slept with a wet handkerchief over his mouth to keep out the smell. In the morning, when he woke, the wet handkerchief was dry and in his mouth there was the gritty taste of chalk. (Otsuka, 2002, p. 77)

<< • >>

> "I have seen the smoky fury of our factories—rising to the skies," said President Eisenhower pridefully as he addressed the people of Seattle last night. Well, I can see the smoky fury of our factories driving right into this room this very minute; the fury sits in my throat like a bundle of needles, it explores my nose, chokes off my breath, and makes my eyes burn. The room smells like a slaughterhouse. (White, 1999, p. 116)

<< • >>

> And so on this particular night as the crier's voice was gradually swallowed up in the distance, silence returned to the world, a vibrant silence made more intense by the universal trill of a million million forest insects. (Achebe, 1995, p. 7)

Ask students to find excerpts in their complex text of appropriate examples and identify the types of figurative language and infer meaning from them. Students can also find excerpts that rely solely on one type and expand them to include more or switch an author's form of figurative language to another (like a simile to a metaphor or a metaphor to an example of personification).

Summary

Authors' work is replete with different types of literary devices and figurative language. For example, they might write comparisons using similes or metaphors, create visualization with imagery, or use allusion by referencing ancient literature. Although readers might struggle to interpret these devices and figures of speech, authors intentionally infuse their writing with them to make passages more meaningful, engaging, and sometimes profound. Teaching students these techniques can contribute to their expanding expertise as both readers and writers.

Appendix D

Sentence Structure: Complex Sentences

This appendix provides a synopsis of the mechanics of clauses and the complex sentence as an aid in teaching sentence variety. For more in-depth information about clauses and other sentence structures and to address pertinent content-area standards, you might access grammar resources like Grammar Monster (www.grammar-monster.com), the Purdue Online Writing Lab (https://owl.english.purdue.edu), or Walden University Writing Center (http://academicguides.waldenu.edu/writingcenter/composition).

A complex sentence includes one *independent* clause, one or more *dependent* clauses, and perhaps other words and phrases like modifiers or prepositional phrases. An *independent clause* is essentially just a simple sentence, such as the following: *The dog barked. Mrs. Rothmann adheres to a regimented schedule. My son, Marshall, was accepted into a master's program.*

A *dependent (or subordinate)* clause, as the word denotes, depends or relies on something else. It cannot stand alone as a sentence unto itself since it does not represent a complete thought, such as the following: *When Kimmie returned from Newport Beach . . .; After Mom played bridge . . .; Even though Wendy loves Indiana. . . .* A dependent clause by itself is a sentence fragment or incomplete sentence; it requires at least one independent clause to make it complete, so it becomes either a complex or compound-complex sentence, which contains at least two independent clauses and at least one dependent clause.

There are three types of dependent clauses—(1) adjective, (2) adverbial, and (3) noun. The focus here centers on the adverbial clause, a group of words that act as an adverb and part of a compound or compound-complex sentence. These dependent clauses answer the questions, *How? When? Where? In what manner? To what degree?*

There are three main parts in adverbial clauses in this order: (1) subordinating conjunction, (2) subject, and (3) verb. Often, people confuse clauses with phrases. All clauses contain a subject and verb; phrases, on the other hand, do not. To illustrate, review the following dependent clause and prepositional phrase examples and notice the underlined verbs in the clauses. Also read the deconstructed examples of complex sentences with dependent (adverbial) clauses in figure D.1 (page 150).

- **Dependent clause examples:** *When I <u>turned</u> eight, . . .; Since immigration <u>is</u> such a controversial issue, . . .; If Mr. Tuchman <u>hired</u> new managers, . . .; While Kimmie <u>danced</u>, . . .*

- **Prepositional phrase examples:** *Around a corner, . . .; Behind the wooden fence, . . .; Before the verdict, . . .; After school, . . .*

Complex Sentence Examples			
Dependent Clause			
Subordinating Conjunction	**Subject**	**Verb**	**Independent Clause**
When	I	matured,	I realized the errors of my childish ways.
Once	the devastating storm	subsided,	we assessed the damage and made a game plan for repair.
If only	the situation	changed,	I could have some peace of mind and continue carefree and unencumbered.

Figure D.1: Dependent clauses deconstructed.

*Visit **go.SolutionTree.com/literacy** for a free reproducible version of this figure.*

Adverbial clauses can be flexibly placed either at the beginning or end of a sentence. When the clause starts a sentence, add a comma; otherwise, omit it, as shown in figure D.2. When targeting the skill of beginning sentences in a different way, emphasize the former configuration like those in the figure.

Begin With a Dependent Clause	**End With a Dependent Clause**
After she tried unsuccessfully to fall back to sleep, Michelle finally turned on the light and read a book.	Michelle finally turned on the light and read a book ***after she tried unsuccessfully to fall back to sleep***.
Since the Warriors have enjoyed a string of winning games, fans are packing the stadium.	Fans are packing the stadium ***since the Warriors have enjoyed a string of winning games***.
When narratives include a compelling plot and intriguing characters, readers typically find a story engaging.	Readers typically find a story engaging ***when narratives include a compelling plot and intriguing characters***.

Figure D.2: Complex sentence structure.

*Visit **go.SolutionTree.com/literacy** for a free reproducible version of this figure.*

Appendix E

Professional and Student Resources

The resources in this appendix are for your use while designing (or redesigning) a writing unit and to share with students, as appropriate. Visit **go.SolutionTree.com/literacy** for live links to these resources.

General Writing

The following links provide an inventory of useful writing resources for any unit, such as researching, genre elements, writing process, audience, grammar, sentence structure, and more. Navigate around each site to search for materials that will support you in designing your narrative unit. You might also discover some handouts are excellent tools that you can embed within instruction and share with students.

- **Dartmouth's "Institute for Writing and Rhetoric"** (http://writing-speech.dartmouth.edu/learning /materials-first-year-writers/attending-grammar)
- **Duke (University) Thompson Writing Program** (http://twp.duke.edu/twp-writing-studio)
- **Google differentiated search lessons** (www.google.com/intl/en-us/insidesearch/searcheducation/lessons .html)
- **King's College—CORE 110: Effective Writing Resource Page** (http://departments.kings.edu/effwriting /second%20level/process.html)
- **Purdue Online Writing Lab** (https://owl.english.purdue.edu/owl)
- **UNC School of Education's "LEARN NC"** (www.learnnc.org/lp/editions/writing-process)
- **University of Washington's (Tacoma) "Teaching and Learning Center"** (www.tacoma.uw.edu /teaching-and-learning-center/writing-resources-0)
- **The Writing Center at UNC–Chapel Hill** (http://writingcenter.unc.edu/handouts)
- **Writing@CSU's "The Writing Studio"** (https://writing.colostate.edu/learn.cfm)

Grammar and Conventions

Although some sites in the preceding section provide support with grammar and conventions (punctuation, capitalization, and spelling), the following links focus squarely on these skills should you need to augment your expertise.

- **GrammarBook.com** (www.grammarbook.com/english_rules.asp)

- **Grammar-Monster.com Grammar Lessons and Tests** (www.grammar-monster.com)
- **Purdue Online Writing Lab** (https://owl.english.purdue.edu/sitemap)
- **Walden University's "Grammar and Composition: Overview"** (http://academicguides.waldenu.edu/writingcenter/grammarly)

Literary Devices and Figurative Language

For resources related to literary devices and figurative language beyond what appears in appendix C (page 137), these links contain a host of information and examples. Also search YouTube for videos to embed in lessons that can appeal to students when you are teaching these topics.

- **Literary Terms** (www.tnellen.com/cybereng/lit_terms)
- **Literary Terms and Devices** (http://eienglish.org/literms.html)
- **Literary Devices and Terms** (http://literarydevices.net)
- **Literary Devices** (http://literary-devices.com)

Performance Assessment Tasks

The following resources help you create performance assessments.

- **K–12 performance tasks across content areas** (www.performanceassessmentresourcebank.org/bin/performance-tasks)
- **LDC: Literacy Design Collaborative Task Template Collection 3.0: Templates for Grades K–12** (https://ldc.org/resources#LDC-Task-Template-Collection-3.0)

Student Writing Models

Writing samples can help clarify expectations for students. They serve as an effective instructional tool by asking students to identify evidence of strong skills to emulate in their writing and to pinpoint avoidable weaknesses in their work. Access examples of student writing models across grade levels for various genres from these links. Search specifically for your targeted narrative genre.

- **Achieve the Core's Student Writing Samples** (http://achievethecore.org/category/330/student-writing-samples)
- **Common Core State Standards for English Language Arts and Literacy in History/Social Studies, Science, and Technical Subjects: Appendix C—Samples of Student Writing** (www.corestandards.org/assets/Appendix_C.pdf)
- **Holt, Rinehart and Winston's Holt Online Essay Scoring—Writing Prompts** (https://my.hrw.com/support/hos/host_models_list_Fall_2006.html#MSExpository)
- **Oregon Department of Education's Writing Scored Student Work**
  - Grades 3–8 (www.oregon.gov/ode/educator-resources/assessment/Pages/Writing-Scored-Student-Work.aspx)
  - High School (www.ode.state.or.us/search/page/?=527)

- **Roane State Community College sample essays for narrative and descriptive writing** (www.roanestate
  .edu/owl/Describe.html)
- **Teachers College Reading and Writing Project (TCRWP): Student Writing** (http://readingandwritingproject
  .org/resources/student-work/student-writing)
- **Thoughtful Learning** (https://k12.thoughtfullearning.com/resources/studentmodels); for various student
  models with ratings of strong, good, okay, or poor (https://k12.thoughtfullearning.com/resources
  /writingassessment#Grade6–8)

Rubrics

Rubrics can help you assess impartially and clarify expectations for students. Focusing on the assignment you will issue, access these links to augment the resources and information in chapter 2 for rubrics and adapt, as needed.

- **6+1 Trait Rubrics** (http://educationnorthwest.org/traits/traits-rubrics)
- **Edutopia's Resources for Using Rubrics in the Middle Grades** (www.edutopia.org/rubrics-middle-school
  -resources)
- **Kathy Schrock's Guide to Everything: Assessment and Rubrics** (www.schrockguide.net/assessment-and
  -rubrics.html)
- **RubiStar** (http://rubistar.4teachers.org/index.php) offers an online tool to help instructors create rubrics.
- **University of Wisconsin-Stout's "Rubrics for Assessment"** (www.uwstout.edu/soe/profdev/rubrics
  .cfm#writing)
- **"Using Rubrics to Promote Thinking and Learning"** article by Heidi Goodrich Andrade in *Educational
  Leadership*, *57*(5), pp. 13–18.
- **"What Are Rubrics and Why Are They Important?"** (www.ascd.org/publications/books/112001
  /chapters/What-Are-Rubrics-and-Why-Are-They-Important¢.aspx) is the first chapter from Susan M.
  Brookhart's (2013) *How to Create and Use Rubrics for Formative Assessment and Grading*.

Calibrating to Student Work

These calibration tools will aid you in scoring student work.

- **Center for Collaborative Education's "Calibration Protocol"** (http://centerforcollaborativeeducation
  .org/internal/documents/Tool4_CalibrationProtocol.pdf)
- **The Rhode Island Department of Education's "Writing Calibration Protocol"** (www.ride.ri.gov
  /Portals/0/Uploads/Documents/Common-Core/RIDE_Calibration_Process.pdf)
- **Stanford Center for Assessment, Learning, and Equity's "Calibration Protocol"** (www
  .performanceassessmentresourcebank.org/system/files/QPA_Tool4_CalibrationProtocol_4.pdf)

Peer Review and Feedback

Peer review and feedback can be prudent instructional tools to improve the quality of students' writing. Use the following resources to help students review each other's work to give and receive effective input.

- **Eli Review** (http://app.elireview.com)

- **Peerceptiv** (www.peerceptiv.com)
- **PeerMark** (http://guides.turnitin.com/01_Manuals_and_Guides/Student/Classic_Student_User_Manual/19_PeerMark)
- **"The Reliability and Validity of Peer Review of Writing in High School AP English Classes"** (http://onlinelibrary.wiley.com/doi/10.1002/jaal.525/full) by Christian Schunn, Amanda Godley, and Sara DeMartino (2016) in *Journal of Adolescent and Adult Literacy, 60*(1), 13–23

Sources for Complex Text

Peruse any of the following publications to find text you might want to use to teach specific writing skills by featuring published and student samples. Make sure to vet selections for challenge level based on readability. Additionally, verify that the material is suitable for your student population, as some include graphic portrayals of personal experiences or the themes might be inappropriate or too sophisticated. Publications that hold contests and welcome submissions are also listed in the Essay Contests and Submissions section (page 157).

- **Aesop's Fables Online Collection** (www.aesopfables.com) has over 655 of Aesop's fables as well as 127 of Hans Christian Andersen's fairy tales.
- **Ebooks:** Access these websites to find free ebooks to download. You might locate a text excerpt and use it as the basis for classroom discussion or individual annotation or to highlight a writer's style or target a skill.
  - **Project Gutenberg** (www.gutenberg.org) provides free epub books and Kindle books to download or read online. You can browse books by author, title, language, or those recently posted.
  - **Eastoftheweb** (www.eastoftheweb.com/short-stories/indexframe.html) hosts a compilation of short stories across genres to print out or read online. Stories include age ratings so you can select those appropriate for your students. Writers can also submit stories for publication consideration. Teacher resources are available for vocabulary, questions, and ideas for discussion, plus accompanying activities and games for selected stories. The site also includes interactive opportunities.
  - **The Literature Network** (www.online-literature.com) features online books, short stories, and poems along with a quiz system and a database of quotes. It also provides summaries of classical literature, such as works by Jane Austen and Charles Dickens.
  - **Fullreads** (http://fullreads.com/literature) includes full-length online classic stories divided into easily readable pages. You can find a range of literature—for example Aesop's fables, and works by Isaac Bashevis Singer, James Thurber, Jack London, Herman Melville, and many more.
  - **Gleeditions** (http://gleeditions.com/index.asp) is another online library for editions of early-to-modern classics as full-text ebooks. They feature plays, stories, poems, memoirs, essays, documents, speeches, and video performance clips.
  - **LibriVox** (https://librivox.org) makes all books in the public domain available in audio format on the Internet. You or your students can volunteer to read books in any language or with any accent providing the reading is understandable.
- **Hippocampus** (www.hippocampusmagazine.com): This is a monthly online publication with various texts, including memoirs, essays, interviews, and more.
- **The Moth** (https://themoth.org/stories): This site is an extravaganza of storytelling accessible in different ways—*The Moth Radio Hour*, the weekly Moth Podcast, and a library of stories going back to 1997.
- *The New York Times Magazine*'s **"Lives" section** (http://goo.gl/vM9R3P): This site features stories about meaningful personal experiences.

- **Storycenter** (www.storycenter.org): This site includes a venue for listening to and sharing stories worldwide, including intergenerational ones of civil rights and first-person narratives of struggle, courage, and transformation. Users create and access stories via Storywork, digital storytelling, and other forms of digital media production.

- **Storyline Online** (www.storylineonline.net): The Screen Actors Guild Foundation BookPALS produces this website where you can access and show videos of different actors reading stories aloud, such as *Wilfrid Gordon McDonald Partridge* by Mem Fox; *The Rainbow Fish* by Marcus Pfister; and *Thank You, Mr. Falker* by Patricia Polacco. Participating actors include Bradley Whitford, Jane Kaczmarek, Elijah Wood, and others.

- **The Sun** (http://thesunmagazine.org): This monthly online magazine features personal essays, short stories, interviews, poetry, and photographs.

- **Teen Ink** (www.teenink.com/Contests/Winners1516): Read and use any of the writing from teenage contest winners for their magazine, including fiction, nonfiction, and poetry, plus topical writing products on community service, environment, and travel and culture. There are also art winners featured on the magazine's cover.

- **USC's Shoah Foundation** (http://sfi.usc.edu): This site features audiovisual interviews with survivors and witnesses of the Holocaust and other genocides, plus accompanying student videos, discussions, and lectures.

- **Wattpad** (www.wattpad.com): People around the world can participate and collaborate on content in this multiplatform entertainment company for culturally relevant stories based on local trends and current events.

Autobiography, Memoir, and Personal Narrative Resources

When students have the opportunity to read and critically examine published work, it strengthens their own writing. These resources for autobiography, memoir, and personal narrative can assist students in this way.

- **Born in Slavery: Slave Narratives From the Federal Writers' Project, 1936 to 1938** (www.loc.gov/collections/slave-narratives-from-the-federal-writers-project-1936-to-1938): This collection contains more than 2,300 first-person accounts of slavery and 500 black-and-white photographs of former slaves.

- **Hippocampus** (www.hippocampusmagazine.com/category/creative-nonfiction/memoir): This monthly online publication has various nonfiction texts, including memoirs, essays, interviews, and more. Students can read examples and also submit their own entries.

- **How to Write Your Own Memoir** (www.oprah.com/omagazine/How-to-Write-Your-Memoir-by-Abigail-Thomas): Instruct students to read this article as a springboard to a memoir unit. Or, use the probing questions on the last page of the article for students to brainstorm ideas for writing.

- **The Moth** (https://themoth.org/stories): This site includes an extravaganza of storytelling accessible in different ways—*The Moth Radio Hour*, the weekly Moth Podcast, and a library of stories going back to 1997.

- *The New York Times Magazine*'s "Lives" section (http://goo.gl/vM9R3P): This site features stories about meaningful personal experiences.

- **Ranker's "The Best Memoirs Ever Written"** (www.ranker.com/list/best-memoirs/ranker-books): This site features a list of popular memoirs that includes historical accounts that were written from personal knowledge.

- **Storycenter** (www.storycenter.org): This site includes a venue for listening to and sharing stories worldwide, including intergenerational stories of civil rights and first-person narratives of struggle, courage, and transformation. Users create and access stories via Storywork, digital storytelling, and other forms of digital media production.

- **The Sun** (http://thesunmagazine.org/about/submission_guidelines/readers_write): This site provides the opportunity for students to read different kinds of text and also submit their own writing for publication.

- **USC Shoah Foundation's Visual History Archive Program** (http://sfi.usc.edu/vha/vha_program): The Visual History Archive includes a digital collection of audiovisual interviews, with fifty-three thousand testimonies of survivors and witnesses of the Holocaust plus other genocides that provide a compelling voice for education and action. Scroll down in the link to see offerings under "Watch," such as sample clips and student videos.

- *Your Life Is a Book: How to Craft and Publish Your Memoir* by Brenda Peterson and Sarah J. Freymann

Unit and Lesson Examples

Although this book asks that you design or redesign your own unit, it is helpful to see others' examples. Peruse and cross-reference those featured here; each includes a host of resources that you can embed in your own unit. Adapt or use lessons in these sites that align to the learning outcomes of your unit.

- **Achieve the Core ELA and Literacy Lessons** (http://achievethecore.org/category/411/ela-literacy-lessons): Peruse hundreds of teacher-developed, standards-aligned lessons for K–12 by navigating around this site starting with the provided link. Filter your search to find what you need.

- **Bill and Melinda Gates Foundation** (http://k12education.gatesfoundation.org/resource/#?initiative= common-assignment-study): The Common Assignment Study (CAS) is a research and development project in which teachers collaborate across districts and states to develop and implement high-quality curricular units across disciplines. The CAS was led by the Colorado Initiative and the Fund for Transforming Education in Kentucky with support from the Gates Foundation.

- **EDSITEment!** (https://edsitement.neh.gov/about): This site, a project of the National Endowment for the Humanities and the National Trust for the Humanities, provides a wealth of high-quality materials in literature and language arts, foreign language, art and culture, and history and social studies. All websites linked to any lesson have been reviewed for content, design, and educational impact in the classroom.

- **EngageNY** (www.engageny.org): This site includes extensive, robust curricular units for grades preK–12 in both mathematics and ELA. The ELA modules, which address the Common Core standards for ELA as well as social studies and science content, provide eight weeks of instruction and include assessments.

- **EQuIP** (Educators Evaluating the Quality of Instructional Products; www.achieve.org/equIP): This site features quality ELA and mathematics lessons and units aligned to the CCSS or NGSS (Next Generation Science Standards). EQuIP's resource bank includes other materials, such as rubrics to assess the quality of curricular units, annotated student work, and more.

- **LearnZillion English Language Arts Guidebook Units** (https://learnzillion.com/resources/81666 -english-language-arts-guidebook-units): The Louisiana Department of Education in cooperation with LearnZillion has created and made available ELA units that include daily lessons, assessments, texts, blank and completed handouts, and student writing samples. There is also a portal to purchase published books aligned to classroom texts. The units adhere to Louisiana's standards, which are based on the Common Core, but address a variety of subjects.

- **Literacy Design Collaborative** (LDC; https://ldc.org/sample-curricula): LDC's library houses hundreds of nationally vetted, teacher-created lessons across content areas.

- **PBS LearningMedia** (http://ca.pbslearningmedia.org/standards/0): This site offers more than one hundred thousand videos, images, interactives, lesson plans, and articles drawn from PBS programs and expert content contributors. Users can browse the collections by searching for resources by the subject, grade, and alignment to national standards, Next Generation Science Standards, and Common Core standards.

- **Project Exchange** (http://goo.gl/tvhG9Y): This website for grades 9–12 is designed for high school teachers to share curriculum, resources, and materials, and also to collaborate about best practices in project-based design and implementation. Envision Schools, a nonprofit charter organization, hosts the site.

- **Reading Like a Historian by Stanford History Education Group** (http://sheg.stanford.edu/rlh): The curriculum in this site engages grades 9–12 students in historical inquiry that can support them in writing historical fiction. Each lesson includes primary documents intended for differentiation purposes. This curriculum teaches students how to investigate historical questions by employing a host of reading strategies. Instead of memorizing historical facts, students evaluate the trustworthiness of multiple perspectives on historical issues. They learn to make historical claims backed by documentary evidence.

- **The Learning Network** (www.nytimes.com/section/learning): This site offers a broad compilation of materials and resources for teaching and learning across content areas using material from *The New York Times*, such as articles, photographs, podcasts, and graphics. It offers free lesson plans, quizzes, essay contests, vocabulary acquisition ideas, and more.

Essay Contests and Submissions

Collectively these sites listed hold writing contests across all text types, among them narrative and descriptive. Be mindful to heed the contest deadline dates, submission guidelines (word count, formatting, and other information) for entries, and required fees (if any). Some are geared to students only; others are open to anyone, including you!

- **Eastoftheweb** (www.eastoftheweb.com/short-stories/indexframe.html): This site hosts a compilation of short stories available online across genres. It also accepts story submissions for publication consideration.

- **Hippocampus** (www.hippocampusmagazine.com/submissions): This online magazine accepts submissions for memoirs, personal essays, and flash creative nonfiction (a work of creative nonfiction in an experimental format).

- **Letters About Literature** (www.read.gov/letters): This site holds a contest for students in grades 4–12 in which they are asked to read a book, poem, or speech and write to the author (living or dead) about how the piece affected them personally.

- **Scholastic Art and Writing Awards** (www.artandwriting.org/the-awards/categories): Students in grades 7–12 can submit writing in all sorts of categories, such as critical essay, drama script, flash fiction, poetry, science fiction, and more. There are also entries for art categories including ceramics, fashion, jewelry, painting, and other creative endeavors.

- **The Sun** (http://thesunmagazine.org/about/submission_guidelines/readers_write): This online magazine accepts submissions for essays, interviews, fiction, and poetry.

- **Teen Ink** (www.teenink.com/Contests): This site offers a variety of contest opportunities including cover art, fiction, nonfiction, and poetry. It also sponsors writing contests on topics such as environment (solutions and ideas about a problem facing the planet), educator of the year (students can nominate an amazing teacher in their life), community service (how students make the world a better place), and more.

- **Winning Writers** (https://winningwriters.com): This clearinghouse site for writing contests and services provides links to the best literary contests along with their rules. By subscribing to its free email newsletter, you'll learn more about each contest, including which ones are suitable for writers at the beginning, intermediate, and advanced stages of their careers. Plus, it cautions writers about contests and services to avoid lest they be taken advantage of or scammed.

Graphic Organizers

Graphic organizers support student learning in myriad ways as a reading and writing tool. Students can use organizers to classify information, make connections, structure their writing, record and organize research notes, brainstorm topics, and more. These sources provide a collection of graphic organizers that students can use for different purposes across content areas.

- **BrainPOP Educators** (https://educators.brainpop.com/printable/?printable-type=Graphic+Organizers)
- **edHelper.com** (www.edhelper.com/teachers/graphic_organizers.htm)
- **Education Oasis** (http://educationoasis.com/curriculum/graphic_organizers.htm)
- **EverythingESL** (www.everythingesl.net/inservices/graphic_organizers.php)
- **Freeology** (http://freeology.com/graphicorgs)
- **Houghton Mifflin Harcourt Education Place** (www.eduplace.com/graphicorganizer/)
- **Teacher Files** (www.teacherfiles.com/resources_organizers.htm)
- **TeacherVision** (www.teachervision.com/graphic-organizers/printable/6293.html)
- **TeAchnology** (www.teach-nology.com/web_tools/graphic_org)

Organizations and Associations

The following organizations and associations post useful resources on an ongoing basis. Access these sites to find support for what you might need when building your narrative unit.

- **International Literacy Association** (ILA; www.literacyworldwide.org): Originally International Reading Association, the ILA has worked since the 1950s to enhance literacy instruction through research and professional development. This membership organization is involved in a host of literacy efforts that include research journals, publications, professional development, conferences, and advocacy efforts. It also offers annual annotated reading lists of recently published books that children, young adults, teachers, and librarians select as their favorites. Visit www.literacyworldwide.org/get-resources/reading-lists to access *Choices* reading lists.

- **National Council of Teachers of English** (NCTE; www.ncte.org): This professional association, which has been in existence since 1911, comprises educators in English studies, literacy, and language arts. To support its membership, NCTE provides professional learning, programs, interest groups, publications, resources, research support, and projects.

- **National Writing Project** (NWP; www.nwp.org): NWP provides professional development, develops resources, generates research, and acts on knowledge to improve writing curriculum and instruction. It has a variety of sites and serves teachers across content areas from early childhood through university level.

- **ReadWriteThink** (www.readwritethink.org): ReadWriteThink, which partners with ILA and NCTE, provides free standards-aligned resources and materials for reading and language arts instruction to parents, educators, and other professionals.

- **Stanford Center for Assessment, Learning and Equity** (SCALE; http://scale.stanford.edu): SCALE creates and develops performance assessments and solutions for states, districts, and education foundations. It serves students and teachers from early childhood through college and career.

Appendix F

List of Figures and Tables

*Visit **go.SolutionTree.com/literacy** for free reproducible versions of these figures and tables.

References and Resources

Achebe, C. (1995). *Things fall apart*. New York: Everyman's Library.

Ackerman, D. (2007). *The zookeeper's wife*. New York: Norton.

Anderson, L. H. (1999). *Speak*. Madeira Park, British Columbia, Canada: Douglas & McIntyre.

Anderson, L. H. (2000). *Fever 1793*. New York: Simon & Schuster.

Andrade, H. G. (2000). Using rubrics to promote thinking and learning. *Educational Leadership, 57*(5), 13–18.

Angelou, M. (1997). *I know why the caged bird sings*. New York: Random House. (Original work published 1969)

Asher, J. (2007). *Thirteen reasons why*. New York: Penguin Random House.

Asimov, I. (1959). *Rain, rain, go away*. Accessed at www.scribd.com/document/103382368/Rain-Rain-Go-Away on September 1, 2017.

Atwell, N. (2015). *In the middle: A lifetime of learning about writing, reading, and adolescents* (3rd ed.). Portsmouth, NH: Heinemann.

Avi. (1995). *Poppy*. New York: HarperCollins.

Babbitt, N. (1975). *Tuck everlasting*. New York: Farrar, Straus and Giroux.

Bradbury, R. (n.d.). *All summer in a day*. Accessed at www.btboces.org/Downloads/6_All%20Summer%20in%20a%20Day%20by%20Ray%20Bradbury.pdf on May 8, 2017.

Bradbury, R. (1951). *The pedestrian*. Accessed at www.riversidelocalschools.com/Downloads/pedestrian%20short%20story.pdf on August 31, 2017.

Bradbury, R. (1995). *Fahrenheit 451*. New York: Simon & Schuster.

Brookhart, S. M. (2013). *How to create and use rubrics for formative assessment and grading*. Alexandria, VA: Association for Supervision and Curriculum Development.

Brown, J. (2009). *Hate list*. New York: Hatchette Book Group.

Capote, T. (1967). *Counterpoint in literature*. Glenview, IL: Scott Foresman.

Chernow, R. (2004). *Alexander Hamilton*. New York: Penguin.

Cisneros, S. (1991a). *Eleven*. Accessed at www.stjohns-chs.org/english/nwixon_courses/english-9-111/eleven-by-sandra-cisneros.pdf on September 1, 2017.

Cisneros, S. (1991b). *Woman hollering creek: And other stories*. New York: Random House.

Coleridge, S. T. (1834). *The rime of the ancient mariner*. Accessed at www.poetryfoundation.org/poems/43997/the-rime-of-the-ancient-mariner-text-of-1834 on September 11, 2017.

Cooper, S. (1973). *The dark is rising: The complete sequence.* New York: Simon & Schuster.

Dahl, R. (1975). *Danny, the champion of the world.* New York: Puffin Books.

Dahl, R. (1988). *Matilda.* New York: Puffin Books.

Dickens, C. (1843). *A Christmas carol in prose: Being a ghost story of Christmas.* Accessed at www.gutenberg.org /ebooks/46?msg=welcome_stranger on May 8, 2017.

Dickens, C. (1850). *The personal history of David Copperfield.* Accessed at www.gutenberg.org/files/766/766-h/766-h .htm on May 8, 2017.

Dickens, C. (2016). *David Copperfield.* London: Macmillan Collector's Library.

Doerr, A. (2014). *All the light we cannot see: A novel.* New York: Scribner.

Emerging Technology from the arXiv. (2016, July 6). Data mining reveals the six basic emotional arcs of storytelling. *MIT Technology Review.* Accessed at www.technologyreview.com/s/601848/data-mining-reveals-the-six-basic -emotional-arcs-of-storytelling on January 31, 2017.

Fisher, D., & Frey, N. (2014). *Better learning through structured teaching: A framework for the gradual release of responsibility* (2nd ed.). Alexandria, VA: Association for Supervision and Curriculum Development.

Foner, E. & Garraty, J. A. (Ed.). (1991). *The reader's companion to American history.* New York: Houghton Mifflin Harcourt. Accessed at www.history.com/topics/davy-crockett on September 7, 2017.

Forbes, E. (1971). *Johnny Tremain: A story of Boston in revolt.* New York: Houghton Mifflin Harcourt. (Original work published 1943)

Fountas, I. C., & Pinnell, G. S. (2012). *Genre study: Teaching with fiction and nonfiction books.* Portsmouth, NH: Heinemann.

Frost, R. (n.d.). *The road not taken.* Accessed at www.poetryfoundation.org/poems/44272/the-road-not-taken on October 30, 2017.

Gilbert, E. (2006). *Eat, pray, love: One woman's search for everything across Italy, India and Indonesia.* New York: Riverhead Books.

Glass, K. T. (2012). *Mapping comprehensive units to the ELA Common Core standards, K–5.* Thousand Oaks, CA: Corwin Press.

Glass, K. T. (2017a). *The fundamentals of (re)designing writing units.* Bloomington, IN: Solution Tree Press.

Glass, K. T. (2017b). *(Re)designing argumentation writing units for grades 5–12.* Bloomington, IN: Solution Tree Press.

Goodwin, D. K. (2005). *Team of rivals: The political genius of Abraham Lincoln.* New York: Simon & Schuster.

Graham, S., & Perin, D. (2007). *Writing next: Effective strategies to improve writing of adolescents in middle and high schools* (A report to Carnegie Corporation of New York). Washington, DC: Alliance for Excellent Education.

Green, J. (2012). *The fault in our stars.* New York: Penguin Random House.

Haddon, M. (2003). *The curious incident of the dog in the night-time.* New York: Random House.

Hammond, M. (2008, April 18). *Tone and mood words* [Video file]. Accessed at www.youtube.com/watch?v=jDUh DV-72S0 on July 19, 2017.

Hastings, S. (1987). *Sir Gawain and the Loathly Lady.* New York: HarperCollins.

Hattie, J. (2009). *Visible learning: A synthesis of over 800 meta-analyses relating to achievement.* New York: Routledge.

Hattie, J. (2012). *Visible learning for teachers: Maximizing impact on learning.* New York: Routledge.

Hawthorne, N. (1835). *Young Goodᵐan Brown.* Accessed at www.online-literature.com/poe/158 on May 8, 2017.

Herriot, J. (1994). *James Herriot's cat stories.* New York: St. Martin's Press.

Hiaasen, C. (2002). *Hoot.* New York: Random House.

Hillenbrand, L. (2014). *Unbroken: A World War II story of survival, resilience, and redemption.* New York: Random House.

Hillocks, G., Jr. (2007). *Narrative writing: Learning a new model for teaching.* Portsmouth, NH: Heinemann.

Isaacson, W. (2013). *Steve Jobs.* New York: Simon & Schuster.

Jackson, S. (1949/2010). *The lottery.* Accessed at http://lgdata.s3-website-us-east-1.amazonaws.com/docs/1500/343509/The_Lottery.pdf on August 31, 2017.

Jackson, S. (2010). Charles. In J. C. Oates (Ed.), *Shirley Jackson: Novels and stories* (pp. 73–77). New York: Library of America. Accessed at https://loa-shared.s3.amazonaws.com/static/pdf/Jackson_Charles.pdf on May 9, 2017. (Original work published 1949)

Jacobs, W. W. (1997). The monkey's paw. In *Elements of literature: Second course* (Annotated teacher's edition; pp. T185–T195). Austin, TX: Holt, Rinehart and Winston.

Kipling, R. (1993). *Just so stories.* Hertfordshire, England: Wordsworth Editions.

Kittle, P. (2008). *Write beside them: Risk, voice, and clarity in high school writing.* Portsmouth, NH: Heinemann.

Kohn, A. (2006). *The homework myth: Why our kids get too much of a bad thing.* Cambridge, MA: Da Capo Press.

Konigsburg, E. L. (1973). *A proud taste for scarlet and miniver.* New York: Bantam Doubleday Dell.

Krakauer, J. (1996). *Into the wild.* New York: Random House.

Leach, M., & Fried, J. (Eds.). (1972). *Standard dictionary of folklore, mythology, and legend.* New York: Harper & Row.

Lee, H. (1960). *To kill a mockingbird.* Philadelphia: Lippincott.

London, J. (1908). *To build a fire.* Accessed at www.classicshorts.com/stories/firelndn.html on September 12, 2017.

Marquis, D. (n.d.). *freddy the rat perishes.* Accessed at www.donmarquis.org/freddy.htm on May 11, 2017.

Martin, G. R. R. (1999). *A clash of kings.* New York: Random House.

Marzano, R. J. (2017). *The new art and science of teaching* (Rev. and expanded ed.). Bloomington, IN: Solution Tree Press.

Mathabane, M. (1986). *Kaffir boy: The true story of a black youth's coming of age in apartheid South Africa.* New York: Touchstone.

McCullough, D. (2001). *John Adams.* New York: Simon & Schuster.

Mistry, R. (1995). *A fine balance.* New York: Random House.

Myers, W. D. (1997). The treasure of lemon brown. In *Elements of literature: Second course* (Annotated teacher's edition; pp. T93–T101). Austin, TX: Holt, Rinehart and Winston.

MysteryNet.com. (n.d.). *Mystery vocabulary worksheet.* Accessed at www.mysterynet.com/learn/lessonplans/vocab-worksheet on May 11, 2017.

National Governors Association Center for Best Practices & Council of Chief State School Officers. (2010). *Common Core State Standards for English language arts and literacy in history/social studies, science, and technical subjects.* Washington, DC: Authors. Accessed at www.corestandards.org/assets/CCSSI_ELA%20Standards.pdf on July 5, 2017.

Nielsen, J. A. (2015). *A night divided.* New York: Scholastic.

Ontario Ministry of Education. (2006). *The Ontario curriculum grades 1–8: Language* (Rev. ed.). Accessed at www.edu.gov.on.ca/eng/curriculum/elementary/language18curr.pdf on November 5, 2016.

Otsuka, J. (2002). *When the emperor was divine: A novel.* New York: Knopf.

Palacio, R. J. (2012). *Wonder.* New York: Random House.

Pearson, P. D., & Gallagher, M. C. (1983, October). *The instruction of reading comprehension* (Technical report no. 297). Champaign: Center for the Study of Reading, University of Illinois at Urbana–Champaign.

Picoult, J. (2016). *Small great things.* New York: Penguin Random House.

Poe, E. A. (1843/2002). *The tell-tale heart and other writings.* New York: Bantam Dell.

Popham, W. J. (2008). *Transformative assessment.* Alexandria, VA: Association for Supervision and Curriculum Development.

Probst, K. D. (1997). *Elements of literature: Second course* (Annotated teacher's edition). Orlando, FL: Holt, Rinehart and Winston.

Randazzo, L. [Laura Randazzo]. (2015, September 4). *Teaching irony: Help students understand verbal, situational, and dramatic irony* [Video file]. Accessed at www.youtube.com/watch?v=XCU9ytiiN4U on July 5, 2017.

ReadWriteThink. (n.d.). *Lesson plan: What's in a mystery?: Exploring and identifying mystery elements.* Accessed at www.readwritethink.org/classroom-resources/lesson-plans/what-mystery-exploring-identifying-865.html on September 12, 2017.

Robinson, E. A. (n.d.). *Richard Cory.* Accessed at www.poetryfoundation.org/poems/44982/richard-cory on September 11, 2017.

Rohmann, E. (1997). *The cinder-eyed cats.* New York: Random House.

Rowell, R. (2013). *Fangirl.* New York: St. Martin's Press.

Rowling, J. K. (1997). *Harry Potter and the sorcerer's stone.* New York: Scholastic.

Ryan, P. M. (2000). *Esperanza rising.* New York: Scholastic.

Sachar, L. (1998). *Holes.* New York: Yearling.

Schunn, C. D., Godley, A. J., & DeMartino, S. (2016). The reliability and validity of peer review of writing in high school AP English classes. *Journal of Adolescent and Adult Literacy, 60*(1), 13–23.

Scieszka, J. (1989). *The true story of the 3 little pigs!* New York: Viking Kestrel.

Shakespeare, W. (2017). *Othello.* New York: Simon & Schuster.

Sloane, W. (1979). *The craft of writing.* New York: Norton.

Soto, G. (n.d.). *The jacket.* Accessed at http://teachersites.schoolworld.com/webpages/AThomson/files/The%20Jacket.pdf on September 12, 2017.

Stanford Center for Assessment, Learning and Equity. (n.d.). *Spreads like (exponential) wildfire.* Accessed at www.performanceassessmentresourcebank.org/resource/8036 on October 30, 2017.

Steinbeck, J. (1968/1994). *Of mice and men.* New York: Penguin. Accessed at www.alanreinstein.com/site/213_Of_Mice_and_Men_files/OMM.Full.Text%281%29.pdf on September 11, 2017.

Stevenson, R. L. (1886/1991). *The strange case of Dr. Jekyll and Mr. Hyde.* Mineola, NY: Dover.

Swift, J. (1729). *A modest proposal.* Accessed at www.gutenberg.org/files/1080/1080-h/1080-h.htm on September 11, 2017.

Taylor, M. D. (1976). *Roll of thunder, hear my cry.* New York: Scholastic.

Teachers TryScience. (2015, July 9). *Urban heat island effect NGSS.* Accessed at www.teacherstryscience.org/ngsslp/urban-heat-island-effect-ngss on May 4, 2017.

Texas Education Agency. (2010). *§110.20. English language arts and reading, grade 8, beginning with school year 2009–2010. Chapter 110. Texas essential knowledge and skills for English language arts and reading: Subchapter B. Middle school.* Accessed at http://ritter.tea.state.tx.us/rules/tac/chapter110/ch110b.html#110.20 on September 9, 2017.

TheedofNaboo. (2011, October 30). *What if—Why educators should teach science fiction* [Video file]. Accessed at www .youtube.com/watch?v=gOHM9qeNcRE on October 30, 2017.

Thomas, A. (2017). *The hate u give*. New York: HarperCollins.

Tolkien, J. R. R. (2004). *The lord of the rings*. London: HarperCollins.

Tolstoy, L. (2001). *War and peace*. New York: Random House.

Tomlinson, C. A., & Moon, T. R. (2013). *Assessment and student success in a differentiated classroom*. Alexandria, VA: Association for Supervision and Curriculum Development.

Van Allsburg, C. (1984). *The mysteries of Harris Burdick*. New York: Houghton Mifflin.

Vidal, G. (1995). *Palimpsest: A memoir*. New York: Random House.

Virginia Department of Education. (2010). *Standards of learning (SOL) and testing: English*. Accessed at www.doe .virginia.gov/testing/sol/standards_docs/english/index.shtml on November 5, 2016.

Vonnegut, K. (2014). Harrison Bergeron. In *Welcome to the monkey house* (Special ed.). New York: Dial Press.

Warner, C. [Christopher Warner]. (2012, December 13). *Situational irony: The opposite of what you think* [Video file]. Accessed at www.youtube.com/watch?v=tqg6RO8c_W0 on July 5, 2017.

Warner, C. [Christopher Warner]. (2013a, January 29). *In on a secret?: That's dramatic irony* [Video file]. Accessed at www.youtube.com/watch?v=RZFYuX84n1U on July 5, 2017.

Warner, C. [Christopher Warner]. (2013b, March 13). *What is verbal irony?* [Video file]. Accessed at www.youtube .com/watch?v=IiR-bnCHIYo&list=PL57ovddpcLCfdcBJNUDp6GUM5UL1QdPn on July 5, 2017.

Welty, E. (n.d.). *Petrified man*. Accessed at http://storyoftheweek.loa.org/2013/07/petrified-man.html on August 31, 2017.

White, E. B. (1999). *Essays of E. B. White*. New York: HarperCollins.

Wiesner, D. (1988). *Free fall*. New York: HarperCollins.

Wiesner, D. (1991). *Tuesday*. New York: Clarion Books.

Wiesner, D. (2001). *The three pigs*. New York: Houghton Mifflin.

Wiggins, G., & McTighe, J. (2005). *Understanding by design* (2nd ed.). Alexandria, VA: Association for Supervision and Curriculum Development.

Wright, R. (1967). *Counterpoint in literature*. Glenview, IL: Scott Foresman.

Yep, L. (n.d.). *Breaker's bridge*. Accessed at http://arvindguptatoys.com/arvindgupta/breakers-bridge.pdf on January 3, 2017.

Yep, L. (1989). *The rainbow people*. New York: HarperCollins.

YourDictionary. (n.d.). *Analogy examples in literature*. Accessed at http://examples.yourdictionary.com/analogy-examples -in-literature.html on May 9, 2017.

Zinsser, W. (2006, Spring). How to write a memoir. *The American Scholar*. Accessed at https://theamericanscholar.org /how-to-write-a-memoir/#.WV5evYTyvIU on July 6, 2017.

Zusak, M. (2005). *The book thief*. New York: Random House.

Index

(Re)designing Argumentation Writing Units for Grades 5–12
Kathy Tuchman Glass
Developed for teachers, curriculum designers, and literacy coaches, this user-friendly guide offers practical recommendations, strategies, and tips for establishing argumentation units of instruction that empower students to artfully and logically present and convince others of their position.
BKF708

The Fundamentals of (Re)designing Writing Units
Kathy Tuchman Glass
Perfect for teachers, curriculum designers, and literacy coaches, this title provides guidance for designing new writing units and revising existing ones across content areas for grades 5–12. Discover practical strategies for teaching skills in drafting, editing, revising, feedback, and more.
BKF711

Blended Vocabulary for K–12 Classrooms
Kimberly A. Tyson and Angela B. Peery
Discover a research-based model you can implement to help all students master tiered vocabulary. With greater understanding of how to teach vocabulary effectively and incorporate digital tools, you can develop a blended approach to word learning that makes a significant impact on achievement.
BKF630

200+ Proven Strategies for Teaching Reading, Grades K–8
Kathy Perez
This easy-to-use reference guide provides K–8 teachers with practical strategies to motivate all students to develop their reading abilities across grade levels and content areas and to help students who are struggling with reading make great strides in literacy achievement.
BKF663

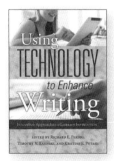

Using Technology to Enhance Writing
Edited by Richard E. Ferdig, Timothy V. Rasinski, and Kristine E. Pytash
Sharpen your students' communication skills while integrating digital tools into writing instruction. Loaded with techniques for planning and organizing writing, this handbook troubleshoots issues students face when writing in a printed versus digital context and teaches them how to read in multiple media.
BKF607

Wait! Your professional development journey doesn't have to end with the last pages of this book.

We realize improving student learning doesn't happen overnight. And your school or district shouldn't be left to puzzle out all the details of this process alone.

No matter where you are on the journey, we're committed to helping you get to the next stage.

Take advantage of everything from **custom workshops** to **keynote presentations** and **interactive web and video conferencing**. We can even help you develop an action plan tailored to fit your specific needs.

Let's get the conversation started.

Call 888.763.9045 today.

 solution-tree.com